Markets of the Sixties

Books by the Editors of FORTUNE

Markets of the Sixties

by THE EDITORS OF *Fortune*

HARPER & BROTHERS *Publishers* NEW YORK

Contents

The following members of FORTUNE's *Research Staff assisted in the preparation of this book: Louise Bacon, Eleanore Carruth, Lorraine Carson, Shirley Estabrook, Marjorie Jack, Claudine Knight, Edith Roper, Betsy Stilwell, Haynes Winton.*

Jacket design and all charts by Alexander Semenoick

Acknowledgments

THE twelve chapters of the present book appeared originally, in somewhat different order, as articles in FORTUNE's fifty-ninth and sixtieth volumes (January-November, 1959). The extensive research that produced them enlisted the talents, in its various phases, of a score of members of FORTUNE's editorial staff, as well as the consulting services of many outside specialists. To many hundreds of businessmen, economists, statisticians, and ordinary consumers who were interviewed in the course of preparing this book, the Editors of FORTUNE owe thanks. Special mention must be made of Pascal K. Whelpton and Arthur A. Campbell of the Scripps Foundation for Research in Population Problems, on whose population projections FORTUNE relied heavily; Alan Greenspan of Townsend-Greenspan, Inc., who developed detailed estimates of productivity for the postwar period; Dr. Paul Boschan of New York City, for estimates and projections of income distribution; and Dr. Louis Winnick, Executive Director of New York State's Temporary Commission on Economic Expansion (on leave from the New York City Planning Commission), for his assistance in the chapter on housing. The basic approach to the problems of economic analysis throughout was the responsibility of Sanford S. Parker, FORTUNE's chief economist.

THE EDITORS

Introduction

THIS book describes coming transformations in the American way of life. Thus it also describes in depth what to producers of goods and services appears as the domestic consumer market. Like its predecessor, *The Changing American Market,* sponsored six years ago by the Editors of FORTUNE and now out of print, it is "an attempt to combine in one inquiry the best standards of journalism and the most rigorous standards of original economic analysis." But the present book seeks systematically to cast its light forward over a full rather than a half decade, as did the earlier one.

The hardihood to do so derives in part from the warm reception given to *The Changing American Market* by economists, the business press, and reviewers in general. Arthur Upgren, then Dean of the Amos Tuck School of Business Administration at Dartmouth, for example, described the book in the New York *Times* as "monumental in breadth of approach and the care with which the rapidly growing income stream of the American people is examined." And, as appreciative comments have revealed, the book proved useful to many businessmen in their forward planning.

The present volume is offered to the professional reader—the businessman, the market analyst, the economist—and also to all serious students of that endlessly astonishing social phenomenon, modern capitalist America. It is in part a source book in statistics, many developed originally by FORTUNE and its consultants, and used to deepen our understanding of an endlessly changing society. Of course, the most exciting are the projections for the future. These will naturally prove to embody some element of error, as did those in *The Changing American Market*. On the whole, however, the latter turned out to be exceedingly realistic. This should reassure the reader as he is brought up short by some of the astonishing forecasts in the present volume.

THE MARKET FRAMEWORK

The first four chapters endeavor to delineate the framework of the consumer market of the Sixties. This will reflect a new American way of life, yeasty with new Americans. Its consumer market will be increasingly shaped by teen-agers who will demand vast amounts of food and will enter massively into the market for "seconds"—the family's second car, its second TV set, its second telephone instrument.

The technology of the Sixties will once again increase man's mastery of energy and matter and thus give a new increment to the prodigious variety and thrust of the American market. This book attempts to specify the shots, long or sure, of a research and development effort in basic science and engineering that will be of unexampled magnitude. The prospects for biology, astronomy, medicine, nuclear science, space technology, are all breath-taking.

Technological gains, in turn, will stimulate American productivity, the real source of gain in national well-being. FORTUNE points to developments that seem to assure in the Sixties continuation of the 3 per cent average annual gain in productivity that characterized the fabulous decade that followed World War II.

The result of having more producers working with improved technology and so turning out more per hour throughout the Sixties should be an expansion of the economy at an average annual rate of 4.2 per cent (combined gains in labor force and productivity). The potential for containing inflation is promising and the implication for 1970 is staggering: a gross national product of $750 billion, 56 per cent more than the all-time high thus far ($480 billion in 1959). This achievement would be without historic parallel for such an extended period and starting from so lofty a base as that of the U.S. economy of 1959.

THE TREND OF AMERICAN SOCIETY

The next three chapters sketch the development of the society of the Sixties in such a transformed, expanded economic framework. The decade may complete the inversion of the traditional income pyramid in which a few were in clover at the top, most were barely subsisting at the bottom. There may come to pass nothing less extravagant than an annual after-tax income of over $7,500 for 45 per cent of all U.S. families. True poverty will be hard to find. As the decade closes, more than half of all disposable personal income is likely to be "discretionary," that is, over and above the amount required for the indispensables of life. The decade will see the blue-collar worker naturalized in suburbia, ancient class lines more blurred than ever before, "status symbols" rising, becoming well-nigh universalized, and passing. A college education will become nearly as routine as high-school education now is. And the growing American population with its rising discretionary income and its improved education is likely to be more discerning than ever as to "fitness, beauty, order, and congruity" when it goes to market. The "new masses" of America will demand better quality, greater variety, the uncommon, the striking, in the goods and services on which they lavish their vast resources.

DIVIDING THE PIE

The last five chapters treat some specific markets of the Sixties. First comes housing, around which revolves the biggest of American markets. The Sixties will be that industry's biggest decade and one with a revolutionized market—for rental construction, vacation cottages, small "retirement houses," and more large houses than ever for the increasing numbers of large families. The subdivision developer is likely to give way to the large land-development corporation and to the mobile construction company that applies to homes the efficient, cost-cutting techniques already standard in heavy construction. Where will all the mortgage money come from? In considerable part, perhaps, from pension funds and other novel sources. And thus the amounts spent on construction, upkeep, household goods, and household services will rise dramatically, to a total of $160 billion or even $165 billion by 1970.

On food, clothing, liquor, tobacco, and a wide variety of other "ordinary" necessities and luxuries, Americans will spend $175 billion annually by 1970, a 40 per cent gain over the 1959 total and a rise of 1.5 per cent annually in per capita expenditures under this heading. The market will be broadly in a state of flux as consumers demand more and better convenience foods ("boil-in-bag" preparations, and the like), chic apparel, wines, and a host of new products which their older brothers cannot now anticipate.

There may, by 1970, be a U.S. car market of close to ten million units, produced in an unprecedented range of sizes and models. As early as 1965, the market may reach the record-breaking level of eight million. Compact and small cars will account for a big part of the expansion, but if Detroit is right the big car will still be a U.S. commonplace. And the upgrading of compact-car equipment may help the industry to maintain its accustomed average revenue per car. The 1959 $36-billion market for new purchase, maintenance, and operation may rise above the $60-billion level by 1970. The basic factor in the expansion will be the doubling of the proportion of families with disposable incomes over $7,500. As the simultaneous improvement in highways and deterioration in public transport facilities make personal car use ever more attractive, the future of public transport on rails for private profit grows ever dimmer, while that for intercity air travel brightens measurably.

The final chapter examines what Americans do with the income that goes neither for taxes nor for housing, food, clothing, or transportation. There emerge strong general reasons supporting the earlier conclusion that consumers will show striking discernment and prudence in allocating their soaring incomes. Notwithstanding the popular notion that Americans are devoting ever more time and money to enjoyment of the good life, spending for recreation since World War II has barely kept pace with gains in consumer income. Leisure spending in general will be increased through the Sixties by rising incomes and by the growth of a new leisure class of retired men and women, but if it grows no more than disposable income that will be because too many other outlets make a stronger claim: medical care, private education, insurance, financial charges, and the like, which have been growing faster than recreation spending and which grow with special rapidity once the disposable family income tops $7,500. By 1970, for example, consumers will probably be laying out about $33 billion annually for medical care or about twice the current total. Spending for private education will at least double.

And "personal business"—insurance, interest on personal debt, and service fees to bankers, brokers, lawyers, etc.—will rise sharply from the current level of around $17 billion. In spite of the vast postwar democratization of the use of credit, personal savings have stabilized at a rate that should mean a rise from today's $24 billion to perhaps $37 billion in 1970. Already 12,500,000 Americans own stock and the practice of investing in securities will proliferate. Indeed, there is in the making a new kind of society, composed of employees vested with highly individualized, well-paid skills, freed by private and social insurance from fear of catastrophe, and possessed of a stake in the economy through security ownership.

TO WHAT END?

The prospect is vast. Assuming that the projections are translated into reality, what of it? Here it seems relevant to pose again a question raised in a FORTUNE editorial a year ago. After pointing out that the developments now forecast in this book were not to be realized without the investment of effort and common sense, the Editors asked: "What shall we do with the growth, what do we want to grow *into*?" And they offered this reply:

"Here is where American society possesses, to borrow a word from the Wall Street analysts, a truly enormous leverage. For in a society where the basic material wants have been met for almost everybody, and met in real abundance for many, relatively modest increases in income and leisure can produce quite startling changes in the whole style and quality of life. We have seen the process at work, almost year by year, all through the postwar period: in the tremendous growth of travel, sports, hobbies, do-it-yourself; the spread of popular interest in music, art, the theatre; the improvement of taste in houses and home furnishings; the pouring-out of energy for civic and charitable causes; the intense concern (credit Russian technological achievements with a large assist) for American education. Even the much-discussed 'religious revival' may be related in some degree to America's material triumphs. For there is nothing quite like material satisfaction for convincing a people that material satisfaction is not enough.

"The Sixties could be immensely exciting. The highest excitement will lie in Americans' decisions about the uses of abundance."

Markets of the Sixties

CHAPTER ONE

The Future Population "Mix"

THROUGH most of the 1950's the U.S. heard almost nothing but good news about its fabulous baby boom. The totals kept getting bigger and bigger, and the size of the totals was consistently interpreted as better and better news—for U.S. society in general, and for the U.S. economy in particular. The pessimism of the 1930's, which foresaw a "mature" U.S. economy enfeebled first by a static population, then a declining population, was in complete rout. The aura of high spirits enveloping the whole subject was aptly symbolized in an amiable little celebration—it consisted mostly of soft drinks and heady rhetoric—held by the Commerce Department in the fall of 1958, when its "census clock" proclaimed the population of the U.S. to be 175 million. (The clock is an electrical device, conspicuously situated in the lobby of the department's Washington headquarters, whose multicolored flashing lights tirelessly signal a birth every seven and a half seconds, a death every twenty seconds, the arrival of an immigrant every minute and a half, and the departure of an emigrant only once every twenty minutes, the net of all this being an increase in the population of one person every eleven seconds.) Considering the bullish construction that Commerce always puts on high population figures, it may seem surprising that the department let it

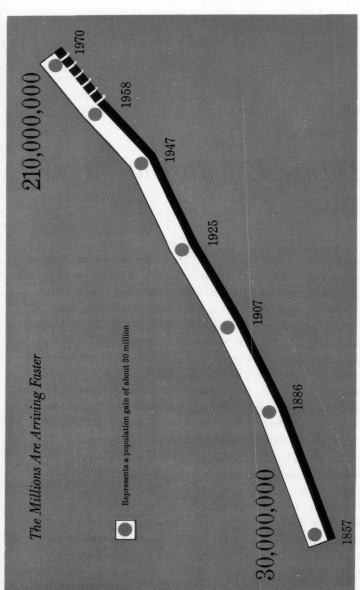

The Millions Are Arriving Faster

Just between 1947 and 1958 the U.S. grew by 30 million—which was the nation's total population on the eve of the Civil War. The U.S. will have grown by about 30 million more by the end of the 1960's, when the population should reach 210,000,000 or even more. Then the growth rate will accelerate again.

go at 175 million. Many of its experts in the Census Bureau believe this figure should be "adjusted for underenumeration"—a bureaucratic locution that refers to persons missed in the last census—and maintain that the U.S. actually had about 185 million people at the beginning of 1960, rather than the reported 179 million.

Just in the past two or three years, however, the ebullient talk about U.S. population growth has been invaded by an undertone of doubt. It is not that any sharp downward turn in the birth rate has suddenly come into view. The common assumption that U.S. population is going to grow very rapidly in the next twenty years is entirely accurate; if anything, the projections that most businessmen and market-research experts have been using are probably too conservative. What is somewhat changed is the tone of voice in which these prospective increases are discussed. Perhaps the turning point came one day when the sales manager of some Manhattan baby-food firm learned that the school taxes on his Long Island home were to be raised for the tenth year in a row. However it came about, there is a new disposition in the U.S. to look on people as being costs as well as customers. There is a new uncertainty whether all the squalling millions of new babies represent unalloyed good news.

THE VITAL STATISTICS

First let us consider the immediate trends in births, in marriages, in family growth, and in deaths.

The great postwar baby boom is leveling off—at a very high level. Nineteen fifty-eight was the first year in the past decade in which births did not set a new record high. The decline was by only 1.3 per cent, and there were still 4,250,000 babies born that year, about twice as many as were born annually through most of the 1930's. The decline was at least partly related to the 1957-58 recession, for births recovered all of the loss in 1959. Now, there are reasons for supposing that there will be a near plateau in the number of births for the next few years.

The next baby boom will start sometime soon after 1965. Like all population "schedules," this one has some large caveats attached: no prolonged depression, no major war, no major improvement in contraceptive devices. (For a report on current research into the prospects of improving contraception, and also minimizing sterility—oddly enough, the same steroid compounds show promise in both lines of inquiry—see "The Birth-Control 'Pill,'" in the April, 1958, FORTUNE. The article suggests that this research is not likely to lead to any widely marketed new products before 1970, at least.) If the birth levels are not depressed by any of these events, then the annual totals might well hit five million by 1970. The precise timing and magnitude of the next boom depend on the age at which the postwar children marry one another, and the rapidity with which they begin to raise families. It is hard to make specific predictions about either of these patterns, because the trends affecting them have, as we shall see, been fluctuating oddly in recent years.

More and more Americans get married, but the trend toward earlier marriages has finally been halted. One of the most interesting features, and principal causes, of the baby boom during the first postwar decade was the abrupt hastening of the age at which women married. Before World War II, about 53 per cent of all women between twenty and twenty-four were married; by 1955, the proportion was 71 per cent and has remained there. As FORTUNE pointed out in 1954 in *The Changing American Market,* this sharp decline in the age of marriage created a temporary increase in the number of new families—just as a sudden reduction in the draft age would create a temporary increase in the supply of draftable men—and when the age of marriage stopped declining, there would be a fall in the number of new families. FORTUNE erred in its 1954 assessment of the extent to which this would happen, and this error was in part responsible for FORTUNE's mistaken prediction that the baby boom would subside in the mid-1950's.

Actually, although the age at marriage has stopped falling, the number of marriages remains relatively high. A major reason is that the proportion of all women who marry continues to rise. In FORTUNE's 1954 analysis of population trends, it was remarked that 94 per cent seemed to be a kind of "practical upper limit" on the proportion of women in any generation who would ever marry. But today just about 94 per cent of women *in their early thirties* have married—and since the others' prospects are not totally dimmed at thirty-five, the limit plainly has to be raised, perhaps to as high as 98 per cent. (The proportion of men who ever marry appears, by the way, to be substantially lower than for women— a discrepancy explained by the interesting fact that divorced men

Ordering Children

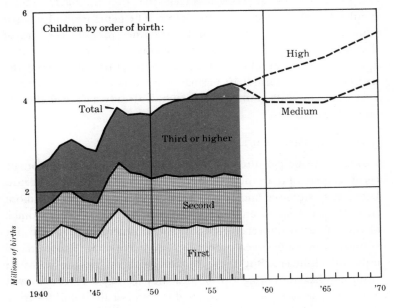

The first great wave of children, in the years just after World War II, con- sisted principally of first and second births to parents rather recently married; the "higher-order" births accounted for only about a third of the total then, and many of these—probably about a million in all—were babies "postponed" by families who had been unwilling to have children during the depression. In recent years the higher-order births have been almost half the total. The annual birth totals in the years ahead will probably fall between the two projections shown. (A low projection—which would pertain only to seriously depressed business conditions—was omitted.)

are more likely to marry single women than divorced women are to marry single men. The number of women who are divorced and have not remarried is 42 per cent higher than the number of men in that situation.)

American families are getting larger. This might seem, at first glance, to be a most unstartling piece of news, coming after thirteen years of a widely heralded baby boom. But actually it has not been at all clear, until quite recently, whether (*a*) Americans were increasing the size of their families, or (*b*) simply having small families earlier in life. Now it is clear that they are having larger families—and also having them earlier. The generation of women who were between forty-five and forty-nine (roughly the end of the childbearing period) in 1955 had averaged less than 2.3 children apiece. This was an all-time low, and apparently represented the nadir in the long-term drift to smaller families in the U.S. Women who were ten years younger in 1955 had already averaged slightly more children.

WHAT DO MOTHERS WANT?

But the principal question about family size in the 1960's concerns women who are now in their twenties. The generation now between twenty-five and twenty-nine has already averaged about two children apiece—an average considerably higher than women of this age group have ever attained in this century. In 1920, for example, women between twenty-five and twenty-nine had averaged only 1.6 children. But these women kept on having a lot of children after they were thirty, and they averaged three children apiece by the time they had reached the end of their childbearing years (around 1940). What are the prospects that today's young matrons will continue to enlarge their families during the 1960's? And how large will their families be?

Because these are momentous questions whose answers will provide important clues to the future size of the U.S. population, and to the dimensions of the U.S. market, some strenuous efforts to obtain preliminary answers have been made recently. The most ambitious of these efforts is a study begun in 1955 by Pascal

K. Whelpton and Arthur A. Campbell of the Scripps Foundation
for Research in Population Problems, in Oxford, Ohio, and
Ronald Freedman of the University of Michigan. Their findings,
which were published in 1959,* comprise the most exhaustive
report ever issued on the hopes, expectations, plans, and practices
of American wives and husbands. (But only wives were interviewed
for the study: the Whelpton team believes, in general, that wives

*Family Planning, Sterility, and Population Growth, McGraw-Hill.

How U.S. Family Size Is Changing:

The Actual and the Ideal

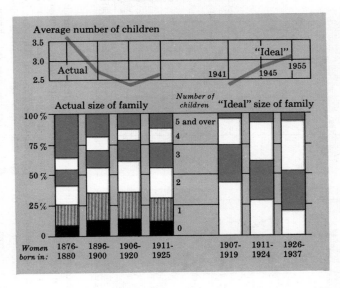

Among families that are "completed"—i.e., in which the mother has reached
her late forties—there has been a long-term decline in family size followed
by a recent turn upward. The turn reflects in part a rise in what women
consider the "ideal" number of children. Their ideals, measured in Gallup
Polls in 1941 and 1945, and in a 1955 survey supported by the Scripps
Foundation and the University of Michigan, show a shift away from two
and in favor of four.

Education and Income Make Less Difference...And Religion Makes More

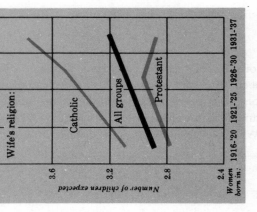

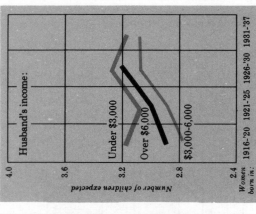

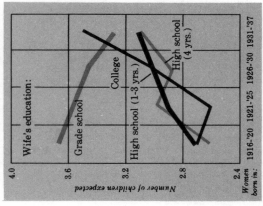

Historically, larger-than-average families have been associated in the U.S. with less-than-average education and income, rural background, unskilled occupations, etc. The 1955 survey undertaken by the Whelpton team confirmed from the size of existing families of all ages that these have indeed been the trends. But the sur-

vey also showed that the differentials seem to be rapidly disappearing, i.e., among the *younger* families they were dramatically reduced or nonexistent. The one important differential that persists is religious: Catholic families are still larger than Protestant families. Taking the two groups as a whole, it appeared that the Catholics

will average about "half a child" more than the Protestants. Moreover, the gap is likely to widen—to about one child per family—in the younger groups. (Survey data on Jewish families were not entirely adequate, but the figures suggested that these families will be smaller than the Protestant.)

THEY KNEW WHAT THEY WANTED

The Scripps-Michigan study of American family-planning habits is based on detailed interviews with 2,713 married women between the ages of eighteen and thirty-nine. (Women in this broad age band have had about 94 per cent of all children born in the U.S. in recent years.) The women interviewed were a "scientific probability sample," representative of the 17 million white married women in their age group. (The sample was unrepresentative only in being restricted to white women—who account for about 86 per cent of births in the U.S.) The questioning was conducted, in 1955, by women interviewers from the University of Michigan's Survey Research Center. (The cost of the survey was defrayed mostly by a grant from the Rockefeller Foundation.)

The interviewers reported that virtually all the wives they spoke to were remarkably cooperative, and were willing to discuss frankly even such intimate subjects as their contraceptive practices. (Many wives who freely answered several dozen questions about contraception said the interviewer was getting "too personal" when she asked questions about the family's income.) Some of the findings:

About 60 per cent of U.S. couples expect to have the number of children they want.

About one couple in six expects to have more children than it wanted, and about one in four to have fewer. About a third of all couples are limited, because of some physical impairment, in their ability to have children.

Ten per cent of the women were childless (after fifteen years or more of marriage), but almost all of these had wanted to have children. "Voluntary childlessness," the Scripps-Michigan scholars concluded, "is virtually nonexistent in this generation." The survey made it clear that ability to bear children begins to decline even in the twenties.

Nine per cent of all married women under forty have had an operation that precludes further conception.

About 70 per cent of American couples take some measures to limit the number of children they have, and another 10 per cent plan to do so in the future. These figures include Catholics using methods approved by the Church, i.e., the rhythm method and complete abstinence. (It appears that about 30 per cent of Catholic couples sometimes use methods not approved by the Church.) Principally because the use of contraception is so widespread, American wives are now having only a little over one-third as many children as they might. Students of fertility problems have estimated that a couple who married fairly early in life and took no steps at all to limit family size would bear, on the average, nine or ten children. In the U.S. the only cohesive group fitting this description are the Hutterites, a communal religious group living in South Dakota—and in fact averaging about nine children per couple.

Over one-quarter of all "planners" have had at least one unintended pregnancy. "Accidents," in fact, account for about 12 per cent of all births in the U.S., and for about 20 per cent of all fourth children. But children conceived accidentally are not usually "unwanted"; about two-thirds of them simply arrived ahead of plan.

give more thought to the subject, have more influence in the decision, and are, besides, more likely to be home when an interviewer calls.) Some of the attitudes encountered are charted on pages 7 and 8, and additional details are reported on page 9. At this point it is sufficient to note that the "medium forecast" of the Whelpton team points to a continued rise in the size of completed families: by 1965 there will be 2.5 children for the average woman between forty-five and forty-nine; by 1970 the average should be around 2.8; and in the years after that the average should level out at around 2.9. These figures are for *all* women, including those who are single and childless. (Children born to unmarried women apparently comprise about 5 per cent of all births in the U.S.—i.e., there are about 200,000 illegitimate births a year.) If only married women are considered, the final average should be a little over three. The "high forecast" puts the final average at 3.35.

The death rate is still falling sharply—or, at least, it would be falling sharply if the continuing gains in medicine were not being offset by the slow, steady increase in the proportion of Americans at higher age levels. Specifically, the crude death rate has declined only from 10.8 in 1940 to about 9.5 (per thousand). But if the U.S. today had the same age composition it had in 1940, then the rate would show a decline to 7.8. Recently the National Association of Insurance Commissioners issued revised mortality tables to account for the tremendous improvements in longevity since before World War II—improvements which, according to the chairman of the committee that worked out the new tables, were as great as all those between 1858 and 1941.

The recent reductions in the death rate have substantially raised life expectancy at all ages, but they do not seem to have cut into the differential between the male and female rates. In recent years there have been 105 boys born in the U.S. for every 100 girls; but the higher male death rate has brought the sexes to parity at about age twenty-five, and at higher ages there are more women than men. Women continue to have lower death rates than men at all ages, and at higher ages the differentials seem to be widening.

To summarize all these trends briefly, then, it appears that the U.S. is moving into a period in which the total number of births will probably remain around today's very high levels, and then (in the late 1960's) rise sharply. Women will continue to marry relatively young; they will continue to have children early and to have more of them than recent generations have had. And finally, there may be a small addition to total population gains from some further reductions in the death rates—which are likely to be reduced most at the higher ages.

The upshot of these trends is a probable slowing in the over-all rate of U.S. population growth—from about 1.6 per cent a year to about 1.4 per cent a year or a bit better for the 1960's. The recent growth rate is about the average for the world as a whole, but it is a fantastic rate in an urban, industrialized society like the U.S., and it was not matched in the 1950's by any European nation—not even, so far as one can tell from the sketchy figures that are available, by the Soviet Union. A 1.4 per cent growth rate, in other words, is not to be sneezed at: if that growth rate were maintained, U.S. population would double itself within the lifetime of most students now in high school. Even for the 1960's, it is important to note that the rate will be on a higher base, and so the total population increase (about 28 million) will equal the terrific gain for all of the 1950's. And as the baby boom of the late 1960's begins, the growth rate as well as the base will be rising; total births in the 1970's might well be 25 per cent higher than in the 1960's.

THE POWERFUL CHILDREN

The tremendous growth rates of recent years have wrought some profound social and economic changes. More are in prospect.

The most striking effect of the boom has been to make the U.S. a remarkably young nation and this in itself is a sharp reversal of historical experience. High proportions of children have almost

invariably marked societies rural or only semi-industrial in character; the advanced nations of the Western world have generally
been characterized by declining birth and death rates, both of
which tend to increase the average age of the population. But in
the U.S. today there are over 50 million children (i.e., fourteen and
younger), comprising over 30 per cent of the entire population—
a proportion not attained in this nation since around 1910. As
recently as 1940, children comprised only 25 per cent of the U.S.
population. Or, to look at the figures from another perspective,
children in the U.S. are now more numerous than the entire
population of the country was in 1881.

WHO'S IN CHARGE?

In many nations a sudden increase in the number and proportion of children might not be of such great consequence. But the
U.S., as many sociologists have pointed out for many years, is a
peculiarly child-oriented society—one in which children are treated
with a deference that many Europeans find astonishing. American
children spend money, or determine how it is to be spent, to a
degree unknown in any other part of the world; there is certainly
no other nation in which an appreciable amount of television time
(or television advertising) is pitched directly at children, nor is
there any other nation in which the "consumer preferences" of
six-year-olds are explored so rigorously. David Riesman has written,
with what appears to be a trace of sadness, that "the twentieth
century is not likely to be the Century of the Common Man, but
it may well be viewed as the Century of the Child. . . . The child
has been brought into the United Nations, given access to news
and opinion, and permitted to make his voice heard long before
he himself is ready to arm himself and take on adult . . . roles. The
paradoxical result is that one can go into many modern homes and
get the feeling that it is the parents, and especially the fathers,
who are marginal, who are in a precarious position, who are the
frightened conformists, while the children hold the strategic
initiative."

CHILDREN AS DURABLES

Another arresting, and perhaps more piquant, commentary on children was made by Gary S. Becker, a Columbia University economist. In a paper delivered at a conference sponsored by the National Bureau of Economic Research, Becker noted that, through much of history, children may have been considered, in effect, a "producer durable"—i.e., the net cost of raising them was less than the income they were able to provide their parents, and so they represented an intelligent economic investment.

In recent times, however, and especially in the U.S., children have become a "consumer durable"; their costs clearly outweigh any income they provide, and so, where parents have the freedom of choice implied in available contraceptives, the only reason to have any children is the pleasure ("psychic income") they afford. With rising incomes, parents can afford to spend more on children: by increasing either their quality (i.e., by spending more on their food, clothing, education, etc.) or their quantity, or both. Becker regards the prospect of qualitative improvement as the more likely in the U.S.—because, in general, American families passing up through the middle-income levels tend to want a few high-quality consumer durables, rather than a lot of low-quality durables. So far as children are concerned, this analysis was confirmed, in part, by the wives who, when interviewed by the Scripps-Michigan team, made such remarks as, "I can't see the right in bringing children into the world that you can't take care of properly."

THE NEW IDEAL

Becker's hypothesis also seems to be confirmed by the fact that the number of children American women regard as "ideal" seems to be stabilizing, despite the steady postwar rise in incomes. Previous Gallup polls showed an increase in the ideal from an average of 3.0 children in 1941 to 3.3 in 1945; the Scripps-Michigan survey raised this average only to 3.4. Even when these ideals are adjusted to exclude women who do not marry or who do not bear children (i.e., who are unable to translate the ideals into realities), the figures still suggest a new stabilization: the rise is from 2.4 children in 1941 to 2.8 in 1945, and to only about 3.0 in 1955. (See the chart on page 7.) This last ideal figure is very close to the 2.9 children per woman the Whelpton team anticipates as the future reality—barring, of course, some further drastic, unforeseeable changes in ideals—i.e., in the "style" of American family life. When women marry as early as they do today, they have, obviously, more years ahead of them in which to revise their ideals.

THE TEEMING TEENS

Between now and 1970, the emphasis on children in American life will become somewhat altered: we are moving now into an era in which marketing opportunities, school problems, and doubtless much of our cultural life will revolve around teen-agers. Since these children are already here, and just now beginning to enter the teen years, this is one population projection that can be ventured with complete confidence: the number of persons between fifteen and nineteen will increase by almost *63 per cent* by 1970. The magnitude of spending by teen-agers is largely a matter of conjecture, with estimates running mostly around $10 billion a year; however, it is no secret that their spending is almost entirely "discretionary," and is confined principally to nondurable consumer goods. The teen-age spender has traditionally been associated with low-cost products like soft drinks and phonograph records, but recently a number of major merchandisers—e.g., Shillito's department store in Cincinnati—have tried to expand the field by opening up "teen-age centers" in which the callow customers are exposed to a wider range of temptations, including relatively expensive items like overcoats.

Spending *for* teen-agers is still a much more important matter, however. One basic market that will certainly expand with the teen-age population is the food market; teen-agers are prodigious consumers of food, requiring, on the average, about 20 per cent more calories than normally active adults. A country teeming with

The Babies of the 1940's and the Households of the 1960's

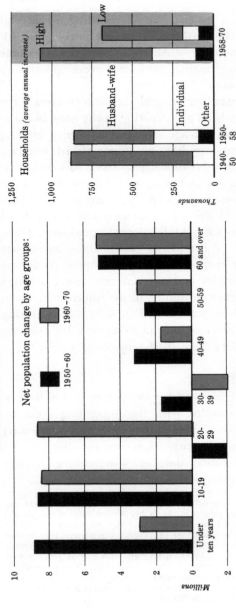

The age composition of the U.S. has been transformed in the last three decades. The sparseness of the generation born during the 1930's resulted in a decline during the 1950's of two million in the number of people in their twenties (bar below the line); in the 1960's people in their thirties will be scarcer. The sharp rise in births after the war will result, naturally, in a tremendous increase in the 1960's in the number of people in their twenties.

Households have recently been increasing by about 900,000 a year. During the 1940's almost all the gains were accounted for by new marriages. During the 1950's a considerable part of the increase was in "individual" households—i.e., persons living alone or with people who aren't relatives. Husband-wife households will increase more rapidly in the 1960's (high projection) if many of the postwar children marry one another early (i.e., when girls are about twenty).

teen-agers also implies a tremendous burgeoning of several "second" markets, e.g., the markets for second telephones, TV sets, and autos. George Romney of American Motors has become persuaded that the teen-age market presents a great opportunity for expanding small-car sales.

But perhaps the most startling thing about the teen-agers is the extent to which they have been participating in the baby boom as parents. Traditionally, the teen-age mother has been a kind of tragicomic figure in American life: an impoverished illiterate living in the backwoods who occasionally creates a fuss by marrying a man three times her age. A few squalid cases of this sort are still reported. But the modern prototype is the urban high-school girl of respectable antecedents who marries a boy a couple of years older, and sometimes has a child, before she graduates. These occurrences can scarcely be considered oddities any more: one eighteen-year-old girl in every four is married now, as is one seventeen-year-old in every six and one sixteen-year-old in every sixteen. Marriages and births to women in the fifteen-to-nineteen age group attained levels unprecedented in U.S. history during 1950-55; and though the rates are now tapering off a bit, they are still much higher than they were in the 1940's or earlier.*

THE BOOM IN HOUSEHOLDS

A continuing high rate of marriage for teen-agers and women in their early twenties, coupled with the impending great increase in the number of these women, has some very interesting implications for the U.S. economy—especially for those sectors of it, like housing and consumer durables, that depend for their growth on new household formation.

* There is, by the way, no very good evidence to support the widely held suspicion that teen-age marriages are related to the higher divorce rates of the postwar years. There is about one divorce today for every four new marriages (as against a ratio of about one to six in the 1920's and 1930's). But the present high rate of divorces is at least perceptibly lower than it was in the late 1940's (when, presumably, a lot of wartime marriages were breaking up); and this decline actually took place in the years just following the surge in teen-age marriages. It seems probable that the still-high level of divorces can be explained principally by higher postwar incomes: divorces are expensive, in several different ways, and a lot of Americans simply could not afford them in earlier years.

In recent years the number of households, now about 52 million, has been increasing by almost 900,000 a year. (See the chart on page 15.) The Census Bureau anticipates that this figure will decline sharply this year. The bureau's "medium-high" forecast shows the annual increase in households currently running at only about 600,000. But this dip will be short-lived—principally because the next couple of years will be the last in which the "hollow generation" born in the 1930's is coming of marriageable age, and because so many of the women in this generation have already married.

Beginning around 1963, there should be a dramatic increase in new household formation, with the annual gains averaging over a million in the remaining years of the 1960's, and total households reaching nearly 64 million by the end of 1970.

The character of U.S. households is likely to undergo some important changes over these years. Right now, a high proportion of households are headed by men or women in their "middle years"; over 60 per cent of household heads are between twenty-five and fifty-four. During the 1960's, this proportion will be reduced appreciably, for about three-quarters of the increase in households will be accounted for by those whose heads are at the younger and older ends of the age scale. One type of household that is almost certain to increase sharply is that headed by women living alone—chiefly widows and divorced women. All the census projections show a sharp increase in such households; and most of the increase is based on the assumption that wives will continue to outlive their husbands.

The upshot of these trends, so far as most marketing men are concerned, is that the new households formed during the 1960's will be somewhat smaller than the present average, and average income for these heads of households will also be somewhat smaller. The most rapidly expanding demand will be in the market for smaller homes and apartments; and so the demand for new appliances and home furnishings is likely to reflect the formation of these modest-sized homes.

THE PRODUCTIVITY DRAIN

The U.S. labor force showed only a modest growth in the 1950's, and what growth did occur stemmed less from population gains than from the entry of women into the job market. Specifically, the civilian labor force—which the Census Bureau defines as all civilians over fourteen who are either employed or looking for work—grew by five million, to about 68 million. Four million of this gain was represented by newly employed women; in fact, the increase in women workers was four times the increase in women keeping house during these years.

It is a noteworthy fact, and one of considerable economic import, that the increase in the labor force has been much less than the population increase during the 1950's: the figures are about 8 per cent and 15 per cent, respectively. This means, in effect, that consumers have been increasing more rapidly than producers, and to some extent draining away the productivity gains of U.S. industry. Furthermore, the women who have expanded the labor force have, on balance, a lower productivity than workers as a whole—or, to state the case somewhat more charitably, women workers have moved principally into white-collar occupations in which productivity is low.

The extent to which these trends will continue into the 1960's depends principally on whether women continue moving rapidly into the labor force, and on the specific job markets they move into. It is at least clear that our productive capacity will not grow much from population gains alone. Between 1960 and 1970, the number of Americans in the most productive ages—twenty to sixty—will not grow by much more than 10 per cent, against a likely increase of over 20 per cent for those older and younger.

FRIGHTENING PEOPLE

Among those who view our population growth, recent and prospective, with loud cries of alarm, three main lines of argument may be discerned. The first is a twentieth-century restatement and refinement of Thomas Malthus' familiar position, advanced in the late eighteenth century, that population growth tends to outrun natural resources. The second argument holds that a rapid growth rate requires an uncomfortably high level of savings and investment. Finally, there is a popular conviction, ordinarily based on personal experience rather than scholarship, that there is already too much crowding and congestion in modern life.

Unlike Malthus, who believed that only wars, famines, and pestilence could limit population growth, and that even these could leave mankind permanently condemned to a subsistence level, most of the "Neo-Malthusians" believe that birth control, if encouraged and practiced worldwide, can save mankind from itself. But most of the Neo-Malthusians are glum about achieving this salvation in the near term; and since, like Malthus, they regard population pressure as a major cause of wars, their pronouncements tend to be decidedly gloomy. Fairfield Osborn, head of the Conservation Foundation, has said, for instance, that "the hope for world peace is remote, or even unattainable, until the pressures resulting from population growth are relieved."

But the principal thrust of the Neo-Malthusians' argument is directed at the dwindling gap, as they see it, between our finite resources and the growing demands placed on them by population. Shortages of fuels, foods, and water are the ones most commonly discussed—often with an urgency that seems wildly inappropriate in the U.S. (In late 1957, Osborn warned that our farm surpluses would probably be "a thing of the past, even within the next few years"; the cost of farm price supports in fiscal 1959 hit an all-time high.) Except for water, which is in short supply right now in some heavily populated areas, none of these problems is apt to be serious during the 1960's. Most of the businessmen and farmers whose business it is to supply the U.S. with fuels, fibers, minerals, and food are still much more concerned about domestic oversupply and foreign competition than about shortages.

THE PRICE OF GROWTH

The argument that rapid population growth puts too heavy a strain on our capacity to save and invest has been put forcefully by Joseph Spengler, a Duke University economist. In a widely quoted article in the *Harvard Business Review* of January, 1956, Spengler ridiculed the view, popular among businessmen, that population growth is an important underpinning of our prosperity. The heart of his argument is this calculation: "When a country's population is growing 1.5 per cent per year, it must save and invest 6 to 7.5 per cent of its national income; otherwise the amount of productive wealth available per capita is likely to decline. Here is money being spent just to maintain a given living standard, money that in a stable population might go toward progress and even better consumption possibilities."

Other economists have quarreled with Spengler's arithmetic, and have pointed out—as he does himself—that the problem in the U.S. is long run rather than immediate. And in the long run, of course, it is possible that some decisive new technological breakthrough (e.g., the harnessing of fusion power) might require a thorough overhauling of all present calculations about U.S. investment policy.

Of all the fears expressed about U.S. population growth, the one about simple overcrowding commands the most popular support—doubtless because it is the only one visibly justified by present trends. Americans living in and around large cities are already overcrowded, or at least their schools, hotels, hospitals, subways, roads, restaurants, beaches, and other public facilities are often jammed uncomfortably. If more people imply a greater potential market for housing and automobiles, they may also imply worse slums and traffic jams.

IS CONNECTICUT CROWDED?

It is true that, by the standards of most highly developed nations, the U.S. is not overcrowded today, nor will it be in the 1960's. The U.S. could have a population of one billion—and would have, by around 2050, in the rather unlikely event that the growth rate of recent years were the norm in the next century (see the chart opposite)—and be no more crowded than Connecticut is now. Nevertheless, it is clear that *any* growth rate, if projected far

enough into the future, would imply insupportable crowding
eventually. By way of illustrating that fact, Harold J. Barnett of
Resources for the Future Inc. has cited a calculation which showed
a thousand-fold increase in world population by A.D. 8900—
even if the average growth rate until then were only 0.1 per cent.
Barnett also noted that if the 3 per cent rate of growth Malthus
feared had in fact been sustained, then eleven centuries from
now the world's population would actually weigh more than the

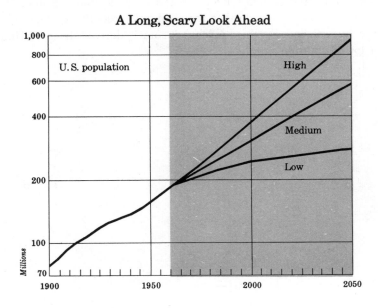

A Long, Scary Look Ahead

The notion that the U.S. might have a population of a billion by 2050—i.e.,
within the lifetime of some Americans now living—is one that some other
Americans now living may find a little terrifying. Pascal K. Whelpton and
Arthur A. Campbell, who prepared these projections for FORTUNE, think
it more likely that U.S. population in 2050 will be much lower, probably
under 600 million. This "medium" projection assumes that over the years
about 94 per cent of U.S. women will marry, on the average, and that they
will bear just about three children apiece—a figure based on the Scripps-
Michigan findings about future trends in family size. But the U.S. could
reach almost a billion by 2050 if these assumptions are raised just a little: if
98 per cent of women marry, and if they average 3.35 children apiece.

earth mass itself—an impossibility, of course, unless additional mass to provide food and materials for this vast additional population were imported from elsewhere in the universe.

Of course, in any calculation about the "optimum" population of the U.S., the relevant criteria are not only economic—not even when that word is understood to include the whole problem of crowding. It might be that Americans would finally decide that rapid population growth threatened their living standard—but still want rapid growth for other reasons, e.g., military reasons. Or they may simply decide that the economic costs of rapid growth are outweighed by the "psychic income" derived from having a lot of children around.

CHAPTER TWO

The 1960's: A Forecast
of the Technology

IN THE decade of the Sixties man will finally soar beyond the thin film of the earth's atmosphere in which he and all his ancestors have been imprisoned for a billion years or more. History will record the event with appropriate wonder and solemnity. Before 1965, almost surely, one of the satellites thrown aloft by Project Mercury, or its Soviet counterpart, will carry not a mouse or a monkey but a human being. The next goal will be placing a man on the moon. Whether anyone lands there before December 31, 1969, is relatively unimportant. Men will build the great moon rocket as soon as their technology permits and take off as soon as their curiosity drives them to it. No one can believe that the machinery or the desire will long be lacking.

Meanwhile, throughout the Sixties, space technology will keep feeding back a wealth of engineering ideas that can be put to use in hundreds of unforeseen ways throughout industry. Like the atomic-energy quest, the space venture will confront scientists and engineers with a host of new and baffling problems. The effort to solve them will broaden and deepen man's understanding of nature and extend his control over the materials and forces of the physical world.

	1950-52	1953-54	1955-56	1957-59
Basic Science	Discovery of colliding galaxies ('51) Discovery of radio emission from cold hydrogen in space ('51) *Total synthesis of cortisone ('51)* New estimates doubling size and age of universe ('52) Discovery of brain's arousal mechanism ('52)	*Total synthesis of oxytocin, pituitary-gland hormone ('53)* *Proposed structure of DNA, key genetic substance (U.S.-U.K., '53)* *Detailed structure of insulin (U.K., '54)* Discovery of reward centers in brain ('54)	Further upward revisions in size and age of universe ('55; revisions continuing) Creation of antiproton ('55) Creation of antineutron ('56) Confirmation of neutrino's existence ('56) *Total synthesis of reserpine, hypotensive and tranquilizer ('56)*	Fall of parity principle ('57) Discovery of cold fusion ('57) Creation of element 102, nobelium ('57) Discovery of intense radiation zone in nearby space ('58)
Inventions and Experimental Achievements	Junction transistor ('51) "Area rule" for design of supersonic aircraft ('52) Bubble chamber for tracking elementary particles ('52) Heart-lung machine used on a human ('52)	Bevatron in operation ('54) Solar battery ('54) Maser, ultrasensitive electronic amplifier ('54)	*VTOL (vertical take-off and landing) jet aircraft ('55)* First "proof" of rainmaking ('55) Cryotron, low-temperature electronic switch ('56) *Experimental use of oral contraceptives ('56)*	Thermionic (heat to electricity) converter ('57) VTOL jet "tail-sitter" ('57) Sun photographs from unmanned balloon ('57) *Test-tube creation of DNA-like molecules ('58)* VTOL flying "jeep" ('58)
"Practical" and Commercial Achievements	Orlon ('50) Extensive cloud seeding ('50) Antibiotics used to stimulate animal growth ('50) Coast-to-coast TV ('51) Large electronic computer delivered to Bureau of Census ('51) Start of "automation" in auto industry ('51) Zone-refining of metals ('52)	Dacron ('53) Wide-screen movies ('53) Chemical "milling" of metals ('53) Color TV ('53) Tranquilizers ('54) First large computer delivered to industry ('54) Silicon transistor ('54)	*Mass use of Salk polio vaccine ('55)* All-transistor radios ('55) First turboprops in U.S. ('55) Polyurethane foams ('55) Weather forecasting by computer ('55) Transatlantic telephone cable ('56) *Television tape recording ('56)*	Linear polyethylene ('57) *Synthetic diamonds ('57)* Use of giberellin in agriculture ('58) Stereophonic records ('58) Super insulators for storing liquefied gases ('58) *Transatlantic jet service ('58)*
Nuclear Technology	First electric power from U.S. reactor ('51)	First demonstration of fuel "breeding" ('53) Boiling-water reactor ('53)	First nuclear power to a U.S. utility ('55) *Disclosure of U.S.S.R. research to control thermonuclear reactions ('56)*	Portable package power plant ('57) First U.S. underground nuclear explosion ('57) Large Shippingport power reactor in operation ('57)
Military and Space Technology	*First U.S. thermonuclear explosion ('52)*	*First U.S.S.R. thermonuclear explosion ('53)* Nike missile ('53) First supersonic flight by a military aircraft ('53)	*Nuclear-powered submarine ('55)*	Completion of DEW Line ('57) First U.K. thermonuclear explosion ('57) *First Russian ICBM; Sputniks I and II ('57)* *First U.S. satellites and ICBM ('58)* Flight of X-15 ('59) *Russian unmanned probe to moon ('59)* *Russian and U.S. operational ICBM's ('59)*

Key: [ ] Totally unpredictable   Italics: Achieved sooner than expected

Two fabulous decades of science and technology, the one closing and the one just beginning, are charted above in retrospect and prospect. The left-hand portion of the chart records, primarily, the more memorable American achievements of the Fifties, but also includes several foreign accomplishments of outstanding significance. In all, fourteen of the achievements listed (tinted) were totally unpredictable; twenty-one

And a Prospectus for the Sixties

EARLY SIXTIES	MID-SIXTIES	LATE SIXTIES	LONG SHOTS FOR THE LATE SIXTIES
Total synthesis of chlorophyll	Radiotelescopes probe "edge" of observable universe	Total synthesis of insulin	Comprehensive theory of elementary particles Test-tube creation of a living cell Detailed understanding of the aging process
Completion of 25-bev accelerators at Brookhaven and Geneva Completion of super computers Animal kept alive with internal artificial heart Machine translation of languages Predetermination of sex in humans	Borehole to "Moho," boundary between earth's crust and interior	Controlled mutations in plants and animals	Computers with brainlike attributes Substantial control over tornadoes and hurricanes
Electronic telephone exchange Ultrasonic dishwasher Applications of fuel cell Appliances using thermoelectricity	New family of ultrahigh-capacity computers Significant advances in weather forecasting Panel lighting for homes Gas-turbine trucks and buses Introduction of irradiated foods VTOL or STOL aircraft for short-haul routes	Major advances in treating atherosclerosis, cancer, mental illness Major advances in structural materials: polymers, metals, ceramics Electronic safety devices for cars and highways Mural television	Cure for cancer 2,000-mph VTOL airliner Small VTOL flying car Accurate ninety-day weather forecasts Fresh water from sea water at acceptable cost
Nuclear-power merchant vessels, aircraft carriers, and aircraft	Experimental use of nuclear explosives for nonmilitary purposes Demonstration of 100-million-degree fusion temperatures	Direct conversion of nuclear energy to electric power (experimental)	Nuclear power competitive in most of U.S. Atomic explosives in practical use Fusion power technically feasible
Unmanned probes to Mars and Venus Satellites as navigation and meteorological aids Million-pound-thrust rocket engine	Man in satellite and return VTOL military aircraft Anti-missile missile	Communications using satellites Man in flyable space ship	Man on the moon Rocket mail and freight service

(italics) were achieved sooner than most experts would have expected.

The right-hand section of the chart attempts a forecast for the Sixties, but as the Fifties have proved, the hazards of prophecy are formidable. It is predictable, however, that a tremendous R. and D. effort will be aimed at reaching the goals listed at far right as "Long Shots for the Late Sixties."

It is this growing mastery of energy and matter that gives the American market so much of its prodigious variety and thrust. Some of the topics discussed here may seem remote from the market place, but the gap between a laboratory achievement and commercial application is getting shorter and shorter.

The market's future vitality is guaranteed by the huge sums—federal and private—being invested in research and development. In 1950 the nation's R. and D. expenditure was less than $3 billion. In 1958 total R. and D. spending (including all industrial and nonindustrial research) had zoomed to $10 billion, with half the funds provided by the government. For the entire Fifties, the R. and D. expenditure added up to $60 billion. In the Sixties the U.S. will easily spend twice that sum. This is exponential growth in precisely that area of human activity that exerts the greatest impact on the economy and on society as a whole.

The nation's R. and D. outlay has grown so huge, indeed, that one leading economist, Fritz Machlup, has suggested that part of the money might more profitably be spent elsewhere—on education, for example. There is no doubt, in any case, that the division of the total expenditure between basic research and development has become inexcusably lopsided. Out of 1958's $10 billion, no more than $750 million went for basic research in all fields—and even this sum was heavily skewed in the direction of nuclear and subnuclear physics. Meteorology, geophysics, oceanography, and the various life sciences (e.g., biochemistry, genetics, psychology) have all been seriously underfinanced. Leading American scientists are determined to see that U.S. science develops in a much more balanced fashion over the next decade than it has in the past. This determination was expressed in a report conveyed to the White House in late 1958 by the President's former Special Assistant for Science and Technology, James R. Killian Jr. The report offered thoughtful recommendations for strengthening U.S. science, many of which were later acted upon by the Administration.

If fundamental research is indeed pursued more diligently in the years immediately ahead than in the past, the Sixties can scarcely fail to produce more scientific surprises than the Fifties. Both science and technology, however, present a curious mixture of the predictable and the unpredictable. The business of science is discovery, and discovery requires penetration of the unknown. But as the accompanying chart indicates, basic science also includes "discovery" of such things as the antiproton, the antineutron, and the neutrino, which had been predicted to exist. On the other hand, technology is not easily predictable just because it rests on the application of established science. As the chart also shows, the technology of the Fifties—both commercial and military—contained many surprises. Ten years ago few scientists expected a U.S. thermonuclear explosion as soon as November, 1952, and the U.S. was totally unprepared for a Soviet duplication of the feat less than a year later.

In nonmilitary technology, some developments moved faster, others slower than expected. Ten years ago it was clear that electronics was on the threshold of great advances. The transistor had been announced in 1948, and the first electronic computer— the ENIAC—two years earlier. On balance, the transistor came along at just about the rate that cautious engineers would have predicted—meaning the transistor had its troubles—but the commercial and industrial demand for computers outstripped all sober estimates. In 1949 anyone could have predicted color TV in the Fifties, but many experts were betting on the wrong system and the impatience of the public for color was grossly overestimated. Ten years ago few U.S. airline executives foresaw that the jet age was so close at hand, and that jet transports making scheduled flights in 1958 would have greater range and payload than any prototype jet bomber flying in 1949. And in 1949 only science-fiction fans—and a few scientists—were prepared for artificial satellites in the Fifties. Russia's launching of Sputnik I on October 4, 1957, was the most stunning technological news of the decade.

On retail shelves there was nothing so unexpected as Sputnik, unless it was the tranquilizers, which suddenly appeared in drugstores in the mid-Fifties. The tranquilizers were first reported in medical journals in 1954 and within three years had been used by at least twenty million "normal" Americans—with precisely what benefit no one will ever know. Some anxieties, no doubt, were allayed, but the greatest impact of the new drugs seems to have been in the mental hospitals, where the number of patients has been declining since 1956.

In consumer goods of the more tangible sort, the Fifties held few surprises. In 1949, Americans could already buy TV sets, air conditioners, dishwashers, clothes dryers, power lawn mowers, high-fidelity phonographs, LP records, tape recorders, Polaroid Land cameras, and automobiles with automatic transmissions. It is true, of course, that the Fifties added power steering (1952) and power brakes ('53) to the automobile, and stereophonic sound ('58) to phonograph records, but these were relatively modest accomplishments, from a technical point of view.

THE INVISIBLE FRONTIER

It would be wrong to conclude, however, that the R. and D. billions of the Fifties did little more than polish existing products and produce new military weapons. What did happen was that industrial technology deepened its insights and changed its emphasis from the obvious and macroscopic to the subtle and submicroscopic. Manipulation of the invisible has always characterized research in chemicals, drugs, petroleum, and electronics, but even these industries have found exciting new frontiers at the level of precise molecular and interatomic design.

Advances at this deep level have already had a profound effect on the market and will have still more in the future. In 1949 there was only one wholly synthetic fiber of consequence, nylon. Today there are a variety of synthetics: the acrylics Orlon, Acrilan, Dynel, Verel, Creslan, Darvan, and Zefran, and the polyesters Dacron, Kodel, and Teron. These fibers have transformed whole industries. In the Fifties, polyethylene (first produced in volume in World War II) became a household word. Latex-based paints, introduced in 1949, ran off with the do-it-yourself market; fiberglass revolutionized pleasure-boat building; and handsome, long-wearing vinyl plastics cut sharply into the market once dominated by linoleum and asphalt tiles.

The transistor provides a similar example of what to expect as technology deepens its insights. By itself, the transistor does nothing that could not be done before. But because of its tiny size, ruggedness, and low power consumption, its influence has now extended to every corner of electronics. All-transistor hearing aids were on the market by 1953 and all-transistor radios by 1955. During the Sixties there will be more and more transistors in the home, in the family car, and elsewhere, doing jobs for which vacuum tubes are hopelessly impractical. The tremendous impact of the transistor on the telephone system was described in detail in "Tomorrow's Telephone System," FORTUNE, December, 1958.

The lesson in all this is immensely reassuring. Manufacturers of consumer products enjoyed a fabulous decade in the Fifties without a single innovation comparable to the automobile (which became commercially important about 1910), the radio (early 1920's), mechanical refrigerator (mid-1920's), automatic washing machine (late 1930's), or home air conditioning and TV (late 1940's). The Sixties may fail to bring forth any single new consumer product (none is in sight) of impact comparable to the automobile, radio, or TV, and still be a decade of huge economic growth.

Meanwhile, during the Sixties, Americans may show an increasing desire for technological advances other than the kind that can be bought at retail. Indeed, most Americans doubtless would prefer for 1969 a cure for cancer rather than a family flying car; clean air to breathe rather than a Picturephone, carrying images as well as speech; many might even prefer a "push button" in Washington to prevent tornadoes and control hurricanes, rather than a push button to perform every imaginable household chore. And, in fact, the first choice in each pair may represent the more readily attainable scientific or technological goal in the light of present knowledge.

THE ULTRASONIC KITCHEN

The Sixties should make crystal clear to every industrial research laboratory—if any are still in doubt—that there is no way to isolate technology from basic science. The two form a continuous spectrum ranging from the most prosaic product engineering to the most esoteric basic research. In the pages that follow, we shall work our way backward from the consumer market to basic technology, thence to outer space and basic science, and conclude with the outlook in health and medicine.

During the Sixties the technological subtlety of synthetic polymers and transistors will begin to be felt in a wide variety of consumer products. There will be home appliances using ultrasonics, refrigerators with no moving parts, and lighting systems without heated filaments or glowing gases. Most of the big electrical and electronics firms are working intensively on one or more of these developments, and there should be important commercial results in the early Sixties.

Ultrasonics—the use of sound vibrations above the audible range—is already at work in industry solving difficult cleaning problems. Westinghouse indicates that an ultrasonic dishwasher— employing an ultrasonic generator or vibrator immersed in a detergent bath—will appear in the early Sixties, and presumably other firms are working toward the same goal. Ultrasonic clothes washers should follow soon after.

HOT AND COLD LIGHT

"Electronic" or "solid-state" refrigerating devices should reach the market within the next year or two. They will exploit the fact that an electric current will force heat to flow from one side of a metallic junction to the other, if the junction is formed of suitable materials of the semiconductor family. In this way heat can be driven out of a box that is to be cooled. Both R.C.A. and Westinghouse have built experimental electronic refrigerators with capacities of four to ten cubic feet. But the method's immediate usefulness should lie in smaller special-purpose cooling units—possibly portable and battery operated.

In 1958 Westinghouse demonstrated a simple, plug-in wall panel that could heat or cool and also provide light, using electroluminescence. This lighting method employs special phosphorescent substances that glow when energized by electricity. The three-way panel may be many years off, but panel room lighting should be moving swiftly by the mid-Sixties. By the late Sixties, electroluminescence should lead to mural TV screens of almost any desired size for both black-and-white and color.

ELECTRONIC HIGHWAY SAFETY

Here are a few other commercial developments that look reasonably certain for the early and mid-Sixties:

All-electronic cooking ranges. (In early models, the penetrating radar waves cooked the inside of the roast without browning the surface.)

Tiny high-fidelity speakers of exceptional range and brilliance.

Gas-turbine trucks. But unless Detroit is engineering a massive ruse, enthusiasm for a gas-turbine automobile has seriously waned. Reason: too costly.

Perhaps the mid-Sixties will also see the appearance of foods that have been either sterilized or pasteurized by gamma rays or electron irradiation.

The late Sixties may bring electronic safety devices for automobiles which will warn of cars approaching from behind or that a car ahead is being overtaken too fast. Automatic car guidance on an electronic highway is also being studied, but its appearance in the Sixties seems unlikely.

PLASTICS THAT PRODUCE WATER

During the Sixties much research will go into methods for obtaining fresh water from saline waters, either from sea water itself, or from brackish waters of lesser salinity. Congress has authorized the Department of the Interior to spend up to $10 million building five experimental desalting plants, two of which at least will have a capacity of a million gallons a day.

In 1959, Coalinga, California, operated the first desalting plant to provide municipal water in the U.S. The 28,000-gallon-per-day plant, built by Ionics, Inc., Cambridge, Massachusetts, uses plastic membranes that let fresh water pass through but not salt. The plant processes brackish water from wells. Coalinga has been paying $7 a thousand gallons for fresh water carted in by truck. The new plant produces water for about $1.10 per thousand gallons and Ionics says the process would produce water for as little as 40 cents per thousand gallons if applied on a grand scale. However, neither the Ionics process nor any other yet tested will desalt *sea* water for much under $2 per thousand gallons. Price of most municipal water in the U.S.: under 25 cents per thousand.

ELECTRICITY WITHOUT WHEELS

While municipal water companies are watching the progress of desalting, electric utilities will be following closely the progress being made in thermoelectricity. This process turns heat directly into electricity by exactly reversing the principle of the electronic refrigerator.

Westinghouse has developed special alloys and ceramic-like materials that convert heat into electricity with claimed efficiencies of 10 per cent and with 15 per cent in sight. While 10 per cent is only one-quarter the efficiency achieved in large steam-power plants, it compares favorably with that of small prime movers and auxiliary power plants. Westinghouse expects to show in the Sixties that thermoelectricity will be economic as a standby power source in large power plants. Almost certainly the new techniques will be used within the decade to obtain power directly from a nuclear reactor.

G.E. does not share Westinghouse's enthusiasm for thermoelectricity, but has conceived a rival principle embodied in a "thermionic converter." In this device, electrons "boiled out" of a heated metal surface provide an electric current.

Still a third method of generating electricity from a device containing no moving parts is under development in the "fuel cell." A clean fuel such as hydrogen or alcohol is passed over a catalytic surface where combustion occurs with a direct yield of electric current. Union Carbide has built cells of 1-kw output that have the remarkable efficiency of 75 per cent. Possible early application: supplying electric power at remote military bases.

The efficiency of the fuel cell is so high that it could serve as the equivalent of a very-high-capacity storage battery. The British have suggested that electric-generating stations might produce and store hydrogen (by decomposing water) during periods of low power demand. The peak power demands could be met by burning the hydrogen in fuel cells. Such possibilities will be carefully explored during the Sixties.

Meanwhile, U.S. utilities will be participating in the nation's costly atomic-power program. Proof that the atom can compete with fossil fuels in most of the U.S. is no better than a long shot for the late 1960's.

WHEN WILL THE ATOM PAY?

After years of optimistic speeches and press releases, the AEC disclosed in late 1958 that it had begun an "agonizing" reappraisal to learn why the nuclear-power program was lagging. This news was given to the Atomic Industrial Forum by AEC Commissioner John F. Floberg, who pointed out that utilities were currently building 318 conventional generating stations, compared to a handful of nuclear-power plants.

Modern steam plants, even those not especially favored by nearby coal supplies, can produce power for 6 to 7 mills per kwh. Estimated cost of power from the most efficient nuclear-power plants now building in the U.S. is 50 to 100 per cent higher, with large uncertainties as to actual fuel and maintenance costs. The principal uncertainties are two: how much power can actually be obtained from a given type of reactor, and how long will the fuel last? The Sixties should answer these questions for the several types of plants now building and under design.

"By any scheme now in sight," says W. E. Shoupp, technical director of the atomic-power department of Westinghouse, "6-mill nuclear power is just not in the cards. Eventually, conventional power and nuclear will cross in the region of 8 to 10 mills."*

The "agonizing" reappraisal of nuclear-power progress is being accompanied by a similar appraisal of the outlook for early harnessing of fusion or thermonuclear energy. The Second Conference on Peacetime Uses of Atomic Energy, held at Geneva in August of 1958, brought out a spectacular display of U.S. apparatus for fusion research. But the conference papers on fusion disclosed that Russian, British, and U.S. scientists are all up against thorny problems for which no answers are in sight. The basic difficulty is that the plasma—a hot, rarefied "soup" of dissociated deuterium nuclei and electrons—resists heating to fusion temperatures by undergoing oscillations that radiate energy away from the plasma at a high rate. "We'll be lucky now," says one fusion expert, "if we can just get some 100-million-degree plasma to study, without worrying whether we can get any net energy out of it."

Edward Teller, credited with the stroke of invention that made the U.S. H-bomb feasible, has said that the only way he sees to get useful power from the fusion reaction in the near future is to explode an H-bomb underground. The heat released into the earth could then be extracted in the form of steam and used to generate power. Teller also suggests using nuclear explosions to create new harbors, to release oil from shale and tar sands, and even to create vast aquifers to serve as underground reservoirs for river water that would otherwise flow to the sea. The AEC is exploring such possibilities in Project Plowshare.† Routine use of nuclear explosives can be considered no more than a very long shot for the late 1960's.

* The outlook in Britain is considerably different, according to Sir John Cockroft, of the U.K. Atomic Energy Authority. His forecast: "We expect nuclear power to cost the same as coal power by about 1963, and to be 30 per cent cheaper than coal power by 1970." The predicted 1970 cost of U.K. atomic power: $5\frac{1}{2}$ mills.

† Harry Wexler, director of meteorological research for the U.S. Weather Bureau, has proposed a method of changing the world's weather by "the explosion of ten really 'clean' hydrogen bombs" in the Arctic Ocean. This would throw enough steam into the air to produce a vast "quasipersistent" ice cloud that would blanket most of the Arctic north of latitude 65°. The result: melting of the arctic icecap; milder winters from latitude 35° to 50°N (the northern two-thirds of the U.S.); but heavier winter snows—reminiscent of the ice age—between latitude 50° and 65°N (meaning much of Canada, Europe, and Russia); and a rise of two to five degrees Fahrenheit in equatorial regions. Wexler's conclusion: "The cure [may be] worse than the ailment."

NEEDED: BETTER METALS

If any one factor were to be singled out as holding back progress in atomic power and other advanced technologies, it would be lack of suitable engineering materials—particularly, metals and alloys. The materials situation is regarded as so serious that a number of worried scientists have urged that the government establish a major new research institute wholly devoted to the problem. The proposal has been studied by the President's Science Advisory Committee. There are, however, serious objections to the institute concept, the chief being that faster progress could be made by supporting more materials research in universities, in existing institutes, and in government laboratories.

The problem in metallurgy is easy to state: there has as yet been no major breakthrough in metals comparable to the transistor in electronics, nylon in high polymers, or nuclear fission in energy creation. The quest for newer and better alloys goes on in empirical fashion, with relatively little scientific understanding to quicken the search. The result is that each year alloys get a little stronger and tougher, a little more heat resistant, and sometimes a little lighter, but no sensational advance can be expected until development is guided by deeper scientific understanding.

There is good evidence that the Russians are seeking this understanding more diligently than anyone else in the world. In the U.S. the metallurgical industry has never felt inclined to support very much basic research. As a result, some of the country's most promising metals research is going on at General Electric, Westinghouse, du Pont, Union Carbide, and at a few government laboratories, notably those of the AEC. Out of this, eventually—though perhaps not in the Sixties—will come the science needed for some real metallurgical progress. Better metals would lead to cheaper electric power, to lower capital costs in oil and chemical plants (which use lots of pressure vessels), and to wholly new processes using high pressures and temperatures.

In the field of high-polymer chemistry, another aspect of materials technology, the U.S. has relatively great strength. The

Fifties closed with the tough new linear polyethylenes in volume production, and with polypropylene not far behind. These two plastics derive their strength and toughness from new principles of molecular ordering discovered in the U.S. and Europe within the last six or seven years. Polymer experts believe that the full impact of these discoveries will not be felt until later in the Sixties, when plastics will take over more and more jobs now performed by metals.

COMPUTERS: NO LIMIT IN SIGHT

It is safe to say that few technical programs in the Sixties will be held back by lack of suitable electronic mechanisms. Solid-state devices (transistors, diodes, cryotrons, masers, magnetic amplifiers and memory devices, and new "parametric" amplifiers) will increase the speed, sensitivity, reliability, and versatility of electronic equipment of all types. At the same time the urge—and the means —to make everything smaller and smaller will continue unabated.

R.C.A. has a sizable Signal Corps contract to built electronic circuits in the form of "micro-modules," built up from "micro-wafers" 0.3 inch square and 0.01 inch thick. A cubic-foot box would contain 600,000 circuit parts, or enough to build 1,000 television sets. Pilot lines making micro-modules should be running in 1962. Looking further ahead, R.C.A. is working on methods for packing the equivalent of six million circuit parts into a cubic foot.

At M.I.T., researchers hope within the Sixties to produce cryotrons—electronic devices useful for switching and memory storage —that are no bigger than a grain of photographic emulsion. If successful, they will be able to lay down several million cryotron elements within a square centimeter, and a stack a centimeter high might contain billions.

Such fantastic concentrations, inconceivable a few years ago, make it realistic for the first time to speak of a computer rivaling in complexity the human brain, with its ten billion switching and memory units called neurons. Against the day when such a computer may become available, information theorists and neurophysiologists are cooperating in an effort to unravel the brain's own "wiring" diagram and programing scheme so they can endow computers with brainlike attributes. This is a mind-numbing long shot for the late 1960's.

Pernaps equally startling is the growing belief of some physicists and mathematicians that information theory and computer theory will shed new light on human behavior. "The effort to translate languages by machine," says E. R. Piore, I.B.M.'s director of research, "is forcing us to a deeper understanding of language and its meanings. Since language and human behavior are so profoundly associated, better understanding of language should have important implications for the social sciences."

THE NEW TOOLS OF RESEARCH

The point where technology leaves off and science begins—the distinction between applied and basic research—has become increasingly fuzzy. During the Sixties it will become fuzzier yet, for the great research tools that will dominate physical science in the years ahead will be engineering marvels first and research tools second.

Three prodigious new research instruments are now taking shape, and like Galileo's telescope they cannot fail to provide sights and insights impossible to predict in advance. The powerful new tools are: the 25-bev (billion-electron volt) accelerators now under construction at Brookhaven, New York, and at the CERN laboratory in Geneva; the huge new radio telescopes being built at several sites in the U.S.; and, finally, the satellites and space probes that will be launched by the dozens in the decade ahead.

During the Fifties, scientists reaped a rich harvest from earlier counterparts of each of these three tools: from the Brookhaven Cosmotron (2.5 bev) and Berkeley Bevatron (6 bev); from the 200-inch optical telescope on Palomar, and early radio telescopes; and from high-altitude rocket and balloon flights.

The bevatron produced, on order and as predicted, the previously unobserved particles of antimatter, the antiproton and antineutron. And it provided a rich profusion of puzzling K-meson tracks that led, in 1957, to the overthrow of the physicists' sacred principle of parity. (See "Physics: The Magnificent Riddle," FORTUNE, January, 1957.)

The great Palomar telescope, in less than ten years, has doubled and redoubled the estimated size and age of the universe. And, in collaboration with radio telescopes, it has produced the first evidence of galaxies meeting in titanic collision. Finally, the pre-Sputnik rockets carried measuring instruments to the edge of the earth's atmosphere for the first time. They provided brief tantalizing glimpses of a new frontier of discovery.

PEERING TOWARD INFINITY

The 25-bev machines, scheduled for operation in 1960, should help to establish whether the inventory of elementary particles is now complete at thirty, or whether still more remain to be discovered. The machines, acting like supermicroscopes, will also provide clearer "images" of the elementary particles and thereby guide theorists to a new understanding of the baffling subnuclear universe. Out of the interplay between experiment and theory may come new concepts upsetting all present notions of time and space. But many thoughtful physicists believe that a comprehensive theory of the elementary particles—comparable to quantum theory of the Twenties—will still be eluding man's grasp ten years from now.

Most astronomers are confident, however, that powerful new radio telescopes will be probing—and, perhaps, defining—the "edge" of the observable universe by the mid-Sixties. Astrophysical theory holds that the galaxies in the universe are rushing outward in all directions, and that the more distant the galaxy the faster it will appear to be receding from the earth. Presumably there are galaxies receding so fast that their light (or radio emission, which is the same thing) can never reach the earth. Thus there is an "edge" to the universe beyond which man cannot hope to see.

The discoveries that will be made in the Sixties by satellites and by unmanned space vehicles probing to the moon, Mars, Venus, and to the vicinity of the sun are truly impossible to predict. Whether the probes will detect life of any sort, even the most primitive, is a matter of speculation.

When the satellites are big enough to carry telescopes, of perhaps twenty-inch aperture, they should provide stunning celestial photographs, having a clarity unattainable from earth. And the first view of the earth itself—suspended in space, radiant in the sunlight—will provide the most breath-taking scene ever photographed. It will be hanging on classroom walls in 1969.

THE PAYOFF FOR EARTH

The space vehicles should have an impact almost immediately on daily life. Equipped with simple radio beacons operating on solar batteries, satellites will soon be serving as navigation aids. Their precisely calculated orbits will be handily available in almanacs. Equally soon, satellites will keep the whole world's weather under surveillance. They will transmit to earth simple pictures of shifting cloud patterns, together with a detailed energy survey, showing how much of the sun's heat is absorbed and how much is reflected back into space. Once information of this sort has been correlated with the earth's weather, meteorologists should make dramatic improvements in their forecasting techniques. A target for the late 1960's: accurate ninety-day weather forecasts.

How great a role satellites may play in worldwide communications is the subject of vigorous debate among experts. Some regard the satellites as the cheapest, most effective means for achieving high-capacity international transmission of radio and TV programs, along with private telephone and telegraph messages. They point out that the first transatlantic telephone cable (1956) cost $40 million and could carry only thirty-six conversations (though this is now being raised to seventy-two). To establish a satellite radio-relay network—consisting of three to a dozen satellites—might cost anywhere from $100 million up, but it could have a capacity of 500 to 1,000 phone conversations, plus several FM channels and a TV channel or two. Communications experts who are not impressed by this vision point out that the radio spectrum is already crowded and that filling the air with messages to and from satellites might only make matters worse.

The booster rocket engines of 1,500,000 pounds' thrust, now under development, will be able to put seven to ten tons of payload into orbit with standard fuels, and twice that mass if high-energy fuels are used in the upper stages. Finally—still within the decade—a cluster of million-pound boosters could be used to launch as much as 100 tons into orbit. By that time, a nuclear-powered rocket may be contending for weight-lifting honors. "Depending on luck and the budget," says Herbert York, director of research and engineering for the Department of Defense, "we may get a man to the moon and back by 1970."

WHAT BUDGET FOR HEALTH?

There seems little likelihood that space technology will be starved for funds in the years ahead. One of the biggest unknowns for the Sixties is the level at which the U.S.—especially the government—will support basic research in medicine. By every criterion, the U.S. ought to be spending a great deal more on biological and medical research than 1958's estimated $400 million.

It would be rash to predict for the Sixties fundamental cures or prophylaxis for any of the outstanding medical problems— coronary and atherosclerotic disease, cancer, or mental illness— but the decade should certainly see major advances. And it could well see a substance to control essential hypertension, as insulin controls diabetes.

Cancer, in all its various manifestations, is still a deep mystery, but basic research on the process by which DNA (deoxyribonucleic acid) controls cell growth might suddenly clarify the whole problem of unrestrained cell and tissue growth. Meanwhile, on a less fundamental level, the intensive search for drugs that will disable specific types of cancer cells could have important results in the next few years.

Mental illness, like cancer, appears to consist of a host of disparate ailments that would be unlikely to yield to a single therapy, but again the diversity may be more illusory than real. It may be that the greatest value of the tranquilizers and "psychic energizers" (mood raisers) discovered in the Fifties will have been to open the eyes of psychiatrists generally to the importance of biochemistry in mental health and illness.

THE USES OF $120 BILLION

If, as seems likely, the U.S. spends approximately $120 billion on R. and D. during the Sixties, this will substantially exceed the nation's total investment in science and technology in the 184 years between 1776 and the present date. There is no guarantee that the money will produce another Einstein, or even a Willard Gibbs. (And, more than likely, it will not.) It may not even guarantee the U.S. world leadership in science and technology if the $120 billion is used so that the Sixties—field by field and area by area—is simply the Fifties swollen to double size.

While the recommendations of the Federal Council for Science and Technology—set up by the President as a result of the December, 1958, Killian report—should help to prevent this from happening, government action can, at most, directly influence only half of the total R. and D. effort. It will be up to industry to reexamine its own R. and D. programs to see where they can be strengthened in the years ahead.

There is a clear need for more industrial effort in basic technology—as well as in basic science—to achieve greater productivity gains than the 2½ to 3 per cent typical of recent years. Experts may disagree on the seriousness of the Soviet "economic threat," but there can be no doubt that the U.S.S.R. has large cadres of well-trained scientists and engineers to assign to the productivity problem, as yet undistracted by the need to turn out annual engineering refinements in cars and a host of other consumer products.

Should the cold war somehow be ended during the Sixties, there would presumably be a sharp reduction in the federal funds pumped into R. and D. It would then be imperative for scores of corporations to find nonmilitary outlets for their capabilities. The result could resemble the technological demobilization that followed World War II, which diverted into the civilian economy a torrent of ideas and techniques, and thousands of talented young people at the peak of creativity. Another such torrential release, if it came, say, by 1965, could have an unimaginable impact on industrial technology and on the market before the decade ends.

A NEW AGE OF DISCOVERY

Short of an ending of the cold war—and barring the outbreak of a hot one—science will inevitably take on a more international character during the Sixties, following the pattern of the highly successful International Geophysical Year. Plans are already afoot for an International Public Health and Medical Research Year, to start in 1961, which has the enthusiastic support of both Khrushchev and Eisenhower. Such cooperative ventures can themselves do something to reduce international tension. If wisdom and forbearance prevail, the Sixties could be filled with wonders—not alone for consumers and businessmen, but for everyone who can perceive the beauty and excitement in the great voyages of discovery now going forward in every region of science.

CHAPTER THREE

How the U.S. Can Get 50 Per Cent Richer

THE most sensational piece of news about the U.S. economy and its prospects for the 1960's is contained in a statistic that so far has received surprisingly little attention. The statistic is this: U.S. productivity (measured as private nonfarm output per man-hour) rose more than 7 per cent from the end of the recession in mid-1958 until the steel strike began to hamper production in the summer of 1959. This is the sharpest increase of the postwar and, though no such rate can be sustained indefinitely, this spurt about "made up" for two years of sluggishness, 1956-57, when productivity increased only about 1.5 per cent a year. And there are cogent reasons for expecting that output per man-hour will advance at least as fast over the next decade as it has during the last one— i.e., at a rate considerably above the long-term average.

This means that during the 1960's a 50 per cent increase in national output is well within our grasp, for rising productivity is the principal source of increased output, far overshadowing the gains from an expanding labor force. Productivity, of course, is simply a concept to express the efficiency with which labor is used in the economy, and it is usually measured in terms of output per man-hour. (This in no way implies, however, that labor is the sole or even the chief source of productivity gains.) Productivity, technical though many of its aspects are, can be a fighting word. There is at least one economist who has proclaimed that further increases in U.S. output are no longer an important goal. Harvard's Dr. John Kenneth Galbraith feels that our "Affluent Society" should be concerning itself with other matters. And a number of trade-union officials have voiced their apprehension over the steepness of the current productivity trend, which has kept employment from rising as rapidly as output. But the lag in employment in 1958-59 was no more severe than the lag during the recovery from the 1953-54 recession. In the last analysis, it is the rate at which productivity grows that will determine the size of the markets and the standard of living of the 1960's.

How fast productivity is likely to grow in the 1960's is a subject of fairly heated debate among economists. FORTUNE feels confident that the rate during the 1960's will about equal the postwar average of 3 per cent a year. But a number of economists reject this optimism. The lag during 1956 and 1957, in their view, was a reflection of fundamental changes in the structure of the economy that will restrict future productivity gains. Thus Professor Jules Backman of New York University has predicted that productivity will grow by only 2 per cent a year during the 1960's.

As much as $100 billion is riding on the outcome. If output per man-hour were to expand by 3 per cent a year (and if, as seems likely, the number of man-hours grew by about 1 per cent a year), the gross national product could reach the staggering total of $750 billion by 1970 (in 1959 prices), compared to a 1959 rate of $480 billion. But if productivity were to keep growing only at the average rate recorded in 1956-57—i.e., 1.5 per cent a year—the G.N.P. in 1970 would be $100 billion less—i.e., $650 billion. (At Professor Backman's projected 2 per cent the difference would be $70 billion.) One hundred billion dollars would mean a difference of about $1,300 per family. More is at stake than just the size of the market, however. The difference between 3 per cent and 1.5 or 2 per cent could easily spell the difference between price stability and an inflationary spiral; it might even mean the difference between success and failure in the cold war.

How much of the productivity growth of the 1960's Americans are likely to take in the form of higher output (rather than more leisure), and how an increased output might be split among competing demands—e.g., investment, consumption, defense, and social welfare—will be discussed in the next chapter. Succeeding chapters will analyze the way this allocation will affect specific

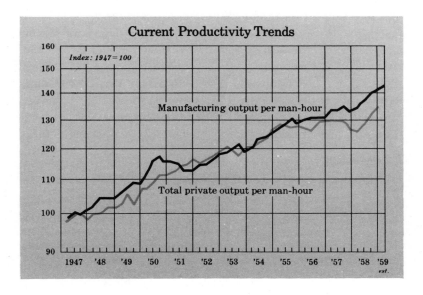

Current Productivity Trends

Index: 1947 = 100

Manufacturing output per man-hour

Total private output per man-hour

Productivity typically grows in spurts and lags, as is indicated in this chart showing the quarterly changes in private nonfarm output and in manufacturing output per man-hour over the postwar. The sharpest fluctuations, as might be expected, occur in manufacturing, where the 1956-58 lag was more protracted than the earlier interruptions in 1951 and 1953-54. Productivity in the nonfarm economy as a whole, on the other hand, grew at a fairly steady rate until the second quarter of 1955, when the lag began. But productivity started rising sharply after the second quarter of 1958 all across the line. And agricultural productivity, which cannot be charted quarterly, rose fantastically in 1958, bringing productivity for the private economy as a whole nearly back on trend.

consumer and industrial markets. But it is productivity that
largely determines the size of the pie to be cut, and thus FORTUNE
first analyzes the factors governing U.S. productivity growth, and
estimates the growth rates that now seem possible for the 1960's.

A good deal of skepticism, it must be acknowledged, has always
surrounded productivity figures, in part because of their free-and-
easy manipulation (by both sides) during wage negotiations. The
soberest economists have been suspicious of many of the measurements of past productivity changes, and they looked upon efforts
at projecting future productivity rates as real blue-sky stuff. Just
in the past three or four years, however, economists in government
and academic circles have greatly expanded and improved the
available statistics, and these have confirmed the conclusions
FORTUNE reached four years ago in an article that struck some
economists at the time as extravagantly optimistic (see "Productivity: the Great Age of 3%," FORTUNE, November, 1955). And
FORTUNE later broadened its own analysis. (For a discussion of the

Where Productivity Growth Comes From

Productivity has been growing at a rate of 3 per cent a year in the private
economy for the postwar period as a whole, but this average reflects widely
disparate trends in individual industries. The six industries charted opposite
have been roughly grouped according to their level of output per man-hour.
(For the actual dollars of output per man-hour, see middle chart page 48.)

The slowest growth in the high-productivity group (top chart) is in manufacturing, where productivity grew by 3.5 per cent a year between 1947 and
1955, when the rate slowed down.

The fastest growth is in the utility sector—communications and electric
and gas companies—which has averaged nearly 6.5 per cent a year. In transportation, productivity has been growing by 4 per cent a year.

The trends are even more divergent in the low-productivity industries
(bottom chart).

Agricultural productivity, though low (output per man-hour is only $2.28),
is growing at a phenomenal 7 per cent a year.

In the trade and service industries, on the other hand, productivity has
been lagging. The growth in trade (retail and wholesale) has averaged 2 per
cent a year, in services only 1 per cent.

problems of defining productivity and a summary of how FOR-
TUNE's figures were computed, see Appendix.)

Three per cent a year is actually a tolerably conservative forecast of the productivity gains that can be expected in the 1960's,
but it is a far higher rate than anything the U.S. was ever able to
sustain over any prolonged period in the past. During the middle

Postwar Productivity Trends by Industry

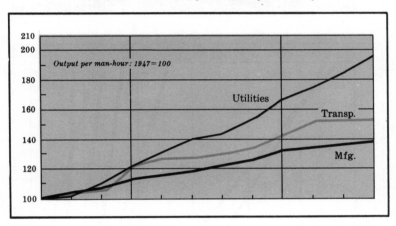

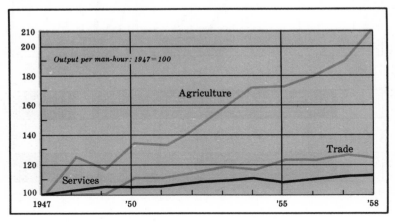

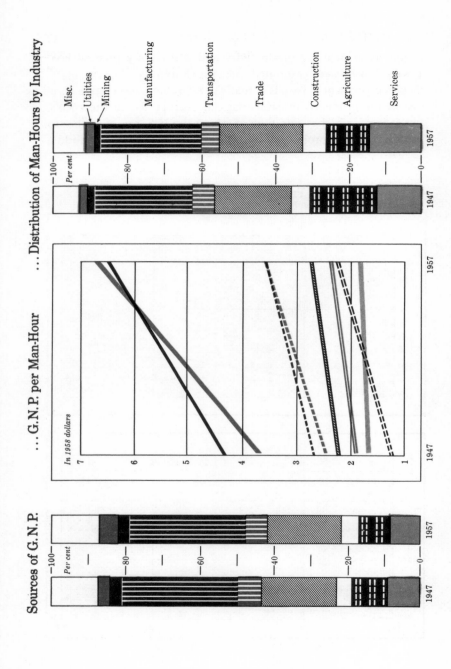

Sources of G.N.P.

... G.N.P. per Man-Hour

... Distribution of Man-Hours by Industry

and later years of the nineteenth century, though the railroads were spreading across the continent and the great industrial complexes of the North and East were growing up, we remained a predominantly agricultural economy, and increases in the national productivity were relatively modest. As the chart on page 54 shows, the annual increase in private G.N.P. per man-hour averaged little better than 1 per cent between 1850 and 1889. Then the shift toward an industrial economy began to be reflected, and from 1889 to 1919 the annual productivity gains averaged 2 per cent. Between World War I and II, the rate rose to 2.5 per cent. From 1947 to 1959 it averaged 3 per cent.

During 1956 and 1957, the rate of productivity increase fell to less than 1.5 per cent a year, and it is this lag that has created a good deal of the uncertainty or pessimism about the prospects for the 1960's. Some slowdown was to be expected in 1956-57, for productivity typically slows down in the later stages of a boom. Firms that had been concentrating on production in the most efficient plants begin using their less efficient standby plants. As the labor supply tightens, marginal workers are attracted into the labor force, labor discipline slackens, and firms begin to hoard

---

The complex relationship between the level of productivity and its rate of growth, on the one hand, and output and employment, on the other, is shown in the charts opposite. They indicate that when productivity lags too badly in one industry, the market acts to keep that industry from dragging down the national productivity. The reason: output tends to grow more slowly in the industries whose productivity is growing slowly.

For example:

Trade and services, where productivity is low and growing slowly, accounted for a smaller share of G.N.P. in 1957 (before the recession temporarily distorted relationships) than in 1947, though their share of man-hours had risen.

Communications and utilities, on the other hand—where productivity is very high and rising sharply—have nearly doubled their share of national output, while increasing their share of man-hours very slightly.

In manufacturing, the level and rate of growth are close to the average for the economy as a whole. Manufacturing's share of output and man-hours has been fairly stable.

(For a description of how the figures were constructed, see Appendix.)

workers against a possible future shortage. And when a boom is characterized by a high rate of capital investment, productivity tends to lag even more severely, for new plants generally require a six to twelve-month shakedown period before they operate at full efficiency.

The slowdown in 1956 and 1957, however, was more severe than usual. But when the changes are broken down by industry, it becomes clear that nothing in the experience of those years suggests any permanent alteration of trend. The lag in productivity was most pronounced in construction, retail trade, and manufacturing, and in the first two the reason was an unusually severe cyclical reduction in sales, and hence in "output per man-hour," rather than any slowdown in actual efficiency. In construction, for example, output per man-hour actually declined in 1956 (from an index of 122 to 121) because home building fell precipitously from its record 1954-55 pace as mortgage money tightened. Now that home building has recovered and the pool of construction labor is more fully employed, productivity has snapped back— to an index of 129 in 1958 and even higher in 1959. Similarly, the lag in trade productivity has been due to the gyrations of the automobile market, where employment of highly paid salesmen has not expanded and contracted in line with the roller-coaster curve of car sales. For trade as a whole, output per man-hour had jumped in 1955 (from an index of 116 to 122) because of that year's abnormal car boom, and the lag in 1956-58 simply reflected the slump in car sales. Productivity has been increasing steadily in most other lines of trade, and so the over-all trade index now stands at a new high as cars show substantial recovery and other products head toward new sales peaks.

In manufacturing, the situation was somewhat more complex. Output per man-hour of manufacturing production workers, as Murray Wernick, an economist for the Federal Reserve Board has pointed out, did not lag at all. The slow-down in over-all manufacturing productivity in 1956-57 was due to an abnormally rapid rise in employment of "nonproduction" workers, whose number rose 11 per cent while output was growing only 3 per cent. (Employment of production workers actually declined in this period.) This rise was largely due to the expansion of defense production and the explosive rise in research and development expenditures. Engineers, scientists, technicians, and managers represented about two-thirds of the increase between 1955 and 1957 in the number of nonproduction workers in manufacturing. The implications of this trend will be discussed more fully below. Suffice it to say here that the man-hours of the engineers and scientists represent a down payment on future productivity gains. Indeed, manufacturing productivity has recently been rising at a record rate, and it is already back on its postwar trend.

THE SERVICE OGRE

Broadly speaking, there are only two ways that a rise in national productivity can come about. Manpower may shift from industries or occupations with a low output per man-hour (e.g., agriculture) to industries or occupations with a higher output per man-hour (e.g., manufacturing); this in itself will bring no improvement in productivity within either industry, but it will raise national productivity. Or national productivity may rise because of real increases in output per man-hour within each industry rather than shifts from one sector to another. Both factors have, in the past, contributed to the steady rise of U.S. productivity.

But manpower shifts are now acting as a drag on productivity, in the opinion of Professor Backman and others who share his pessimism about productivity growth in the 1960's. According to this view, the migration of labor from farm to industry is slowing down, and instead, U.S. workers are now shifting from high to low-productivity industries—i.e., from manufacturing to services; as a result, productivity will slow down rather than accelerate.

This pessimistic view is refuted, however, when the annual changes in productivity over the postwar are broken down into major industrial sectors and when calculations are made as to how much of the over-all productivity change each year has come from gains *within* sectors. The results are striking. The shift of labor away from the farms has accounted for only three points of the

38 per cent gain in the productivity index between 1947 and 1957. Even if the trend slowed down, as seems likely (simply because there are fewer farmers left), the impact on national productivity would be almost invisible. The slowdown would, at most, subtract two-tenths of 1 per cent from the nation's annual productivity growth. On the other hand, the much-heralded shift from manufacturing to services has not served to lower the national productivity trend. Had there been no changes in the industrial distribution of man-hours, the productivity index would have risen by only one-half per cent more than it did over the postwar as a whole. Even if these sector shifts were to increase over the next ten years, the impact on productivity would be insignificant—i.e., less than one-tenth of 1 per cent a year on the most conservative estimate.

The reasons are simple. The fastest growing of the "service" industries are communications and public utilities. In no sector of the economy is output per man-hour so high, and in none but agriculture is it growing so fast. (See chart, page 47.) Productivity has been growing very rapidly in transportation, too—faster, for example, than in manufacturing—and the industry may be on the verge of a real productivity explosion as a result of "containerization." Pan-Atlantic Steamship, for example, a coastal shipping concern, has designed a number of ships to carry cargo in truck-trailer bodies. Pan-Atlantic can completely unload and reload such a ship in fifteen hours, using only two crews; on one informed estimate, conventional dry-cargo handling techniques would probably take seven crews a total of seven days.

MORE EFFICIENT COFFEE MAKING

On the other hand, the trade and service industries, in which productivity has been lagging, have been growing more slowly than the economy as a whole. (They account for a slightly smaller share of G.N.P. now than in 1947; see chart, page 48.) This is contrary to what the pessimists assume—but it is what should be expected in a free-market economy. Where productivity lags, prices necessarily rise relative to other prices, and consumers shift their spending to those industries in which rising productivity keeps prices relatively low. Indeed, if productivity lags too severely, consumers may bypass the industry altogether. A good deal of research and development activity, in fact, is devoted to this end—witness the spread of self-service in retailing and the development of home permanent kits, wash-and-wear fabrics, and a disposable fabric that is being made by Scott Paper for tablecloths, aprons, towels.

What makes the outlook for the 1960's so hopeful, moreover, is that in these lagging industries there is an enormous potential for productivity growth that is just beginning to be tapped. Allied Stores, for example, by moving salesclerks to where the customers are, instead of chaining them to one department, has been able to increase sales per man-hour by as much as 20 per cent in most of its stores. With the aid of an electronic-computer installation for the Bank of America's mortgage and installment-loan operation, 100 employees are now doing the work of 300. The Stouffer restaurant chain has developed an automatic coffee maker that turns out coffee of uniform quality with less supervision. Since the coffee is made cool enough to drink as soon as it reaches the table the technique tends to increase customer turnover and to raise output per man-hour. And so it goes.

The real reason for the increase in white-collar occupations is the profound and far-reaching change that has been taking place in the nature of the productive process. The occupational shift is simply the obverse of the widely heralded trend toward automation, which substitutes engineers, scientists, administrators, computer programers, typists, etc., for men on the production line, whether the production line be a factory, a supermarket, an airline-reservations system, a telephone network, or a life-insurance office.

Since 1940, for example, white-collar employment has increased almost half again as fast as total employment. This growth is not primarily due to the supposed shift from manufacturing to services. On the contrary, the increase in white-collar employment since 1940 has been even sharper *within* manufacturing industries than in business as a whole—i.e., 116 per cent vs. 86 per cent. As a result, more than 20 per cent of all white-collar workers are currently

The Past and Future of U.S. Productivity

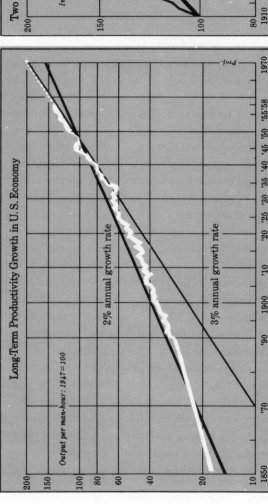

Long-Term Productivity Growth in U. S. Economy

Output per man-hour: 1947=100

2% annual growth rate

3% annual growth rate

Prod.

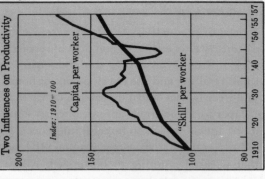

Two Influences on Productivity

Index: 1910=100

Capital per worker

"Skill" per worker

The chart at left above shows the tendency for the rate of productivity advance to accelerate, feeding upon itself. For example, gross private (nongovernmental) output per man-hour grew at a rate of only 1 per cent a year between 1850 and 1889 (according to Twentieth Century Fund figures) and jumped to 2 per cent a year between 1889 and 1919 (according to the new figures developed by John Kendrick of the National Bureau of Economic Research). Between the two world wars, the rate accelerated to an average 2.5 per cent a year, and since 1947 productivity has been

growing by 3 per cent a year. (The chart also shows what the productivity index would have been had the growth rate averaged 2 and 3 per cent, respectively. The growth rate of the actual productivity index may be estimated roughly, therefore, by comparing its slope with the slope of the hypothetical indexes.)

One reason for the acceleration of productivity in the postwar has been the heavy investment in plant and equipment. The gross stock of plant and equipment per worker (right-hand chart) has been growing by 2.5 per cent a year since 1947,

compared to less than 2 per cent between 1910 and 1929. (Capital per worker fell between 1930 and 1944 when depression and then wartime priorities held back capital investment.)

FORTUNE's index of skill per worker shows the rapid upgrading of the labor force in recent years—i.e., the rapid growth in the number of professional, technical, managerial, and skilled workers and the relative decline in semiskilled, unskilled, and farm employment—which is another reason for the acceleration of productivity.

employed in manufacturing, vs. 18.3 per cent in 1940.

But while the number of nonproduction workers increased by 1,500,000 in manufacturing in the postwar, the number of production workers rose by only 116,000.

It is crucial to know why these occupational changes are taking place if we are to understand their implications for productivity. The occupational shifts are vastly more complicated than the usual distinction between white-collar and blue-collar workers suggests. The real question is not what collar a man wears but what kind of work he does. In trade, for example, the white-collar salesclerk is a production worker, and white-collar people are also the production workers in banking and insurance, while telephone operators are the production workers in communications. In these, as in most other industries, production workers are being displaced (see chart, page 56).

THE SCIENTIFIC EXPLOSION

In manufacturing, the recent shift from production to nonproduction employment is due less to the proliferation of paper work than to the explosive growth in the number of engineers, physicists, chemists, mathematicians, and technicians of all sorts. To be sure, clerical employment in manufacturing has nearly doubled since 1940, but most of the increase occurred during the war and early postwar years. Since 1952 the number of clerks, typists, etc., has gone up only 7 per cent. But in the same period the number of "professional, technical, and kindred workers" has risen 60 per cent, to 1,400,000 (there has been a 47 per cent expansion just since 1955); and this accounts for roughly two-thirds of the total increase in nonproduction employment since 1952.

The burgeoning of technical employment comes chiefly from the expansion of research-and-development activity in the last few years. Between 1953 and 1957, for example, industry's R. and D. expenditures nearly doubled, from $3.7 billion to $7.3 billion, and in 1959 they were running at a rate of about $9 billion a year. In the same period, according to a National Science Foundation study, the number of engineers and scientists engaged in R. and D. in

The Professionalization of the Labor Force

The Changing Occupational Structure

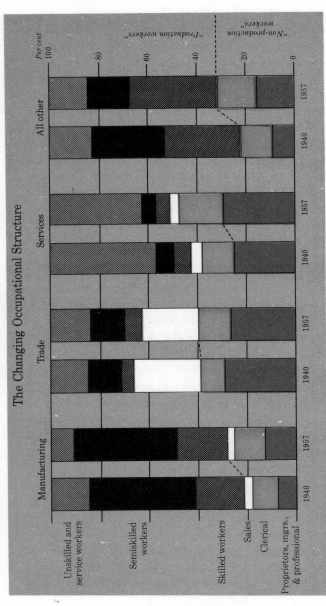

A major redistribution of the labor force has been in process since 1940, which profoundly affects current and future productivity changes. The essence of the occupational shifts is the substitution of indirect or "non-production" for direct or "production" labor in almost every industry. In manufacturing, production workers have dropped from 78.5 per cent to 71.7 per cent of the labor force. The larger part of the rise in non-production workers, moreover, has been due to the expansion of managers and professional and technical personnel, up from 7.4 to 12.7 per cent of total manufacturing employment. In trade, salesmen—the principal production workers—have declined from 27.3 to 23.5 per cent of the labor force. In the financial, business, and personal-service industries, the proportion of service workers (domestics, plant guards, waitresses, etc.) has declined sharply, while the proportion of managers and professionals—teachers, doctors, nurses, accountants, etc.—has gone up. Clerical workers in finance and insurance—the production workers in finance and insurance—are relatively more numerous, but mechanization is beginning to slow their increase. In the "all other" group—mainly communications, utilities, and transportation—the proportion of semiskilled and unskilled workers is down and professional and technical and managerial personnel up.

manufacturing jumped 45 per cent, from 148,000 to 214,000. There was a sharp rise also in the more numerous group of technicians and technical assistants.

R. and D. is the main but not the only reason for the growth in professional employment, however. As a consequence of automation and the spread of scientific management, engineers, scientists, and administrators are becoming ever more important to the production process. The executive vice president of one large chemical company, for example, says he finds it difficult to understand the statistical distinction between production and nonproduction workers. A good process engineer, he points out, can raise productivity 5 to 10 per cent just by changing the product mix slightly. The oil industry is bridging the gap between the plant and the laboratory altogether: several companies are trying to control production through continuous analysis of the chemical composition of the end product instead of by checking on operating conditions like temperature. The number of engineers and scientists employed by manufacturers in activities other than R. and D. jumped 30 per cent between 1954 and 1957, to 376,000.

FEWER "OPERATIVES"

The trend can be seen most clearly, of course, in "process" industries like chemicals and refining, but the same changes are taking place in fabricating industries, too. Ford's publicized "automated" engine plants at Cleveland and Dearborn, for example, use 1,800 fewer direct laborers but nearly 1,000 more skilled maintenance men and technicians than conventional plants turning out the same volume.

These are the underlying factors responsible for the fact that the number and proportion of skilled workers in manufacturing have been rising despite an over-all decline in production-worker employment. More than half of the 3,500,000 skilled workers in manufacturing are foremen, machinists, and skilled mechanics and repairmen. The number of common laborers in manufacturing was declining sharply some years ago, but in recent years most of the displacement has been in the number of "operatives"—i.e., semiskilled workers, who still constitute the heart (42 per cent) of the manufacturing labor force but are being displaced by mechanization. The stock of materials-handling equipment in manufacturing has tripled since 1947, as has the total investment in instruments. And the annual purchases of these tools of automation have been accelerating over the past decade. There is therefore every indication that productivity of production workers will rise even more rapidly in the 1960's than it did during the 1950's.

THE RESEARCH EFFECT

The mushroom growth of R. and D. does raise a number of fundamental questions about the trend of manufacturing productivity, for R. and D. employment of necessity reduces *current* productivity, being an input of man-hours from which there is no immediate product.* But R. and D. is of course designed to increase productivity in some future period. It is, in effect, an investment in future productivity gains, charged to current account.

This means that productivity *will* go up in the future, though for a time the gains may be offset by investment in new research. (If R. and D. does not pay off, firms will simply stop investing in research—and this by itself would raise output per man-hour.) But even in the short term, R. and D. is unlikely to become a serious drag on manufacturing productivity. For one thing, the increases in R. and D. employment probably will not continue at the explosive rate of the past few years. What happened in 1954-57 was that manufacturers suddenly moved up to a whole new level of research activity. Now that the laboratories have been built and staffed, the growth in employment will be more in line with the long-term trend.

One reason is management's growing concern with raising the productivity of research itself. A team of operations-research specialists at Case Institute of Technology, for example, is making a major study of research management and productivity under a grant from the National Science Foundation. A number of

---

* That portion of R. and D. performed under contract for the government— about 50 per cent of the total—does tend to get counted as part of corporate output.

corporations are developing budgeting procedures designed to discover the potential dead-end projects before they eat up too much time, and Union Carbide has even established some automation in its labs. Most important of all, however, there is already abundant evidence that systematic research does vastly speed up the process of discovery and telescope the period between a discovery and its practical application in industry.

Research expenditures by manufacturing companies affect the productivity of the whole economy, moreover, not just of the companies performing the research. The stream of antibiotics, tranquilizers, etc., that have come out of the drug industry's research expenditures have meant gains for the "productivity" not just of the drug industry, but of the whole "medical industry," and to the extent that they have cut down on sickness and absenteeism, have contributed to productivity in many other industries. Or, to take another example, development of new plastics has not only increased productivity in the chemical industry, but has meant tremendous savings in man-hours in production of housewares, and now promises large gains in the construction industry.

Research is not exclusively a preoccupation of manufacturing companies, of course. In the telephone industry, for example, which enjoys a particularly high rate of productivity advance, the number of telephone operators—i.e., production workers—has actually declined since 1949 despite a better than 50 per cent increase in telephone conversations. They have been replaced, in effect, by the Bell Labs scientists. And electric utilities have enjoyed enormous productivity gains through development of larger generators and transmission lines.

CONTAINERS AND MODULES

Where R. and D. may make its largest contribution to future productivity, however, is in its application to the organization of business itself rather than in the discovery of new products or processes. Raising productivity, more and more business managers are discovering, involves far more than just installing more machines or making more time-motion studies. Indeed, the innovations that have had the greatest effect on U.S. productivity in the past fifteen years, as management consultant Peter Drucker has pointed out, have been almost entirely "conceptual" rather than technical.

The most dramatic example, perhaps, is in transportation, which has enjoyed a rapid growth in productivity in the postwar, but which is on the verge of a real productivity revolution as a result of "containerization." Containerization is a conception, not a technology (although it involves a lot of technical changes, too), which requires unified thinking and action by shippers as well as by railroads, truckers, and ocean carriers. It is still too early to judge how quickly containerization will come, but the attitude of railroads and truckers has changed recently from skepticism to enthusiasm or, at the least, grudging admission of its inevitability.

There is a prospect, similarly, of very substantial gains in construction (where productivity gains so far have been below the average for the whole economy) through the adoption of true modular design. Like mass production itself, the basis of this production revolution is a new concept rather than a new product or machine. But the new concept would permit mass production of components, which in turn could be assembled rapidly into an infinite variety of shapes and sizes. According to *Architectural Forum,* there is now hope—for the first time since the early postwar—that modular design may really take hold. In 1957, for example, a Modular Building Standards Association was formed under the auspices of the leading architectural, building-supply, and contracting organizations. To a considerable degree, modular design is being anticipated by the rise of prefabrication and the introduction of many new building materials that sharply reduce construction labor.

THE STIRRINGS IN TRADE

Even apart from manufacturing, transportation, utilities, and construction, there are some astonishing opportunities for improvements in U.S. productivity. There are even signs of substantial productivity gains in trade, which employs over 12,500,000 people (retail and wholesale), through application of the new management methods (including some that are new to trade, although old to manufacturing and other industries).

Allied Stores, as mentioned above, has been able to increase the productivity of its salespeople by as much as 20 per cent; this was done by viewing the store as a flow of transactions, and by scrapping the department-store tradition that salesclerks work for the buyer in favor of the view that they work for the store. Allied studies the flow of transactions over time in each store, discovers predictable shifts in the flow from one department to another. It then trains salesclerks to shift from one department to another within a given area, and maintains what it calls a "flying squadron," able to fill in wherever traffic is particularly heavy.

The growth of self-service has already reduced the number of salesmen from 28 per cent of total trade employment in 1940 to 23 per cent today, and the trend is continuing, in supermarkets and elsewhere. (The number of proprietors, most of whom work in one-man or family stores, is also declining relatively.) Productivity in food retailing is rising by 3 per cent a year (vs. 2 per cent for all of trade), as the self-service principle is applied to meats and fresh produce, and William Tongue, economist of Jewel Tea, thinks productivity will grow as rapidly during the 1960's. "It's hard to see precisely where the gains will come from in the future," he observes, "but I would have said the same thing ten years ago."

One likely source is the humble vending machine (already handling more than $2 billion of retail sales a year), whose use may be extended enormously as the result of the recent perfection by two separate companies of machines capable of handling paper money as well as coins. Vending machines are already being used extensively for mass feeding operations—quite important since restaurants employ roughly 1,500,000 workers. General Electric, for example, has converted the main cafeteria at its Lynn, Massachusetts, plant, which employs 13,500, to vending operation, and the company has added sixteen vending stations for light snacks, such as hot soups and sandwiches. American Motors feeds 10,000 employees from vending machines in its Kenosha, Wisconsin, plant. A number of vending-machine manufacturers—e.g., Automatic Canteen—are developing machines that will hold a choice of frozen meals and cook them to order electronically in twenty to sixty seconds.

There are more than two million skilled and semiskilled workers in trade. About one-fourth of them drive trucks and delivery vans, where productivity gains are hard to come by. But there are large numbers working in gas stations, garages, parking lots, etc., where a good bit of mechanization is going on. Use of materials-handling equipment in stores and warehouses will continue to eliminate many workers, and stores and wholesalers are studying every possible means of reducing the labor required in the physical handling of goods. For example, a number of large department stores—Joseph Magnin of San Francisco, the Broadway Department Store of Los Angeles, Marshall Field of Chicago—are now using a service offered by a subsidiary of Gilbert Carrier Corp., a large trucking firm, which delivers preticketed clothing on racks, thereby eliminating unpacking cartons, putting the clothing on hangers, steaming out the wrinkles, etc.

The relative decline in the number of salesmen and other production workers in trade has been accompanied, of course, by an increase in the proportion of clerical workers (of whom there are now about 1,600,000) from 10 per cent of trade employment in 1940 to 13 per cent in 1959. As a result, mechanization is proceeding quite rapidly. A growing number of department stores—e.g., Woodward & Lothrop in Washington, D.C., and Ohrbach's in New York—now use pre-punched I.B.M. cards as sales tickets. These cards are run through a sorter at the end of the day, so that each morning buyers are given a complete record of sales the preceding day and of the inventory position.

FIGHTING THE PAPER

But the paper-work problem, it goes without saying, cuts across all of U.S. business, even though the specific clerical function may vary from line to line. So much attention has been paid to the paper-work revolution being wrought by computers and other electronic data-processing machines that it is easy to forget how new the trend really is. The first commercial computer installation actually was made only five years ago by General Electric. The first insurance-company installation, by Metropolitan, was not made until 1954, and the first major retailing application was announced only a year ago by R. H. Macy, for handling its credit accounts. The growth in computer sales during the past five years—from $50 million to more than $300 million—has been truly phenomenal. And this is only the beginning. Hardly a week goes by without a full-page ad in the business press announcing the marketing of a new, less expensive, and more flexible computer.

As a result of the boom in computer sales, the stock of office and store machinery, which had been expanding slowly during most of the postwar, is now increasing at more than twice the rate of just a few years ago. This should enormously increase the productivity of clerical workers in the 1960's, and perhaps even reduce their number.

But the key to successful computer installations, as many companies have discovered to their sorrow, is reorganization of the function being performed. Indeed, astonishing gains in productivity frequently can be obtained just from analysis and reorganization of paper work without even installing a computer. One manufacturer, for example, discovered that a certain bit of information required by World War II regulations was still being rubber-stamped on all invoices by hand. Arthur Anderson & Co. did an analysis of a large industrial company's office procedures and eliminated some 42 per cent of the 1,000-odd periodic reports being filed in the company.

When mechanization is joined to rational organization of paper work, the results can be dramatic—either in reducing man-hours or in providing information that had not been available before, or both.

Insurance companies, which employ close to a million people, nearly half of them clerical workers, have probably gone further than any other industry in exploiting the new paper-work techniques. New York Life, for example, has put the bulk of the work of its actuarial department on an I.B.M. 705 computer, with about a 20 per cent reduction in labor time. The computer also provides a mass of information not previously available, e.g., breakdowns of policyholders by state and quarterly projections of sales and earnings, and it permits greater precision in calculating premiums and dividends.

AUTOMATIC BANKING

Bank mechanization is now coming along very rapidly, too. There are over 600,000 people employed in banking, and about one-third of them do work that is susceptible to large-scale mechanization. (The rest deal in one way or another with the public, as tellers, loan officers, etc., and are not so easily replaced.) The largest single bank operation is check processing. And National Cash has sold over 5,000 of its new Post-Tronic bookkeeping machines in less than three years; about 20 per cent of the nation's annual volume of 11 billion checks are already being processed on these machines. The Post-Tronic is just the first stage in a system to which banks can add automatic sorters and computers as they wish to. The possibilities inherent in computer use are such that several leading banks are giving serious thought to setting up divisions that would completely take over (for a fee) the bookkeeping operations of their customers. The prospect is heightened by the number of computers with vastly greater capacity and flexibility now being introduced (see "The Next Generation of Computers," FORTUNE, March, 1959). The real computer boom will come sometime later in the 1960's, however, when machines with a true "random access memory" are developed. The great limitation on the current generation of computers is the fact that they can be used only in a rigidly prestructured way.

THE STUBBORN SERVICES

Not all the service-industry labor force, of course, is subject to productivity improvement in the same way or to the same degree as banking and insurance. There are, for example, over two million people employed in private health and medical care. Though productivity gains for the whole economy have resulted from development of new drugs and new instruments, it is also clear that the rapidly changing medical "industry" can hardly be looked at in conventional productivity terms. What people are willing to pay for medical and dental care is only partially related to the industry's "efficiency." Much the same can be said about private education, which employs over 600,000—although here, too, attempts are being made to raise productivity. And there are nearly 500,000 people employed by religious and welfare organizations, where again the tests of the market place do not apply.

But there is a huge conglomerate of other service industries whose output *is* judged in market terms, and if productivity lags too much, it simply means that the industry will get bypassed—to the benefit of the national productivity figures.

There are more than one million repairmen—in auto service stations, TV repair shops, etc. Productivity gains here come partly from mechanization, partly from redesign of the product to cut repair labor, e.g., replacing parts instead of repairing them. Indeed, development of the printed electronic circuit has cut production costs and prices of TV sets and so has encouraged replacement instead of repair of old sets.

More than 1,500,000 people are employed by hotels, laundries, barbershops, etc. Here productivity is being helped by mechanization, e.g., automatic shirt-ironing machines, as well as by new products.

The number of domestic servants has risen fairly sharply in recent years—from 1,800,000 in 1952 to 2,300,000 now. One reason, of course, has been the increase in working wives, and another is simply the fact that with increases in their "discretionary incomes," more Americans have decided they could afford this luxury. This rise has acted as a drag on the national productivity figures. It would be fascinating, however, to speculate whether the productivity of executives and entrepreneurs is enhanced by a well-staffed home. In any case, it seems unlikely the increase in the number of domestics will continue.

But while the potential for further productivity gains may be limited in the service areas, there is as yet no end in sight for the tremendous growth of farm productivity. Mechanization of the farmyard is just beginning, a lot of work is being done to raise productivity of livestock production, and the science of soil chemistry is still in its infancy.

ON TO 750

To sum up, then, the outlook for productivity gains in the 1960's is excellent. The growth of automation, research, and scientific management (all reflected in the rise of nonproduction employment) will accelerate the growth of productivity among production workers. Even this tendency, to be sure, would not mean higher productivity for the economy as a whole in the absence of productivity gains among the increasingly numerous nonproduction workers. But the productivity of these workers is beginning to rise rapidly, too.

With these crosscurrents at work, of course, there is always the possibility of another temporary lag such as occurred in 1956-57, but the most reasonable expectation is that national productivity will continue to rise at least as fast over the next ten years as it did in the last ten. There is an alluring possibility of a good deal more. All in all, a $750-billion gross national product by 1970 seems like a pretty conservative bet.

CHAPTER FOUR

The Good Uses
of $750 Billion

THOSE who are anxious lest the Soviet Union soon "catch up" with the U.S. can take some comfort in the fact that the prospective *increase* in American production in the 1960's is almost as much as the total current national production of the Soviet Union and West Germany combined. Total U.S. production of goods and services will move on to a new peak in 1960—more than $500 billion. But the "half-trillion economy," once considered such a breath-taking (or unlikely) achievement, will enjoy only a momentary glory. For so rapid is the economic expansion in prospect for the 1960's that by 1970 U.S. production will probably come to about $750 billion (in 1959 prices), up no less than $250 billion or 50 per cent—the largest percentage growth in any decade of our history. A major reason for anticipating such a rise is that national productivity, measured in output per man-hour, can be expected to continue to increase at its record postwar average rate of 3 per cent or more a year. Meantime the U.S. labor force, which grew slowly in the 1950's, is now, owing to the high birth rate that began during World War II, beginning to expand rapidly. With more workers turning out

The Rising Tempo of American Economic Growth

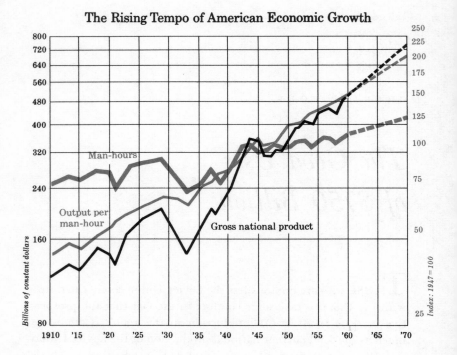

Total output of U.S. goods and services, which has been growing at an average rate of almost 4 per cent a year since World War II, will probably grow by more than 4 per cent a year in the 1960's, and amount to $750 billion by 1970. The basic force in this growth is accelerating productivity, measured in output per man-hour. U.S. productivity, which increased at the rate of 1 per cent a year between 1850 and 1889, 2 per cent between 1889 and 1919, and 2.5 per cent between the wars, has been increasing about 3 per cent since World War II. During the 1960's it will probably equal if not surpass its average postwar rate of increase. What will make total production boom is that man-hours worked will be expanding more than in many decades. For the labor force will grow faster than it has in a generation, and the work week will probably decline only moderately. With man-hours growing at a near-record rate and productivity continuing to grow at a record rate, total production is plainly bound to grow at a record rate.

more per hour, the economy as a whole probably will grow at the unprecedented rate of 4.2 per cent a year. Since the population will be rising steeply, G.N.P.—total national production of goods and services—*per person* will not rise as much. But it will increase at the rate of 2.9 per cent a year or 33 per cent for the decade— or, to put it in 1959 dollars, from $2,700 to $3,600 per person.

To grasp the dimensions and promises of so stupendous an advance, glance at it in historical perspective. During the *two* decades 1910-30, G.N.P. per person increased from $1,250 to about $1,600, or by only 30 per cent. Yet in those two decades mass production and mass consumption transformed the nation's way of life. By the end of the so-called Golden Twenties, food became plentiful and cheap and the automobile was counted a necessity by millions.

During the three following decades, 1930-60, G.N.P. per person increased from about $1,600 to $2,700, or by 70 per cent. (Owing to mounting defense needs, civilian output increased by only 55 per cent.) Yet this growth enabled the country to catch up on the civilian production it lost during World War II, to take the Korean war in stride, to multiply its outlays for research and development, to inaugurate the electronic age, and to overcome more than half of its shortages (as estimated by the Twentieth Century Fund) in health, education, and public works.

During the past fifty years, in other words, U.S. production rose by 1.5 per cent a year or $1,450 per person; just in this decade it will probably increase by 2.9 per cent a year or $900 per person.

MAGNIFICENTLY EASY TO BEAR

Obviously the expansion of the Sixties is going to affect every business and person. Of course, it does not mean a 33 per cent increase for every company and person, across the board. Nor does it mean exactly proportionate increases in each of the major uses of production—defense, investment, and consumption. On the contrary, defense should expand greatly. And the country must pay a certain "price" for its swift growth—a disproportionate rise, for a while, in industrial investment and what might be called social investment, and hence a less than proportionate rise in the output

of purely consumer goods and services. For about five years of the
decade, or till about 1965, the needs of investment and probably
defense may well rise enough to hold the rate of increase in consumption down to about 3.5 per cent a year, which is still a little

Investment Is the Price of Growth

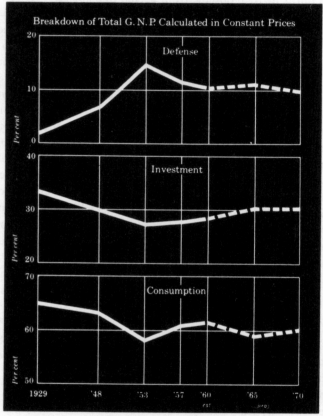

These three charts show the way the U.S. has been allocating its gross national
product over the past thirty years, and the way gross national product may be
allocated over the decade of the Sixties. (Each of the components is indi-
vidually deflated for relative price changes.) Rising defense needs forced both
investment and consumption to take progressively smaller *shares* of the nation's
physical output until 1953, when the trends were reversed. Between 1960 and
1965 consumption's share will again be pressed, but more by investment than
by defense.

higher than the rate of the past ten years. Increase in consumption
per person, since population will be rising, will of course be less—
about 2.2 per cent. What is more, the steady upgrading and "pro-
fessionalization" of the U.S. labor force will mean that a considerable part of the increase in consumption will fall to the people
whose skills have been improved. The disposable income of many
other people may rise by no more than 1.5 per cent a year—
though even this, compounded over five years, works out to an 8
per cent increase.

But for the U.S. as a whole, the price of growth will be magnificently easy to bear; the economic pie will expand so enormously
that almost everybody can get a substantially bigger cut. Although
consumption's *share* of the country's production will probably decline in 1960-65, consumption will still increase by $55 billion—
an amount greater than last year's national production of Italy.

And a still bigger increase in consumption will lie just ahead.
By about 1965, as will be shown later, heavy demands of investment and defense on the economy should be leveling off. Between
1965 and 1970, therefore, output going to consumption should increase by some 25 per cent, or by $90 billion—unless even more
of the productivity increase than assumed here is taken in the
form of a shorter work week. From 1965 on, in other words, the

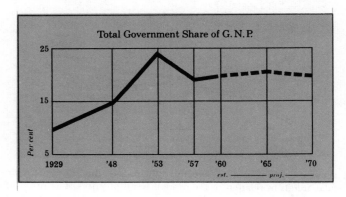

The chart above breaks out government's share of G.N.P., which includes
defense and such "investment" items as public works (but not "transfer" payments, i.e., money paid out for social security, unemployment benefits, interest on debt).

U.S. should enter a new age of abundance that will make even the great days of the 1950's look a little austere.

It is not guaranteed, of course. If the Russians should somehow succeed in breaking our alliances or taking over more of the previously "uncommitted" regions, the U.S. could be forced to accelerate its defense expenditures to the point where they would squeeze everything else unmercifully. The race to space may yet pile egregious burdens on people who would rather be happy on earth than miserable on Mars. Or, at the other extreme, if the cold war were somehow ended, and U.S. defense outlays could be cut back sharply, the U.S. economy might experience a hard jolt before ascending to even higher levels of civilian abundance than those projected here.

Aside from such earth-shaking and unpredictable possibilities, there is the more mundane possibility that the U.S. itself, in the pursuit of higher consumption, may not levy sufficient taxes, or save enough, to put its defense and investment needs on a sound financial basis. Financing them will be doubly onerous because the prices of both defense and investment goods are rising faster than the prices of consumption goods and services. Between 1948 and 1957, for example, their share of the country's physical output

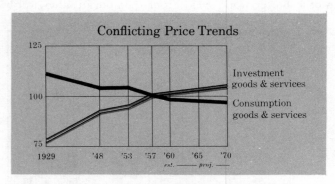

Just about everything is more expensive these days. But the chart expresses particular trends in relation to the over-all trend of prices. The prices of defense and investment goods and services as a group have been rising more than prices in general, and will continue to rise. Relative prices of consumption goods and services have been declining, and will continue to decline. The rate of rise and decline, however, has been slowing up.

rose from 37 to 39 per cent, while their share of the nation's money outlays rose from 34 to 39 per cent. To put it another way, more than $20 billion had to be diverted from consumer spending to investment and defense.

By the mid-Sixties defense and investment will probably have risen from 39 to 42 per cent of G.N.P. This is only a three-point increment, to be sure, but it means that $20 billion more must be diverted from consumer spending—in the form of taxes, personal savings, and corporate depreciation and profits. If these savings are not forthcoming, if the government does not pay for its needs as it goes, and if corporations cannot accumulate their investment needs, the needs will be realized only through inflation—if at all.

WHO TAKES WHAT

To demonstrate the basic trends in the growth of U.S. markets FORTUNE has divided the country's total expenditures into three functional groups:

1) Defense outlays, which in 1957 (the last year of full employment for which detailed data are available) accounted for about 10 per cent of G.N.P.; and international payments (or the excess of exports over imports), which in 1957 accounted for 1.2 per cent of G.N.P.

2) Investment goods and services, which in 1957 took about 28 per cent of G.N.P. These include such familiar items as capital investment (10.3 per cent of G.N.P.) and inventory accumulation (0.5 per cent) by business; house construction (4 per cent), and construction of public works like highways, hospitals, and schools, either public or private (3 per cent). FORTUNE is also including under "investment" several items that are general investments in the nation's well-being or proficiency and hence in its future productivity: expenditures for education, both public and private (3 per cent); expenditures for medical care and hospital services, etc., largely private (nearly 5 per cent). Finally there are government expenses not included elsewhere—i.e., for general administration, police and fire departments, etc. (2.3 per cent).

3) Consumption goods and services encompass everything else. They are all bought out of individuals' income after taxes, and in

1957 accounted for nearly 61 per cent of G.N.P. The chief categories are food, alcohol, and tobacco (18.2 per cent of G.N.P.); rent (8 per cent); clothing (7.9 per cent); auto purchases (3.3 per cent); current transportation, including auto upkeep and fares (5.5 per cent); household and recreation goods (7.2 per cent); and personal and household services and utilities (10.6 per cent).

THE DYNAMICS OF PRICE

To project the country's future expenditures on these groups of goods and services we must first estimate, in current prices, the physical quantities the country will demand. Since prices change, however, the actual amount the country will spend on these various groups almost certainly will not be the same as the estimates of physical demand. For one thing, there is the general upward price movement known as inflation (or what has been practically nonexistent since the 1930's, the general downward movement known as deflation). Since there is no way of telling what general inflation will do to prices, we must disregard it. What we cannot disregard, however, is the *relative* movement of prices. As everyone has observed, prices of all goods and services do not move in the same way. The prices of goods like appliances, whose finished costs benefit from the economies of mass production, can and sometimes do decline even when the cost of everything going into them is rising. On the other hand, the costs and selling prices of goods like machines for factories may rise relatively fast. They rise fast because the machines are virtually hand made and the labor that goes into them is increasingly expensive, inflation or no. Labor in capital-goods industries, even if its productivity does not rise, benefits from the general rise in productivity.

And how does the relative movement of prices affect future sales? If real, i.e., relative, costs and prices of certain goods and services are rising, say, at an average of 2 per cent a year, the country must pay better than 20 per cent more for the same quantity of goods and services ten years from now. And if the country is buying 50 per cent more of these goods and services ten years from now, measured in physical quantity, then it will be spending 80 per cent more on them than it is today.

Of course, goods and services whose prices are rising inordinately fast tend to run into sales resistance, just as goods and services whose prices are falling tend to sell easily. Let anything claim too much of the resources of a market economy, and the country will try to choose something cheaper. Over the short run, however, the country has relatively little option in some purchases, such as defense and certain capital goods. If a particular company is going to need a special machine in 1963 and the price of that machine rises 25 per cent by then, it will usually go ahead and spend 25 per cent more for it. If the nation needs new missiles in 1965, it will presumably lay out the money for them even if the price of those missiles doubles.

But consumers do have a relatively free choice in buying such things as cars and appliances. If the goods become too costly, people will tend to buy less of them. But will this tendency be strong enough to reduce actual dollar sales—or, since population is increasing, per capita dollar sales? If their relative costs and prices are falling, people will tend to buy more of them. But will this tendency be strong enough to offset declining prices and actually raise dollar sales—or again, since population is increasing, per capita dollar sales? To project future markets with any accuracy, questions like these must be considered. Past price movements must be appraised. So must the inherent demand for the goods and services themselves. Although FORTUNE's projections of consumer markets are tentative, all these factors have been taken into account.

DEFENSE NEEDS ARE RISING

The future physical volume of defense needs, depending as they do on domestic as well as international politics, is hardly to be divined by economic insight or statistical method. But to project the economy as a whole, one must make assumptions about defense spending. FORTUNE's assumption is that defense expenditures will rise a little faster than G.N.P., at least until the middle of the decade. In 1959 the country spent $46 billion on defense—mainly Defense Department outlays, but also including the AEC, foreign

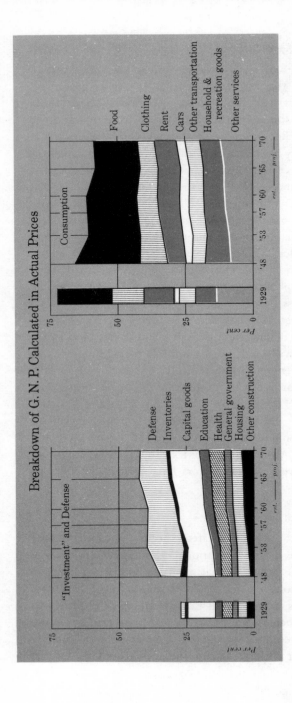

Breakdown of G.N.P. Calculated in Actual Prices

Consumption
- Food
- Clothing
- Rent
- Cars
- Other transportation
- Household & recreation goods
- Other services

"Investment" and Defense
- Defense
- Inventories
- Capital goods
- Education
- Health
- General government
- Housing
- Other construction

Investment's share of the nation's physical output, as shown on page 70, is beginning to rise. Prices of investment goods and services, as shown in the chart on page 72, are also rising. Therefore the share of actual dollar outlays going to investment and defense is rising doubly fast. In 1929 the nation devoted nearly three-quarters of its expenditures to consumption goods and services, and the rest to investment and defense. But today investment and defense together are taking about 39 per cent of G.N.P.; and

they are projected to take about 42 per cent in 1965 and in 1970. This increase will be mainly the result of rising investment expenditures—from 28 per cent of G.N.P. in 1957 to an estimated 29 per cent in 1960, and more than 31 per cent in 1965 and 32 per cent in 1970.

The most important groups in the investment increase (based on price and output projections for each group): capital goods, now about 10 per cent of

G.N.P., are projected to come to 11.5 per cent in 1965 and 1970; "other construction," mainly public works, which now comes to 3.4 per cent of G.N.P., is projected to come to 4 per cent in 1970; and "health," or outlays for hospital care, doctors, dentists, drugs, etc., which comes to about half as much as capital outlays, will be rising just about as fast. But all this, of course, does not mean people will be consuming less. See next chart.

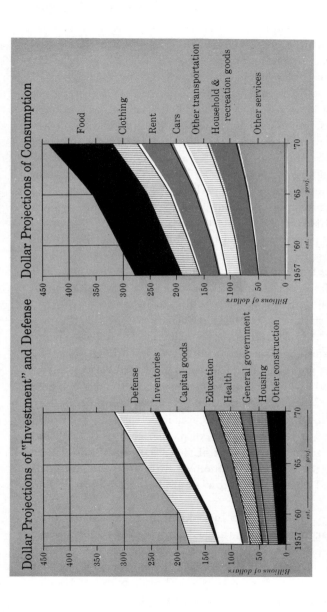

Dollar Projections of "Investment" and Defense

Billions of dollars

- Defense
- Inventories
- Capital goods
- Education
- Health
- General government
- Housing
- Other construction

1957   '60 _est._   '65 _proj._   '70

Dollar Projections of Consumption

Billions of dollars

- Food
- Clothing
- Rent
- Cars
- Other transportation
- Household & recreation goods
- Other services

1957   '60 _est._   '65 _proj._   '70

Investment and defense expenditures together should rise from $177 billion in 1957 to $195 billion in 1960 to $260 billion in 1965 and $315 billion in 1970. Inflation would raise all the figures. Defense expenditures (which on the charts include several billions sent abroad) are projected to rise from $51 billion to $67 billion in 1965 and $75 billion in 1970. Capital-goods outlays are projected to rise from $47 billion

to $71 billion in 1965 and $85 billion in 1970. All other investment outlays are projected to rise from $79 billion in 1957 to $96 billion in 1960, and to $122 billion in 1965 and $155 billion in 1970.

But consumption outlays, though accounting for a smaller *share* of G.N.P., will show an immense actual rise. Total consumption should increase from $275 billion in 1957 to about $355 billion in 1965

and $436 billion in 1970. The breakdown may look something like this: outlays for food, drink, and tobacco will increase from $84 billion in 1957 to $101 billion in 1965 and $117 billion in 1970; for personal services and utilities, from $48 billion in 1957 to $67 billion in 1965 and $89 billion in 1970; for autos, from $15 billion in 1957 to $21 billion in 1965 and $26 billion in 1970.

military aid, and stockpiling. The pressure is rising to ensure our
capacity to deter the enemy by spending a good deal more, and
not only on nuclear retaliatory power.

The question is how much. There is a large and vocal school of
thought that would mount a greatly increased defense program
embodying the main points of the so-called Gaither and Rockefeller committees, including stepped-up ICBM production, heavy
reinforcement of the Strategic Air Command, and a large improvement of "limited-war" capability. Such a program would call for
increasing spending by more than $3 billion a year to $65 billion
by 1965 and then tapering off to perhaps $70 billion in 1970. The
pace of Administration programs, on the other hand, suggests
nothing like this. The Administration has been increasing outlays
for retaliatory power by perhaps $1.5 billion a year. But it has
been meeting some of these costs by trimming limited-war capabilities, such as troop strength. But these savings obviously cannot
go on indefinitely, and a $1.5-billion increase a year would work
out to $54 billion in 1965 and $61 billion in 1970.

Fortune is striking a balance between the "big" defense program and the "Administration" rate of increase in defense spending, and is assuming a physical volume of defense needs at $60
billion in 1965 and $65 billion in 1970. Now, the relative prices
of defense goods held fairly steady between 1948 and 1953, rose
between 1953 and 1957, then steadied again, but will probably rise
somewhat during the Sixties. Thus actual defense outlays would
come to about $61 billion in 1965, or 9.9 per cent of G.N.P., and
$68 billion in 1970, or 9 per cent of G.N.P. In other words, they
would squeeze the rest of the economy a little until the middle of
the Sixties and then might grow somewhat more slowly than
G.N.P.

But as things look now, it is investment, and particularly business' outlays for capital goods, that will provide the major squeeze
on the consumption sector of the economy in the early Sixties. In
1957 capital-goods outlays came to $46.6 billion or 10.3 per cent
of G.N.P. They slumped in 1958, but will probably come back to
$48 billion, or 9.6 per cent of G.N.P., in 1960. But demand for

capital goods, measured in physical volume, should soon rise and reach 11.2 per cent of G.N.P., or $69 billion, by 1965. Then, as the rate of increase tapers off somewhat, physical volume should amount to 10.8 per cent of 1970's G.N.P., or $81 billion.

The average price of capital goods rose 14 per cent, relative to other goods, between 1948 and 1957. Fortunately, the price increases have begun to slow down, and between now and 1970 the increase will probably be not more than 5 per cent relative to other goods. Thus actual dollar outlays for capital goods would come to $71 billion in 1965 and to $85 billion in 1970.

THE PRICE OF GROWTH

Why are capital-goods outlays likely to rise so steeply during the first half of the decade? Replacement requirements, based on FORTUNE's calculations of the survival rate of the existing stock of capital goods, will not be responsible. These have been rising, but they will reach a peak of 5.5 per cent of G.N.P. this year and then decline slightly to 5.4 per cent in 1965, and to 5.1 by 1970.

The answer lies in the rapidly increasing labor force, and the drive for still higher productivity. Both mean large *additions* to plant and equipment, as soon as existing plant and equipment are fully utilized—as they should be by the end of 1960. On the average, U.S. business has to spend about $1.65 on capital goods to increase its capacity by $1—i.e., by $1 a year for ten or twenty years or even more, depending on how long the capital goods last. Thus, business in the 1950's spent the equivalent of 6 per cent of private G.N.P. to realize an increased annual output of 3.7 per cent. In the Sixties it will have to spend the equivalent of 7 per cent of private G.N.P. on capital goods in order to get a 4.2 per cent annual growth in output.

Economists have often argued, it is true, that plant and equipment outlays should increase more slowly than production at capacity because new capital goods are usually more efficient than the ones they replace. But as FORTUNE has pointed out (See "The Coming Boom in Capital Goods," December, 1958), U.S. experience since World War II does not bear this out. Some industrial

groups, such as manufacturing, have not added capital goods quite
so fast as their capacity to produce has increased. But these industries have accelerated their use of energy to increase their efficiency, and this has led to an increase in the capital investment
of the energy-producing industries at a rate rapid enough to offset
the lag in investment of other industries. Notwithstanding the
postwar experience, FORTUNE's projections for the 1960's are conservative, and so allow a little for a possible increase in the efficiency of capital. Therefore additions to plant and equipment
should easily equal or even exceed the projections here.

Research and development outlays, in the sense that they constitute an investment in the future that will swell capital-goods
volume, should be noted here. Owing to the nature of G.N.P.
statistics, only about half of these research outlays of $9 billion
in 1959 were actually classed as research, and these come under the
heading of government defense purchases. The other half are financed by business, and appear as a small fraction of the value
of various goods and services. Private research outlays have risen
from 0.5 per cent of G.N.P. in 1948 to about 1 per cent today and
will doubtless rise between 1.5 and 2 per cent by 1970.

EDUCATION COMES INTO ITS OWN

Investment in the nation's education is, of course, investment in
its future productivity as well as its culture. To Americans exer-
cised about the "lag" in U.S. education it may come as a surprise
that the country's accomplishments in education during the past
decade have already anticipated even the most liberally conceived
tasks of the next. The Twentieth Century Fund, whose *America's
Needs and Resources* was a pioneering effort to define some of the
country's potentials and shortages, defined educational needs for
1950 as more students, more teachers, and higher pay per teacher.
The fund estimated that U.S. education outlays were then meeting only 70 per cent of the needs of elementary and secondary
schools and 50 per cent of the needs of colleges. Since then primary
and secondary-school enrollments have risen 50 per cent. The
average schooling of the labor force rose from 10.6 years in

1948 to twelve years in 1958, a palpable investment in future productivity in a new age of research and automation. Yet more than
half the educational deficit estimated by the fund has already been
made good, and the projections here assume it will all be made
good by 1970.

The country's outlays for education (not including school construction, which will be discussed later) were 3.1 per cent of G.N.P.
or $14 billion in 1957, against only 2.4 per cent in 1948. Half the
increase was accounted for by rising salaries—teachers' salaries
have been actually going up faster than factory wages—and the
other half by more teachers and facilities.

BOOM IN HIGHER EDUCATION

Expenditures for education will probably account for 3.1 per
cent of G.N.P. or $15.5 billion this year. And how will they shape
up during the rest of the Sixties? The big surge will come in advanced education, which is three times as expensive per student
as primary or secondary education. A steadily increasing percentage of the young are attending college. What is more, the
population of college age will increase 50 per cent by 1970.

On the other hand, since the baby boom is leveling off, the
elementary and secondary-school enrollment during the 1960's will
increase only 20 per cent, against 50 per cent in the 1950's. As the
decade ends, the children born in the baby boom of the 1940's will
begin to have children of their own, and enrollment will begin to
rise again. So educational needs will probably level off to 3.1 per
cent of G.N.P., or better than $19 billion in 1965, and nearly $24
billion in 1970. Since the price of education will rise relatively,
actual outlays will probably be something like $20 billion in 1965
and $25.5 billion in 1970.

HEALTH AS INVESTMENT

Another great but unsung social investment in the past decade
has been the improvement of the national health. The Twentieth
Century Fund estimated that medical care was only two-thirds
adequate in 1950. Today, even when full account is taken of the

increased number of people, and particularly of the aged, more than half of this inadequacy has been made good. Expenditures for medical and hospital services (but not hospital construction) increased from 4.1 per cent of G.N.P. in 1948 to 4.8 per cent or $21.6 billion in 1957. At the same time, life expectancy and other measurements of well-being show great improvement. Owing to the unmeasured but doubtless rising effectiveness of new drugs, new medical techniques, less hospitalization time, etc., the productivity of health services may have grown enormously, and therefore expenditure figures do not reflect the true progress the country has made.

It is hard to gauge accurately health standards and needs. But to take care of current demands and at the same time make good the remaining inadequacy in health as estimated by the Twentieth Century Fund, the U.S. will have to spend, as prices stand today, about $30 billion in 1965 and $38 billion in 1970. Since the relative prices of health goods and services (mostly services) will probably be rising by at least 10 per cent during the 1960's—more than prices of all other investment goods and services—actual outlays may come to $33 billion in 1965 and $43 billion in 1970. This latter figure is twice the 1957 figure.

MORE HOUSE PER HOUSE

Although the country's housing "requirements" ought to be easy to meet in the Sixties, needs will change to some extent as standards change. In recent years the U.S. has been building more than 1,300,000 new housing units a year (an additional 150,000 units a year have been created by conversion) for almost 900,000 new households, and thus more than 550,000 units a year have been replacements. By the early 1970's the number of households will be increasing by nearly 1,300,000 a year, so the number of housing starts will probably rise to 1,600,000 a year. But unless people spend more on the houses than they do now, the share of G.N.P. claimed by housing construction will decline from 4.1 per cent in 1960 to 3.4 per cent in 1970.

From the end of World War II to the mid-Fifties, the housing industry failed to persuade Americans to spend as much of their income on houses as they did in the 1920's. Or to put it another way, the country's disposable income rose faster than the value of its stock of houses. The trouble seemed to be the persistently high cost of new houses even when other consumer prices (relative to all prices) were declining.

Several years ago, however, the trend changed. Partly because growing families needed larger quarters, the building industry succeeded in selling more house per house—somewhat as the auto industry sold more car per car. Between 1953 and 1957 the real value of the country's houses rose 17 per cent, while real disposable income rose only 14 per cent. Obviously people are now buying more expensive houses. And as new techniques such as prefabricated modules and new low-cost materials are employed more widely, housing costs and prices may actually decline—relative, that is, to the trend of all prices. So the share of G.N.P. accounted for by house construction should rise to 4.1 per cent this year, and then, with a continued rise in quality, can plausibly be expected to decline to about 4 per cent in 1965 and 1970. This would mean actual outlays of $25 billion in 1965 and $30 billion in 1970.

INVESTMENT IN "PUBLIC WORKS"

A large category of investment needs that will increase faster than G.N.P.—and thus at the expense of consumption—consists mainly of public works such as highways, and schools and hospitals both privately and publicly financed. In 1957 this group (shown as "other construction" in the charts on pages 76-77) took $13.6 billion or 3 per cent of G.N.P. This year, FORTUNE estimates, physical volume will rise to about 3.4 per cent of G.N.P., by 1965 to 3.7 per cent, and by 1970 to 4 per cent. Since construction prices are rising, relatively, actual outlays would come to more than $23 billion in 1965 and to about $31 billion in 1970.

The biggest single factor in the increase is the $40-billion-plus Interstate highway network, whose construction will lift annual outlays on highways by federal, state, and local governments from close to $7 billion now to as much as $12 billion a year by the end

of the decade. School construction now takes more than $3.5 bil-
lion a year as against $2.2 billion in 1950. But despite the heavy
outlays of the past decade, school construction will probably continue to advance faster than G.N.P. Another larger element in
public works is hospital construction, which now takes $1.1 billion
a year and will take $1.6 billion in 1965 and more than $2 billion
in 1970. And there is a miscellany of $5.5 billion devoted to
sewerage, waterworks, etc., which will rise to almost $8 billion by
1970.

Finally, under the general heading of "Investment" there are
three other items: (1) "other government"—general administration expenses and police and fire departments—which over the
years has accounted for 2.3 per cent of G.N.P. and will probably
continue to do so; (2) net exports, included in defense in the
charts on pages 76-77 and partly financed by "national security"
programs, which have been averaging 1 per cent of G.N.P. and
will probably continue to do so; and (3) net additions to inventory,
including farmers' and CCC stocks, which fluctuate widely but
probably will average 1 per cent of G.N.P.

So much for investment and defense needs. Note that all their
prices have been rising relative to consumption prices, and will
continue to do so. If their prices were to remain level, outlays for
them of course would be the same as the estimates of their physical
volume, or a total of $252 billion in 1965 and of $298 billion in
1970. Instead, the country will probably be spending a total of
$260 billion on investment and defense in 1965 and $315 billion in
1970.

$436 BILLION PLUS TO SPEND

The prices of consumption goods and services, compared to
prices of investment goods, have been falling and will continue to
fall. Although the country will probably have $355 billion avail-
able for them in 1965 and $436 billion in 1970, it will be able to
buy more than these sums could buy today. The total "physical"
volume of consumer goods and services in the 1960's, in other
words, will rise faster than consumer's actual dollar payments for

them—assuming, of course, no general inflation.

How consumers will allocate these dollars will depend on a variety of factors that can now be only tentatively appraised: although population will increase less than half as fast as personal income, the number of teen-agers and young adults (up to twenty-five) will increase by 45 per cent; income distributions may well shift, with the largest income gains going not to the unskilled workers, but rather to the skilled and the professionals.

The trend of consumer spending will also depend on relative price movements. Prices of food, clothing, and home and recreation goods have tended to show steady declines, relative to other prices; rents and car prices have been fairly stable; prices of most services have tended to rise. Following are FORTUNE's estimates of the prospects for the major consumer markets:

Per capita volume in the food, drink, and tobacco group fluctuates from year to year with the so-called meat-production cycle, but in recent years it has tended to rise about two-thirds as much as total consumption. This seems only natural, given the limits of man's stomach, though in fact sales of many food products incorporating service features have risen briskly, and more or less static sales of tobacco and alcohol are responsible for the group's sluggishness. The demand for special food products may yet cause that group's volume to rise faster; but its volume will probably continue to rise a third less rapidly than the volume of total consumption. In the latter years of the decade, owing in part to the rapid increase in the numbers of teen-agers and young adults, food consumption will accelerate along with total consumption.

Relative prices of food, which dominate the group, have tended to decline in recent years, and should continue the tendency as farm productivity rises. Actual dollars spent on food, drink, and tobacco, therefore, may rise only 11 per cent between now and 1965 or from $91 billion to $101 billion, and 16 per cent between 1965 and 1970, or from $101 billion to $117 billion.

Clothing volume per capita, while rising, has also tended to rise less than other consumption—even though relative prices have declined substantially during recent years. So actual outlays on clothing should increase by only 10 per cent between now and 1965, or from $39 billion to $43 billion, and by 16 per cent between 1965 and 1970, or to $50 billion.

Rent includes both actual payments for housing space and (in the G.N.P. statistics) imputed payments by homeowners. As the country catches up with the worst of its housing backlog, volume of rental payments and housing costs will probably increase no more, or even slightly less, than total consumption. Much will depend upon the demand for better houses, which is greatly affected by the price of new construction. Prices of housebuilding and of rent have held stable when compared to all prices, i.e., they have not been going down as fast as consumption prices in general. If this continues, actual dollars spent for rent will come to $47 billion in 1965 and $57 billion in 1970.

The volume of household and recreation goods has been rising much more than consumption in general, partly because of the growth in leisure, partly because prices of these items—relative to all prices—have declined sharply. This group encompasses a great variety of products—TV, hi-fi, washers, freezers, air conditioners, cameras, records, sporting goods—and their prices have not declined, nor have their sales risen, in unison. However, the trends toward bigger volume and still lower (relative) prices may be safely projected into the 1960's, and this means that outlays for household and recreation goods would come to $42 billion in 1965, and to $53 billion by 1970.

Car purchases have tended to rise faster than consumption in general for nearly two generations and, despite the auto industry's troubles in recent years, will probably continue to do so in the 1960's. The development of compact cars and the consequent broadening of the market should help sales over most of the decade, and so will the impending large additions to the car-driving population.

Relative prices of cars, as well as they can be measured in the face of major shifts in size, power, and appointments, have fluctuated sharply. They declined, relatively, in the mid-Fifties, and then rose in the last few years. In light of market troubles during the late 1950's and the trend to cheaper compact cars, the relative price trend should be down again during the 1960's. Outlays on cars can be expected to rise 19 per cent in 1960–65 and 24 per cent in 1965–70, or to $21 billion in 1965 and $26 billion in 1970.

Expenditures on "other transportation"—automobile operation, as distinct from car purchases, and fares for public transport—are geared closely to the number of cars on the road. Seventy-five per cent of this total goes for auto operation: gas and oil (42 per cent of the total), tires and parts (10 per cent), and car repair, insurance, etc. (23 per cent). The number of cars has been growing faster than the population and will continue to do so if the accompanying projection of car purchases is realized. During most of the Fifties, relative prices in the transportation category tended to increase, but they dipped a little in recent years. We can assume a very slight rise in the 1960's, owing mainly to the tendency of service costs (repair, insurance, etc.) to mount. So outlays should come to about $34 billion in 1965 and to $44 billion in 1970.

Personal services and utilities are a vast miscellany that totaled $48 billion in 1957. This included $15 billion for gas, electricity, and telephones, and $33 billion for domestic servants, spectator amusements, insurance and bank charges, brokerage commissions, and foreign travel. Growth trends and price trends have been somewhat diverse—e.g., more utilities and fewer servants, more tourists and fewer movie-goers. But there are crosscurrents: recently the number of domestic servants has risen, and utility rates have not been declining as much as they did in the 1940's. The most spectacular volume increases over recent years have been shown by foreign travel—and brokerage charges.

The volume of services, though growing, lagged behind the volume of other consumption between 1929 and the end of the war. But since then it has been making up for lost time, and has expanded far more rapidly than total consumption. More recently, however, the increase slowed down, partly because of rising prices. In the current decade a slow uptrend in relative prices of services may limit the rise; outlays will nevertheless increase at a faster rate than outlays for other major consumption groups. So they

should come to about $67 billion or 11 per cent of G.N.P. in
1965 and $89 billion or 12 per cent of G.N.P. in 1970.

ENOUGH IS NOT TOO MUCH

Such a plenitude of consumer goods and services suggests that
the American people may take a slice of their increased capacity to
produce in the form of leisure. This, as a matter of fact, they
have been doing for a century. A hundred years ago the average
work week (nonfarm) was around sixty-five hours, and at the turn
of the century it was still fifty-six hours. But by 1950 it had been
shortened to less than forty-one hours. It is still about forty
hours. FORTUNE's projections assume that the work week will
shrink more in the 1960's than it did in the 1950's, but less than in
previous decades. There has been no basic change in the standard
nonfarm work week since 1938, when the forty-hour week was
adopted by many industries; the average work week has been
declining by 1.5 hours a decade since then because the nation as a
whole has been gradually adopting the forty-hour week, and
because many women and students have been working part time.
Although there is as yet no sign of a new basic work week, the
thirty-five or thirty-six-hour week (five seven-hour days) is common
in a good many big-city offices and may spread.

Despite such trends, however, the labor force is increasing more
than enough to offset them. In the 1950's it grew by about 8 per
cent. In the 1960's, as the babies of the 1940's come of age, the
population of working age should expand twice as fast as it did in
the 1950's, or by about 16 per cent a year. It is this accelerated
growth in the labor force, coming at a time when the country's
productivity will also be increasing at a record rate, that will
enable the U.S. of the 1960's to meet the demands of defense,
public service, and capital investment, and still have such stupendous quantities of goods and services left for the consumer.

CHAPTER FIVE

The Decade of the "Discretionary" Dollar

As A RESULT of the great income revolution that has transformed U.S. society—and the U.S. market—in the last few decades, some of the changes in prospect for the 1960's are so extraordinary that they sound less like economic projections than like some utopian manifesto. Real poverty will be largely abolished in the U.S. A vast number of adult Americans, perhaps 25 million, will be "making a living" without actually working; most of them, of course, will be retired, and retirement income will be substantial enough so that Americans will be largely free of the old fear of destitution in their late years. Meanwhile, the ancient image of work as something manual and tedious will be fading rapidly: by 1970 a substantial majority of workers will be in white-collar or highly skilled blue-collar jobs—in jobs that characteristically require real training and thought. In part because of this occupational up-grading, personal income will grow furiously during the 1960's; it will, in fact, grow even more rapidly than it grew in the booming 1950's. By the end of the decade, families *above* the middle-income level will constitute the new mass market.

These high-income masses will provide the essential difference between the markets of the 1950's and those of the 1960's. The markets of the 1950's were expanded and reshaped by the emergence of an appreciable new supply of "discretionary" income. While the exact dividing line has to be set somewhat arbitrarily, it is broadly true that families with after-tax incomes under $4,000 are obliged to spend just about everything on the necessities of food, clothing, shelter, transportation, and medical care. As they move over the $4,000 line, they have extra income with which they can exercise a number of options. They can buy better food and drink, or better furniture, or they can take a small flyer in the stock market; or, conceivably, all of the extra income may go for one big fling in the luxury market (e.g., the $5,000 family that saves for years to take a trip to Europe). Right now, about three-fifths of all family units* in the U.S. have some discretionary income.

By the time that families move over the $7,500 line, about half their income is discretionary, and the range of options is now so wide that it is no longer just a question of this purchase or that purchase, but of choosing a whole *style of life*. A skilled mechanic who earns $7,500 after taxes may choose to continue living in "working class" style, meanwhile saving sizable sums for his children's college education; or he may choose to live like a junior executive in his own $17,000 suburban house; or he may choose to live in a city apartment house otherwise occupied by business and professional men. When the American "masses" have options of this breadth, it is scarcely an exaggeration to suggest that we will have arrived at a landmark in all the history of human freedoms.

These extravagant-sounding statements assume that there will be no general war in the years ahead; and they also assume that no large, presently unforeseeable events will send the economy into a recession more severe than those of 1949, 1953–54, and 1957–58. If these assumptions prove correct, it is safe to say that we are in for a gradual, but nevertheless breath-taking, change in the character of life in America.

Another kind of reservation may be expressed. If the marketing

* Except for those who are institutionalized, and some members of the armed forces, every American is counted as belonging to some "family unit." Besides families in the ordinary sense, the term applies to individuals living alone, three bachelor girls sharing an apartment, etc. There were 55 million family units in the U.S. in 1959.

implications of a high-income mass society are exhilarating, the
moral implications of a world in which sizable sums of money
come to millions of Americans easily, almost "automatically," are
somewhat harder to express. It is at least conceivable that the
opulent masses might develop a kind of moral flabbiness over the
years, and that endless preoccupation with problems of consumption might turn us into a race of people poorly equipped to cope
with the realities of the thermonuclear age. In the years just ahead
it is likely that we will be hearing a great deal about this problem.

Perhaps the best way to gain an appreciation of the coming
phase of the income revolution is to consider what has preceded
it. In the first three decades of this century the U.S. began to
develop what was then glorified as a "mass market." It was, at
first, a very impoverished market by modern standards: in 1900,
almost half the family units in the U.S. had less than $2,000 of
income—in terms of 1959 prices. (All income figures are given in
1959 dollars and after taxes.) During the 1920's the most significant
market development was the creation of a sizable "lower-middle-
income" class, based on family units in the $2,000-to-$4,000 income class. It was these families and individuals who made possible the development of a mass consumer market for products
like the Model T; by 1929 there were 14 million such family
units—three times as many as in 1900—and they represented
almost 40 per cent of all the units. But the division between the
mass and the "class" markets persisted: these 14 million, together
with the 12 million below $2,000, had less aggregate spending
power than the 3,300,000 family units with more than $7,500 of
income.

The welfare legislation introduced under the New Deal, and
the higher taxes imposed during the 1930's and the war years,
made up the second phase. These measures tended to equalize
incomes somewhat—i.e., to prop up the mass market and to limit
the growth of the class market—and when World War II finally
ended the depression these measures contributed to the extraordinary growth of a real middle-income class—i.e., of family units
with income after taxes of $4,000 to $7,500. By 1947, family
units in this bracket already had 43 per cent of all the disposable

income in the U.S. But about half of all family units in 1947
were still under the $4,000 line.

In the third phase, which began after the war and is now ending,
the moneyed middle-income class came to dominate the market in
almost every respect. In 1954, when FORTUNE published *The
Changing American Market,* over 40 per cent of all family units
had after-tax incomes between $4,000 and $7,500, and their income
was about 40 per cent of the total. These proportions remained
fairly constant during the 1950's. All together, the number of
family units with $4,000 to $7,500 of income in 1959 was about 22
million (a gain of 30 per cent over 1947), and within this group
there were over seven million family units with more than $6,000.
The number of family units under $4,000 declined both abso-
lutely and relatively: by 1959 only two-fifths of all family units
were under $4,000. Meanwhile, the number of units with more
than $7,500 roughly doubled—to over 12 million—in the years
after 1947.

During the present decade, the market will come to be dominated by this mass high-income class. By 1970 there will be around
25 *million* family units with more than $7,500; they will comprise
nearly two-fifths of all the family units; and they will have over
three-fifths of all consumer spending money. The middle-income
family units, whose spending power dominated the markets of
the early 1950's, will have only 28 per cent of the disposable income by 1970—down from 43 per cent in 1947.

Or look at it another way: If all family units in the U.S. are
divided into a low (under $4,000), middle ($4,000 to $7,500), and
high (over $7,500) income class, then the income pyramid that
has traditionally characterized all societies is now being stood on
its head in the U.S. Even in 1947 about 50 per cent of family
units were low income, about 40 per cent were middle income,

The next American market will be dominated by family units with more than
$7,500 income (after taxes), just as the market of the early 1950's was dominated
by families in the middle range ($4,000 to $7,500). By 1970, families over the
$7,500 line will actually outnumber families in the middle, even though these
too will grow a little during the 1960's. Meanwhile there will be a steep decline, both absolutely and relatively, of families under the $4,000 line (who
will be only a sixth of the total by 1970).

The High-Income Masses

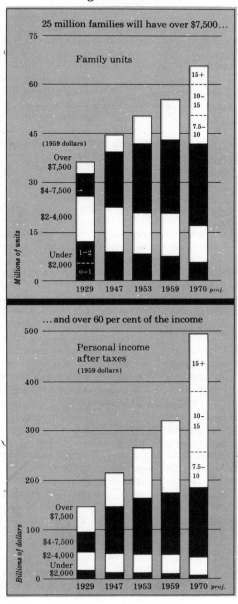

25 million families will have over $7,500...

Family units

75

60

45

(1959 dollars)

Over
$7,500

$4-7,500

$2-4,000

Under
$2,000

30

15

0

15+

10–
15

7.5–
10

1–2

0–1

Millions of units

1929   1947   1953   1959   1970 *proj.*

...and over 60 per cent of the income

500

Personal income
after taxes
(1959 dollars)

400

300

200

Over
$7,500

$4-7,500

$2-4,000

Under
$2,000

100

0

15+

10–
15

7.5–
10

Billions of dollars

1929   1947   1953   1959   1970 *proj.*

Not working is the fastest growing of all major "occupations" in the U.S. today. The number of nonworkers has roughly doubled in the past decade, and might well double again by 1970. In the process, the U.S. is forming a new kind of rentier class, which poses some intriguing challenges for marketing men.

In 1949 there were 2,700,000 able-bodied Americans over fourteen who were not working or looking for work, not going to school, and not keeping house. Today there are about 5,500,000 persons over fourteen who are doing none of these things, and a sizable number of them appear to have resources that enable them to "not work" fairly early in life: about 1,500,000 of them are under sixty-five. The remaining four million are predominantly retired men. In all, there are seven million men in the U.S. over sixty-five, of whom 2,200,000 are still working (and half a million are considered disabled rather than retired). Of the eight million women over sixty-five, 6,500,000 are listed as "keeping house"—and more than a million are employed.

By 1970 about eight million men and eleven million women will be over sixty-five, and they will make up about 9 per cent of the U.S. population. The significant marketing fact about these men and women is that, for the first time, they are coming to represent a big sales potential for a very wide variety of consumer products—for more and more leisure products like cameras and fishing gear, but also for furniture, household appliances, etc., since the retired are frequently setting up new homes. They can devote a lot more time to consumption than workers can; and given the swelling income that is becoming available to them, one might conceive of these elder Americans becoming an important new influence on taste and consumption habits generally.

In 1950 the median income of all men over sixty-five was about $1,000 (in 1959 dollars). Over 40 per cent of all these men were then in the labor force—i.e., they were either employed or looking for work. Today, the most recent data indicate, the median income of men over sixty-five is about $1,450—but only a third of them are in the labor force. In 1950 about 15 per cent of men over sixty-five had incomes over $3,500; today the proportion is 20 per cent. These figures, moreover, include only the sums going directly to men over sixty-five, but many of their wives also have pensions and other income. Of the seven million men over sixty-five, about 4,500,000 are living with their wives (and another 400,000 are the heads of families that do not include their wives). About 40 per cent of these families have incomes over $3,500.

Retirement and retirement income will grow rapidly during the 1960's, principally because Americans have been deferring sizable quantities of current income in order to build nest eggs for the future. The eggs will be hatched, in the 1960's, out of income that has been deferred in several different ways: by paying taxes (e.g., social-security taxes, payroll taxes to finance unemployment insurance) that are ultimately transferred to people who are not working; by limiting payrolls in order to build up pension funds for employees; by saving in order to build up annuities or capital that can later be used to produce income. Here are some figures on the recent and prospective payout to the new rentier class:

Social security. In 1940 about a million Americans received old-age and survivors' payments; the annual payout was $24 million. Today about 13 million Americans receive social security (which has included disability payments since 1957); the annual total is about $10 billion—more than double the payroll of the U.S. automobile industry. By 1970, the Social Security Administration has estimated, about 19 million will be receiving payments; and the annual payout will be about $18 billion. In 1970, even with no further changes in coverage, about 80 per cent of all people over sixty-five will be receiving social-security benefits.

Other federal programs. A miscellany of other benefits for civil servants, railroad workers, regular military personnel, and veterans provide regular payments to some 5,200,000 individuals or families. The total annual payout is about $4.7 billion. There has been a fivefold increase in the number of beneficiaries since 1940 and a sevenfold increase in the payout. It is hard to project these totals ahead to 1970—but they will surely continue to rise.

State and local programs. These afford benefits under a diverse and bewildering assortment of laws—which provide for teachers' and policemen's pensions, unemployment insurance, workmen's compensation, public assistance (i.e., "relief"), etc. Not all the payments are made regularly (e.g., unemployment-insurance payments), and the total number of beneficiaries is not known; but the total payout from all these sources has increased from $1.4 billion in 1940 to around $4.5 billion in 1959. Again, future payouts are certain to increase.

Private pensions. In 1940 about 160,000 families or individuals received regular payments under privately financed group pension plans; the figure is up to about 1,300,000 today. Total payments are up from $140 million in 1940 to about $1.2 billion. About 18 million workers are covered by these plans; if we assume that these workers have the same age composition as the labor force as a whole, then it would appear that there will be about three million regular beneficiaries by 1970. The monthly payments will vary considerably, of course, but to cite a possibility under one of the more generous plans, a welder who began at Grumman Aircraft in 1935 and now earns $130 a week might be eligible to retire in 1970 with $300 a month—$425 counting his social security.

Life-insurance payments, not counting payments under group pension plans, rose from $2.6 billion in 1940 to about $7.4 billion in 1959. It is reasonable to expect a further rise to $13 billion by 1970.

Dividends, interest, and rent—the traditional sources of rentier income—have increased from an aggregate of $9.2 billion in 1940 to $29 billion of cash payments last year. Forecasting the future of these payouts is a parlous business, but it is quite possible that by 1970 the total will be more than $40 billion. However, the figures on dividends, interest, and rent include some payments that are not really to individuals—e.g., payments made to pension funds—and so the totals should be reduced somewhat, perhaps by 15 per cent, to avoid an overlap with some of the newer kinds of rentier income.

The significant fact about these newer kinds of income is that they are growing much more rapidly than personal income as a whole, while dividends, interest, and rent have been declining as a share of all personal income—from 12 per cent in 1940 to 8 per cent in 1959. The newer kinds of rentier income are already close to 8 per cent—i.e., they add up to about $28 billion of the total $375 billion in personal income. Something like 15 per cent of all personal income, then, is already paid out for nonwork—which is getting to be an extremely attractive occupation.

and about 10 per cent were high income. During the 1950's, this pyramid began to assume a diamond shape. (The diamond shape is more marked if we consider only actual families and forget for the moment about "family units"; the latter include a number of relatively low-income single individuals just starting their careers and older persons who are not working, e.g., widows.) Right now there are more families in the middle than at the top or bottom. And by 1970 the pyramid will be finally inverted. Families with incomes over $7,500 will be 45 per cent of all families; the middle-income families will be another 39 per cent (and they will still be moving rapidly toward the top group); and those with less than $4,000 will be only 16 per cent.

The basis for the coming income boom has been set forth in previous chapters. The heart of the matter is the very rapid growth of productivity anticipated in the 1960's; the increase is likely to average 3 per cent a year—as it has in the years since World War II. Meanwhile, the total man-hours worked should rise about 1.2 per cent a year, an increase over the growth rate that prevailed during the 1950's. The over-all increase in the output of goods and services, then, will be more than 4 per cent a year compounded, and suggests a gross national product in 1970 of $750 billion. About a third of this total will be absorbed by defense expenditures and by business and "social" investment (e.g., for schools, highways). This would leave about $500 billion of disposable income in 1970, compared to about $330 billion in 1959.

It is not only the sheer magnitude of this figure that compels attention. What may prove even more intriguing, and more challenging, to marketing men is the fact that so much of this money will be in the hands of families able to exercise a wide range of options in spending it. In 1959, there was some $140 billion of discretionary income in the U.S., i.e., of "after-$4,000 income" to the family units that had it—and 60 per cent of U.S. family units had at least some of this after-$4,000 money. By 1970, these discretionary dollars will just about double, *to around $255 billion. More than half of all disposable personal income will be discretionary by 1970. And the overwhelming bulk of this discretionary*

income, perhaps 85 per cent of it, will belong to the 25 million
families with more than $7,500.

In pondering the marketing implications of these imposing
statistics, it is well to retain a firm purchase on the distinction between the spending habits of middle-income families and of those
above the middle. A family whose income goes up from, say,
$4,000 to $5,000 has only a limited range of discretions, as we have
already observed; and within any one community most of the
$5,000 families have to live pretty much alike. On the other hand,
families with incomes over $7,500 have enough discretionary in-
come so that they are free to change their whole style of life—and
to do so repeatedly.

They may, in fact, go off on all sorts of tangents from one
year to the next, and in the 1960's we may well see a succession of
brief, hectic booms in a wide range of markets, with the money-
laden masses conferring their favors alternately on boats, helicopters, original paintings, adult education, champagne-every-
night, and psychoanalysis.

Historically, the spending habits of the American masses have
been heavily influenced by "spending leaders" whose income was
well above the average. As the incomes of the leaders were steadily
increased, and a wider range of goods became available, they
tended to spend their additional income. In following the leaders,
the masses have tended, over the years, to reduce the proportion of
income saved by any one income class, and they have also tended to
build up mass markets for a wide range of consumer products, like
refrigerators, that were regarded as luxuries when the leaders first
began to buy them. Out of this process there has emerged, somehow, a remarkable kind of stability in spending patterns, i.e., the
proportions of income spent on food, transportation, furniture,
etc., have held fairly constant. This constancy may well persist
during the 1960's, even while the new spending leaders continue to
upgrade the country's notions about necessities. But it is also
possible that these families, which have the capacity to *save* in a
big way, will lead millions of Americans to own more common

The New Labor Force: How Far Can the Upgrading Go?

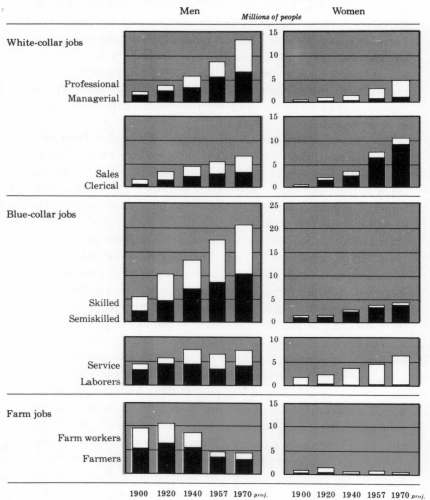

Men   *Millions of people*   Women

White-collar jobs

Professional
Managerial

Sales
Clerical

Blue-collar jobs

Skilled
Semiskilled

Service
Laborers

Farm jobs

Farm workers

Farmers

1900 1920 1940 1957 1970 *proj.*   1900 1920 1940 1957 1970 *proj.*

stocks, say, and fewer physical goods. (Stock ownership is already becoming, for many families, an important symbol of "having arrived.")

These are speculations, of course, not predictions; we can summarize matters by saying that there is a *potentiality*, at least, for an entirely new kind of market, endlessly fragmented by the individualistic spending decisions of millions of well-heeled families; and there is also a potentiality for a cohesive but quite volatile market, dominated by families keeping up (or down) with the Joneses, and moving from one gigantic fad to another. If the spending possibilities cited above sound extreme for many families that have just crossed the $7,500 line, it should be noted that most families over that line will be well over it. More than three-fifths of the over-$7,500 families of 1970 will also be over $10,000.

SEATED EMPLOYMENT

In estimating how Americans are likely to be spending their money in the 1960's, it is important to know something about their occupations as well as incomes.

Perhaps the first point to make about the occupations of the 1960's is that fewer of them will be physical than they have been in the past. Perhaps half of all employed Americans already do their

---

U.S. society will reach an extraordinary milestone by 1970—there will be more white-collar than blue-collar workers. Actually, the jobs of Americans have been undergoing a vast reshuffling ever since the turn of the century. In 1900 more than 40 per cent of all employed men were in agriculture, and a slightly smaller proportion were blue-collar workers, with laborers the largest group among these. By 1920 only 30 per cent of working men were on the farms; the occupational "mix" was heavily weighted with blue-collar workers, who constituted almost half the male labor force. By 1940 more than half of male workers were blue-collars, and the white-collars now outnumbered the men on the farms. Since 1940 the male white-collar workers have increased by 45 per cent, the blue-collars have increased only 15 per cent, and the number working on farms has diminished sharply. By 1970 more than half of all men—including some specialized skilled workers and farmers with technical training—will be largely freed from manual labor (except at home).

Since 1940 women have been pouring into the labor force at a faster rate than men, and they have gone predominantly into white-collar jobs. For men and women as a whole the greatest increase in the 1960's will be in the best white-collar jobs—i.e., in professional, technical, and managerial work.

work *sitting down*. During the 1960's, the trend will continue; an increasing number of jobs will require special kinds of skill, judgment, training, and in turn will offer (along with good pay) challenge and stimulus.

This trend is commonly viewed as the "white-collar revolution," and there is certainly some basis for that view, even if one looks only at the changes in male jobs—the jobs that principally determine the way a family looks at itself. Only about 15 per cent of men held white-collar jobs in 1900 (they were mostly small proprietors). This proportion rose to 25 per cent in 1940 and will rise to 40 per cent by 1970.

But meanwhile, there has been a significant change in farm and blue-collar work. At the turn of the century, more than half of the male labor force in the U.S. consisted of farmers and laborers whose skills were primitive, whose work was arduous, and whose income was not much above a subsistence level. By 1940 only 40 per cent of men were farmers or laborers, and by 1957 only 25 per cent—and they were much better paid. Meanwhile, skilled and semiskilled workers grew from 20 per cent of the male labor force in 1900 to 40 per cent in 1957.

In the coming period, work will be predominantly brain work. By 1970, about two working men out of five will be white collars; there will be about 20 million of them, and two-thirds will be congregated in the very best white-collar jobs—i.e., they will be working, in Census Bureau terms, as "managers, officials, and proprietors," or as "professional, technical, and kindred workers."

Within the blue-collar and farm groups there will also be significant kinds of "upgrading" during the 1960's. In each of these categories, work will not only be less physical, but it will also have a new dignity attached to it. The characteristic blue-collar of 1940 was a man on an assembly line whose work was intensely monotonous. But a high proportion of blue-collar workers are now skilled, and by 1970 over ten million of the blue-collars will be "craftsmen, foremen, and kindred workers," exercising a great deal of judgment and entrusted with the care and operation of some very sophisticated kinds of capital equipment. One modern oil refinery, for example, now requires a high-school education for production workers, and hires only foremen with engineering degrees.

The prototypical farmer of 1970 will also be exercising new kinds of judgment. Indeed, it is already somewhat unrealistic to think of the farmer as a manual worker; a great many of them are beginning to look (and to earn) more like highly trained technicians and entrepreneurs, exercising skills that depend on detailed knowledge of soil chemistry, and even making use of electronic computers, e.g., to determine the best genetic combinations in breeding chickens. The continuing decline in the farm labor force —which had about 8,500,000 men in 1940 and will have about half that many in 1970—has been chiefly at the expense of the least skilled farmers and laborers, e.g., sharecroppers and field hands.

THE HELPMATES

Their flexibility will also be enhanced by the continuing expansion of opportunities for their wives to work, especially in white-collar fields. In 1954, FORTUNE observed that the rapid increase in middle-income families during the 1950's was based in large measure on the growth of supplementary earners; and that about two-fifths of all these families would be *below* the middle 'if they did not have more than one member at work. A similar point may now be made about the growth of over $7,500 families, recent and prospective. During the 1960's there will be more working wives; the wives are already about half of all the supplementary earners.

Jobs that require skills and judgment have, almost inherently, a greater dignity than jobs that are simply manual or repetitive; and the faster growth of "judgment jobs," combined with sharply rising levels of pay, suggests that during the 1960's millions of workers will begin to enjoy something like the status that once was conferred exclusively on certain kinds of professionals and proprietors—traditionally the "individualists" par excellence.

WHO ARE THE POOR?

One corollary of the prospective upgrading of the labor force is that, in the aggregate, the lowest-paid jobs—for service workers, farm and nonfarm laborers—will show no significant growth. Indeed, the attrition in these jobs since 1940, and the rising pay scales attached to them, have already created a situation in which very few Americans can be considered "permanently poor" because they hold bad jobs. In 1957 there were some 3,600,000 families with incomes under $2,000. But more than half of them were either unemployed or retired, i.e., the low income was temporary or it was being bolstered by savings or help from relatives. Only about a million domestic servants, marginal farm operators, and farm laborers and their families still look truly poor.

DISCRETIONARY ANXIETY

By the end of the 1960's, it is manifest, Americans will be free to order their lives in a dramatically new and different fashion. They will have incomes and jobs that offer the prospect of a new kind of human dignity. But the freedoms of the 1960's imply some new kinds of problems too. Masses with high incomes and diverse job opportunities may not only baffle the marketing man, they may baffle themselves. The expanded range of options will call for new and sometimes difficult decisions—how to spend, how much to spend or save, how much, indeed, to work. A man whose career is determined, and whose spending habits are largely determined, by necessity may simply take his position in life as "fixed"—and not worry about it. People with new options about their style of living and position in life may find themselves exposed to new anxieties. Most of them, presumably, will be willing to put up with this.

CHAPTER SIX

The New Masses

ONLY ten years ago, the following description of an American family's style of life would have enabled one to form some fairly firm impressions about the father's occupation and the general social "rank" of the family:

The parents, who are about forty, live with their two boys in a comfortable six-room suburban house outfitted with a full line of appliances, a television set that is in more or less constant use, and a car in which the father drives to work. The car is also used for camping trips during the summer. The mother shops at a local supermarket and at several local department stores; the boys attend the good local public schools; and on weekends the family often goes swimming at a local beach, although recently the father and mother and their older son have begun to take an interest in golf.

Given these facts in 1950, one might have inferred, quite reasonably, that the head of the house was a lower or middle-echelon executive, or salesman, or the proprietor or part owner of some small business, or a professional man, and that the family's position in society was solidly middle class.

Given these same facts in 1960, one could deduce practically nothing about the family's social rank or the father's occupation. For the fact is that in the past few years the broad style of life described above has become available, not only to an identifiable "middle class," but to a great mass of Americans, perhaps even a majority. The family head today might be a truck driver earning $5,500, a college professor earning $7,000, a life-insurance salesman earning $8,000, a skilled production worker earning $9,000, an airline pilot earning $15,000, or an executive earning $18,000. In the new American society, it is increasingly difficult to tell the players apart without subpoenaing their tax returns.

Many otherwise alert Americans continue to think and talk of their countrymen as though all of them could be sorted out into three clear-cut classes. The biggest of these, of course, would be a low-income *working class,* or simply *workers* ("lower class" has never come easily to American lips), symbolized most aptly by the "blue collars" in manufacturing but also including farmers. Then there would be the middle-income *middle class,* whose prototype is the small proprietor, or the professional or white-collar employee. And at the top there would be a small layer of important businessmen, prominent professionals, government officials, etc. Europeans would forthrightly call this the American *upper class;* Americans themselves are more likely to speak of *rich people, society people, big shots,* etc., and of course nobody is more reluctant to say "upper class" than a qualified member.

These traditional class concepts still have a kind of shorthand utility in connoting various styles of life, but when they are used to denote a neatly layered social pyramid they are today simply a source of confusion. For one thing, the shape is all wrong. As noted in the previous chapter, what we have in the U.S. today, by income standards at least, more nearly resembles a diamond than a pyramid—i.e., there are more people in the middle than there are at the top or bottom.

Aside from the shape of the income structure, it is increasingly difficult to "layer" a society of such great flux and diversity. It was never easy to diagram the "class structure" of the U.S. as a matter of fact, and most sociologists have usually been obliged to limit their descriptive efforts to relatively small, self-contained communities like Weirton, West Virginia, or like Newburyport, Massachu-

setts (whose inhabitants were divided, by W. Lloyd Warner and
Paul S. Lunt in a study starting in the 1930's, into *six* classes,
ranging from upper-upper to lower-lower). But as we enter the
1960's it is increasingly difficult to find even small communities in
which classes are clearly separable.

Russell Lynes, a witty amateur sociologist who is an editor of
Harper's magazine, has suggested that we visualize the new U.S.
society as a series of independent pyramids, each with its own
interests, hierarchies, and rewards. That is, one pyramid for
business executives, and others for scientists, labor-union officials,
the military, sports figures, etc.—even one for criminals. (An
ex-convict named Lewis Dent has described the criminal pyramid
in some detail: in prison, the professionals who live entirely by
the criminal code are held in highest regard, then come the gifted
amateurs who can show some genuine antisocial accomplishments,
e.g., rapists, and at the bottom are the "creeps" who are ostracized
because they reject the mores of the underworld.) But the pyramids also present difficulties when one tries to relate them to the
realities of American life. There are too many pyramids, and all
have different shapes. Some of them, in fact, are not really pyramids—e.g., among professional baseball players there are more
men in the major leagues than in class B. Furthermore, too many
Americans have different positions on several pyramids, and on
any one pyramid there is the problem that insiders and outsiders
often evaluate individuals differently; the young "comer" may
have more prestige within a corporation than many of the executives who apparently outrank him.

But the basic reason for the increased confusion about class in
the U.S. is the steady growth in the number of Americans who
can afford at least some of the amenities once associated with the
highest positions in our society. If most "workers" still cannot
afford $110 suits, boats, Thunderbirds, *and* trips to Florida, they
have at least enough discretionary income so that they can have
some of these things some of the time. As much as six years ago, in
The Changing American Market, FORTUNE noted that 43 per
cent of all nonfarm families had become concentrated in the

middle-income range—i.e., they had cash income after taxes of
$4,000 to $7,500 (in 1953 dollars); and it also noted that almost
60 per cent of these families were actually headed by blue-collar
workers. This bunching-around-the-middle has persisted in the
years since 1954, with the noteworthy difference that the "middle"
keeps moving higher up on the money scale. By 1959 about 43 per
cent of all nonfarm families had after-tax cash incomes between
$5,000 and $10,000 (in 1959 dollars).

THE MODERN MAGGIES

The most conspicuous breakdown of class lines is the one that
has taken place just in the past few years as the ex- "proletarians,"
who are now the heart of the middle-income class, began finally to
adopt a middle-class style of life. This phenomenon, portentous in
its implications for the markets of the 1960's, is hard to express
statistically, but there can no longer be any doubt about the broad
facts of the case. Nelson Foote, a distinguished sociologist who
recently left academic life to work for General Electric, says that
he has observed the change even in Detroit, a city where class con-
sciousness dies hard. "During the war," Foote says, "you could
sit on a streetcar and tell at a glance who were the defense workers
and who were the white collars. Then, while the war was still on,
the companies did something which has had a profound effect on
our society: they installed cafeterias and lockers in the plants.
After a while, you stopped seeing lunch boxes and work clothes on
the streetcars, and today you just can't tell who's who. The city is
full of auto workers whose wives shop at Hudson's—who wouldn't
be caught dead buying a pair of shoes at Sears."

Foote is convinced, in fact, that it is the wives of the blue-collar
workers who are instrumental in changing their families' style of
life, and he has observed at least some blue-collar families in which
the familiar old American saga of Jiggs and Maggie is being re-
enacted—though in the modern version Maggie is more concerned
with "bringing up father" to be an active P.T.A. member than to
be a society swell. In some respects, of course, the blue-collar
husbands accept middle-class ways with enthusiasm; many sub-

urban shopping-center proprietors argue that the husband is an easier prospect than the wife when a couple are pondering something of a splurge, especially when the splurge promises greater comfort or just plain fun. The wives, however, are closer to the children, hence closer to the real or fancied social pressures the children are under in the suburban schools. Moreover, many of the wives of blue-collar workers have themselves held white-collar jobs in offices, which brought them into contact with longer-established members of the middle class and their style of life.

A FOOTHOLD IN LEVITTOWN

How many blue-collar families have arrived in the suburbs? Even if no sociologists had observed the phenomenon, it can be inferred from available government data that a sizable number of blue collars* *have to be* in suburban, or semi-suburban, areas. Families headed by blue collars comprise about 60 per cent of non-farm families today. It is manifest that they cannot all be in the metropolitan areas' inner cities (which have about 25 per cent of the nonfarm population) and in the smaller cities and towns (which have about 30 per cent).

In an effort to gauge more precisely the impact of the blue-collar families on suburbia, and vice versa, in 1959 FORTUNE surveyed real-estate agents and developers, bankers, school officials, as well as some sociologists, in the suburbs of seven major metropolitan areas. There was almost unanimous agreement among these observers that the blue collars have moved increasingly into suburban homes, especially those in the $10,000-to-$15,000 price range—though there are sizable numbers of sales all the way up to $21,000. An agent in northeastern Philadelphia guessed that about half the $15,000-to-$20,000 homes he sold in 1958 went to skilled blue-collar workers; and near Dallas there is a development of some 200 homes in the same price range that are almost entirely occupied by production workers for Texas Instruments. On the other hand, an agent near Atlanta who has also sold many homes

* Blue collars include foremen, skilled and semiskilled workers in manufacturing, building, mining, and transportation, service workers, and laborers. In all, there are some 30 million (including 6 million women).

to skilled workers—especially to airline mechanics and Ford assembly-plant employees—finds that not many of them break through the $10,000 price barrier. An estimate by Charles M. Fink, an attorney and realtor who has been directly involved in the sale or rental of some 4,000 homes in the Levittown, Pennsylvania, suburban development, offers this picture of the blue-collar foothold there:

Price	*Number of houses*	*Proportion of blue-collar occupancy*
Over $17,500	1,200	Under 5 per cent
About $15,000	750	About 5-10 per cent
$10,000-$12,500	12,500	About 50 per cent
Under $10,000	2,700	About 65 per cent

This breakdown corresponds closely to the figures and impressions obtained from the other suburban areas. In 1954, FORTUNE estimated that about 30 million Americans lived in communities that were "strictly suburban" in character. The figure is in the neighborhood of 40 million today, and comprises about one-quarter of all nonfarm families. FORTUNE's survey suggests that perhaps a quarter of these are now blue-collar families, and in the newer suburban developments the proportion may be over a third.

BLUE AND WHITE VALUES

In several interesting respects the blue and white collars still play different roles in the suburbs, and still have different reasons for moving there. There have always been some blue-collar families in suburbia, of course, but until recently they tended to be the local service and construction workers who, in middle-class communities, lived on the other side of the tracks. The newer blue-collar suburbanites are characteristically the skilled production workers who man the new industrial plants on the outskirts of metropolitan areas. (Between 1952 and 1957, the suburbs accounted for 80 per cent of all new jobs in the New York metropolitan area.) Unlike the white-collar man, who characteristically moves *away* from his job when he migrates to the suburbs, the blue-collar man is usually moving closer to his job, and is much preoccupied with traffic conditions and driving time between his suburban home and his suburban factory.

The white collar is often acutely conscious of the prestige thought to attach to some particular suburban town or neighborhood. He may load an extra commuting burden on himself to live in such a place—indeed, he may feel that commuting itself is invested with a kind of upper-middle-class prestige value. The blue collar, however, tends to see commuting time simply as an extension of his working day.

The young white collar usually regards his first suburban home as a temporary lodgment on the way to a better one. The blue collar sees it as security for his old age, and for this reason, perhaps, is much more concerned with getting a durable physical property than the white collar is.

But the significant fact is that, while these differences persist, the living habits of the blue and white collars have been converging in many respects; indeed, one might regard the suburbs today as the new American melting pot. A community leader in Royal Oak, a Detroit suburb, notes that the auto workers who followed the plants out of town were "swallowed up" when they lived in Detroit. "When they come out here, they seem hungry for community affairs." Indeed, the fact that they regard their first suburban homes as permanent living places often gives the blue collars a stake in local government that the more transient white collars do not feel they have. A real-estate developer who built a community of $16,000-to-$17,000 houses northwest of Chicago says that about half the community is blue collar, and that he has been "amazed and pleased to see how they've taken hold and run the community. I've sat in on some committees they have, and I'll tell you they make a hell of a lot more sense than some of the junior-executive types I've seen." Even in Park Forest, the Chicago suburb that has been much discussed (in FORTUNE and elsewhere) as a prototypical junior-executive community, there is now a blue-

collar minority verging on 10 per cent, and in two recent years the
Little League baseball chairmen have been blue collars. With a
few exceptions, the people surveyed by FORTUNE reported that the
new blue-collar suburbanites are *not* segregated socially.

The breakdown of the older class distinctions can be seen in an
extreme form in southern California, especially in and around Los
Angeles—an area that is not exactly suburban in character, but
not exactly urban either. Nathan Glazer, a young Bennington
College sociologist who recently spent a year in California, came
away marveling at Los Angeles. "First of all, so many of the
people have come from somewhere else that 'backgrounds' have
less meaning; nobody cares about your family, or your religion,
or the schools you went to. Then the outdoor living tends to
make everyone live alike. Everyone uses the same communal
facilities, especially the national parks and beaches. In the East,
you feel it's kind of immoral to go swimming at four o'clock
Wednesday afternoon, but out there you get used to it pretty fast
—and the people there on the beach with you are aircraft workers,
bellhops, pensioners, intellectuals, and even businessmen. We're
used to defining people in terms of their jobs, but around Los
Angeles there's a strange lack of emphasis on jobs. There's no cen-
tral business district, and working hours tend to be quite irregular,
principally because there are so many part-time workers, so many
service employees who work odd hours, and so many professionals
—and pensioners—who are able to keep their own hours. The
traffic into and out of the city is heavy morning and evening but it
is always going both ways, and you can never be sure who is going
to the beach, to the supermarket, to Disneyland, or to work. The
result of it all is that you don't identify people with their occupations, as you naturally do in the East, and class distinctions become
further blurred."

WHAT THE DIFFERENCE IS

While the older class lines are losing their meaning, it would be
wildly unrealistic to argue that the U.S. is developing into a society
of equals. Instead of having a fairly clear position in an oversim-

plified but still identifiable "class," the American of the 1960's is
seen by the sociologists as a man with a "status." There are dozens
of shadings of status—of a man's standing in the eyes of others.
Status is more easily changed, obviously, than class. A family's
status may jump a notch not only with the father's promotion at
the office, but with the mother's election to the chairmanship of a
suburban charity drive, or the son's enrollment at the state university.

Spending and status are still intimately related, of course, but
in such diverse and sometimes paradoxical ways that novel opportunities and hazards are continually cropping up in the consumer markets. On the one hand, as more and more Americans
have been enabled to adopt some form of the middle-class style of
life, they have also become increasingly aware of, and more finely
attuned to, the nuances that can disclose "the difference"—the
difference between those with more and with less income and responsibility. In an age when millions of Americans live in super-
ficially similar suburban developments, the flagstone walk the
developer has given his more expensive houses is attentively noted.

The nuances involve much more than displays of income and
raw purchasing power, however, since status is importantly bound
up with education—which implies, among other things, the exercise of good taste in consumption. In an age when millions can
travel abroad, the difference between a three-week economy trip
to London-Paris-Rome and a six-week trip taking in Athens and
Istanbul is not just the difference in cost but also in sophistication
of the itinerary. Then there is the "keeping-down-with-the-
Joneses" phenomenon so often seen in modern suburbia, which is
not so much a pressure against heavy spending as a pressure to
spend money as educated men are supposed to spend it—i.e., on
fine high-fidelity sets and good wines rather than expensive fur
coats and cars. And yet—just to complicate things still more—
there has been such a proliferation of interesting, sophisticated,
or chic things to spend money on that it is increasingly difficult
to say that any two or three of these things are *the* badges of status.

The preoccupation with status is a phenomenon whose origins

are interesting—especially, perhaps, to marketing and advertising men who are increasingly obliged to think of products as status symbols. The preoccupation is related in part to the fact that since 1940 over 20 million adult Americans have spent a good deal of time in the armed forces, where one is obliged constantly to think about "rank." It is also related to the fact that more and more Americans work for large organizations: something like 38 per cent of the labor force is employed in organizations that have over 500 employees. The figure (which includes all government employees) was only 28 per cent in 1940. In the nature of the case, large organizations are status-ridden: titles and responsibilities are carefully defined in job descriptions, and relationships are carefully plotted on organization charts.

Of all corporate employees, the blue collars have been traditionally the least concerned about status, because their status seemed quite unambiguous. Their wages, job descriptions, even their vacation privileges and other fringes have generally been matters of public record (in a union contract). And whatever his dreams for his son, the future of the blue-collar man himself has been fairly predictable, for he moves up in accordance with seniority rosters that are posted publicly; he has no important opportunities to advance by pulling wires or gaining favor with his superiors. Hence he has taken his job position as something "fixed"; he has not dwelt on the social implications of his job, but has seen it as a means to make money.

THE NEW STRIVERS

There are some signs, however, that the blue collars are becoming more preoccupied with status: in part because they are now living with white collars in the suburbs, and having their first prolonged exposure to the latter's values; and in part because of the changing nature of blue-collar work. To some extent, the skilled blue-collar worker, eating now in the same company cafeteria as the white collar, working now in shirtsleeves instead of "work clothes," driving home from work to a middle-class suburban community, is beginning to feel the first twinges of concern about his status in society. Nelson Foote, commenting on these changes, says that "it would be a shame, in a way, if the old hard-headed blue-collar values disappeared, and nothing were left in this country except success-strivers."

The corporate white-collar workers, especially the men in the middle and higher reaches of the corporation, have a more ambiguous and volatile status position, and they are prone to develop what the sociologists call "status anxieties." (A number of sociologists have demonstrated that "upwardly mobile" families have a disproportionately high incidence of psychosomatic diseases.) Their preoccupation with status symbols—e.g., with the size and physical trappings of their offices—has been a recurrent theme in business fiction and satire in recent years. (In the movie, *A Face in the Crowd,* an advertising-agency executive suffers a heart attack after realizing he will lose a crucial account. He gasps out to the entertainer who is taking the account away from him: "You've seen my office. A corner office with four windows. Do you know how long it takes at Browning, Schlagel & McNally to get a corner office?" And then he slumps to the floor.)

In the years ahead, status will almost certainly hinge on education more than it has in the past. Indeed, the U.S. may now be moving into a period in which education will make and break men in a totally new fashion. It is a well-publicized fact that undergraduate enrollments, now running around 3,500,000, may come close to doubling by 1970. What is not so well appreciated is the fact that the number of living Americans who *have been to college* will also grow furiously during the 1960's—probably by about a third. Right now, something like 16,500,000 Americans have attended college for at least a year. By 1970, the figure will be in the vicinity of 22 million, of whom about 11 million will have graduated. (A rule of thumb that has held up pretty well in recent years is that of all those who go to college about half graduate.) At that point there are likely to be serious difficulties in finding enough "top jobs" for the college-trained.

ROOM AT THE TOP?

The problem can be seen in sharp focus if we limit it to men in their twenties and early thirties. In 1950 there were 2,200,000 men between twenty-five and thirty-four who had completed at least a year of college. Today, the figure is about 2,900,000, and by 1970, the Census Bureau estimates, it will be about 3,800,000, and will represent almost a third of all the men in this age band (vs. less than a fifth in 1950). What kinds of job opportunities are these growing numbers of college men encountering?

It would appear that their opportunities to move toward the top jobs have already been narrowed considerably. At present, the number of men between twenty-five and thirty-four who are employed (in Census Bureau terminology) as "professional, technical, and kindred workers," or as "managers, officials, and proprietors," or as "sales workers," is three million—i.e., it is only a little higher than the number of college men in this age band. Virtually all the jobs that are at the top, or that can lead to the top, are in these three Census categories; but it should be noted that the categories also include a lot of "bottom jobs" we do not normally link with college education—e.g., the proprietors include marginal news dealers, and the sales workers include clerks in the five-and-dime stores as well as high-paid life-insurance salesmen. Hence it is obvious that a fair number of college-trained men must already be working at jobs to which no high status attaches.

The trend can be seen in a study prepared by the Bureau of Applied Social Research at Columbia University, working in co-operation with *Time,* and also in a study of U.S. consumers conducted for *Life* by the Alfred Politz research organization. Though the data in the two studies are not exactly comparable, they suggest that college training is increasingly unlikely to lead automatically to top jobs. The *Time* study, based on 1947 data, showed that 5 per cent of male college graduates were holding blue-collar jobs. The *Life* study, based on 1955-56 data, showed that almost 20 per cent of employed "household heads" (mostly male, of course) who had any college training were blue collars.

One partial solution to the job problems of the "educated many" would be to give professional or managerial status to the broad band of corporate and government employees who at present hover uneasily between the clerical and executive layers or, in manufacturing, between the skilled workers and the technical staff. In an age preoccupied with status, a lot can be done simply by changing titles. A lot is being done already, in fact, and at all levels. The janitors in schools are often designated "custodial engineers," though in some industries the term "sanitors" is preferred. Girls who type letters for $70 a week are billed as "Gal Fridays"— there are usually a hundred-odd listings under this heading in the help-wanted section of the Sunday New York *Times*—and thereby gain a kind of executive-assistant status. The U.S. Labor Department ruled recently that any "executive" who earned less than $80 a week had to be paid time and a half for overtime. A part of the recent and prospective increase in the ranks of the professional and managerial groups represents not a true increase in the number of such jobs, but an inflation of titles. This depreciation of managerial status has contributed further to the blurring of the old class lines, and to the preoccupation with the symbols that help one to determine a man's real status.

THE UPS AND DOWNS

One fairly certain consequence of the great proliferation of college graduates will be an increase in social and occupational mobility. Education has always been the principal path by which sons gained higher positions than their fathers had; and though the Horatio Alger legend dies hard, numerous studies of the American "business elite" make it plain that the top jobs have *always* gone to the relatively well educated. A recent study by S. M. Lipset and Reinhard Bendix shows that even in the first half of the nineteenth century, when only about 5 per cent of Americans went to high school, 22 per cent of the "elite"* had graduated from college, another 10 per cent had attended college, 51 per cent had attended

---

* Any businessman prominent enough to be mentioned in the *National Cyclopedia of American Biography*—the authors' principal source of information on educational backgrounds—was taken to be of the "elite."

some kind of high school, and only 17 per cent had not gone beyond elementary school. The same authors show that in a more recent generation of elite businessmen (those born between 1891 and 1920) 84 per cent had gone to college and only 5 per cent had not gone beyond elementary school.

It is possible that the value of college degrees will undergo some depreciation, as more and more Americans get them. But at the same time, the degree is becoming an almost universal requirement for admission to the managerial group, and the fact that corporate managers are no longer divided into men with and men without a college education makes for greater mobility within the group. This mobility is fostered by the increasing tendency of corporations to select their managers "scientifically," e.g., with the aid of aptitude and personality tests. The tests may represent invasions of privacy, they may be based on misconceptions about managerial qualities, and they may not even be successful in finding the qualities they are set up to detect, but they attempt at least to put promotions on a more *objective* basis, and make the candidate's background (his college, national origins, religion, father's occupation, etc.) much less relevant. In short, they make it easier for a clerk's son to become a vice president—and vice versa. (Talk about social mobility often seems to proceed on the assumption that mobility is only upward, but in any generation there is always a substantial minority of sons whose positions are lower than their fathers'. Data collected by the Michigan Survey Research Center suggested that, in 1952, of all employed persons whose fathers were "managers, officials, and proprietors," 25 per cent were skilled or semiskilled workers, and 8 per cent were actually laborers.)

THE HOMOGENEOUS LIFE

The increased bunching of Americans around the middle-income levels, the increased blurring of occupational distinctions, and the increased adoption of middle-class living styles by families of diverse occupational background, have all tended to make the U.S. a much more homogeneous society. At this point it may be interesting to observe that we have been "homogenized" in several other respects as well:

National backgrounds have less meaning than they used to. About 95 per cent of all Americans today are native-born (vs. 87 per cent in 1920), and about 80 per cent of them are at least "third generation" Americans (vs. 65 per cent in 1920)—i.e., both their parents were also native-born. With immigration averaging only about 250,000 a year, about 85 per cent of the U.S. population will be at least third generation by 1970. And though the point cannot be verified statistically, it is nonetheless clear that Americans are less prone than they once were to think of other Amercians as "Swedes," or "Irishmen," or "Italians"—in part because the old-country ways and languages are largely unknown to the third and fourth generations, and in part because these generations so often have hopelessly *mixed* national backgrounds.

Religious differences are also less meaningful. A number of theologians have remarked, with some bitterness, that while Americans are more interested than they used to be in having a religion, they are much less interested in the *content* of religion, or in religious differences. Americans are increasingly being admonished, on television, for example, to "attend your place of worship this weekend"—and the inference is plain that it doesn't matter which one you attend. In *Religion and the Free Society,* a pamphlet published by the Fund for the Republic, William Lee Miller of the Yale Divinity School has complained of "the drive toward a shallow and implicitly compulsory common creed. . . . The kind of religion that results from this common civic faith is a religion-in-general, superficial and syncretistic, destructive of the profounder elements of faith." William Clancy, educational director of the Church Peace Union, commented in the same pamphlet, "The 'religion' that is accepted as a part of our public life is largely a matter of good fellowship and good works." Where religion once divided Americans on strongly felt sectarian lines, the new good fellowship and good works tend to emphasize nonsectarian activities (e.g., running nursery schools open to children of all religious backgrounds).

Political differences are also becoming blurred. American political debate is increasingly conducted in a bland, even-tempered atmosphere, and extremists of any kind are becoming rarer. The political expression of the new society, in which more and more families are bunched around the middle-income levels and adapting to middle-class ways, is a Congress in which more and more politicians are bunched around the middle of the road, in which both parties are increasingly dominated by "reasonable" liberals who were called, in a December, 1958, article in *Commentary* by Karl E. Meyer, the "Smooth Dealers." Many of them—e.g., Nelson Rockefeller, John F. Kennedy—could fit plausibly into either the Republican or the Democratic party; and as their numbers have grown, American voters increasingly cross party lines to vote for them. In short, the old party divisions are less meaningful.

THE NEW IVY LEAGUER

The net of these "homogenizing" trends is that we all seem to live alike—or, at least, a great many of us live and think and dress more nearly alike than we used to. Many Americans appear to be disturbed by this trend, and to detect in it a threat to their own sense of individuality; they are endlessly complaining about all the "conformity" and "togetherness" in American life.

But the complaints seem to miss a crucial point about the new society—a point that most marketing men have *not* missed. The point is that while our society is more homogeneous, the individual's own opportunities to live in diverse fashions have been expanded considerably. The man in the Ivy League suit may be a millionaire or a skilled machinist, and so may the man at the wheel of the sports car and the man on the beach in Miami. To the spectator, this may look like a new uniformity; to the machinist, it involves a new diversity—a diversity that, it may safely be presumed, he is enjoying immensely.

CHAPTER SEVEN

How American Taste
Is Changing

NOT so long ago American taste was the concern chiefly of the country's architects, artists, writers, and intellectual leaders. Now it is also the concern of its business leaders—of anyone, that is, who sells consumer goods and services. Price is important and always will be, but in a society looking forward to an average family income approaching $7,500 a year after taxes, price becomes relatively less important. Just as a woman who can afford to spend $50 for a frock will pay $65 for one that delights her, but begrudges $35 for one that does not, so American consumers as a group today tend more and more to let their senses make up their minds.

As with price, so with the utility and efficiency of products. In these days when consumer testing services are hard pressed to find important technical differences between brands of similar products, what counts more and more is the aesthetic quality of the products.

Business' growing concern with American taste is intensifying the intellectuals' concern about it. Taste is perhaps best defined as the capacity to discern fitness, beauty, order, congruity, or whatever constitutes excellence. When patterns of taste are dictated by purely commercial considerations, one argument goes, this capacity is stunted, and nearly all taste must conform to the average. Creative talent is diverted from writing novels or composing sonatas into such tasks as confecting advertising slogans; and intellects that are capable of unlocking the secrets of the universe are diverted into such pursuits as designing better cigarette-making machinery.

What *is* the state of American taste? In this essay, FORTUNE puts aside statistics to argue a speculative and controversial thesis: it is that American taste, at least by prevailing standards, is changing for the better, and will continue to do so. The change will be pervasive, encompassing nearly all social and income groups, and will be evident not only in the things people buy, but in the ways people use their leisure. And despite the apprehensions of the intellectuals, the part that business plays in forming tastes will tend not to corrupt but to improve them.

ABOUT TASTE THERE IS MUCH DISPUTE

But is it possible to talk about absolute standards of taste? A lot of cagey thinkers, from the dawn of civilization, have maintained that anybody laying down such standards is simply describing his personal inclinations. It is certainly true that taste cannot be analyzed and graded to close standards, like aluminum alloys, or internal-combustion engines. Moreover, taste is often the cloak of the intellectual snob who automatically defines as bad anything that is popular. Yet there appear to be some fundamentals of fitness, proportion, and beauty. Give a group of people a series of pictures of objects and tell them to pick the best and the worst, and they agree remarkably on the extremes of both good and bad. What is more, a nation's taste is the measure of its culture, and to deny the reality of qualitative differences in taste is to slam the door on all inherited cultural values. If those values mean anything at all, there is an important difference between J. D. Salinger and Mickey Spillane, between the *Eroica* and *Pink Shoe Laces,* between O'Neill and soap opera, between the Parthenon and a hot-dog stand.

Perhaps the most practical approach to taste values is simply to observe that "good" taste is usually the taste of the "upper" classes, the artistically proficient, or the learned. But the arbiters or makers of taste are not only educators, the *avant-garde*, the intellectuals, the writers, the designers. They are also, as we shall see, often manufacturers and merchandisers. These arbiters, of course, don't always agree among themselves, but whether they agree or not, they do set standards. So let us say that "good" taste in the U.S. is represented by the preferences of its tastemakers.

Four major forces are working to elevate American taste: (1) rising real income; (2) more education, both formal and informal; (3) the efforts of the tastemakers to spread their own gospel; and (4) the old American striving for self-betterment.

The effect of rising real income on U.S. taste is not merely that it enables people to buy more. It usually enables business to provide consumers with a steadily wider range of choices, thus making mass production the agent not of uniformity but of constantly widening variety. And along with more money, Americans are getting more leisure in which to develop their taste.

But income and leisure without education are like force without direction. As the excesses of America's own newly rich suggest, more leisure and more money for masses of Americans without more and better education could produce a temporary decline in public taste. Immediately after World War II, for example, war-plant workers splurged on the elaborate, overstuffed "borax" furniture they had set their hearts on years before.

Not that formal education necessarily improves anyone's taste. But it does help; in fact it is probably the most powerful single factor in the improvement process. And never in American history has education expanded so fast as it is now expanding. The number of adult Americans who have completed high school rose from 27 million, or 33 per cent of the adult population, in 1947 to 39 million, or 40 per cent of the adult population, in 1957; during the 1960's it will surely rise to about 55 million, or 50 per cent of the adult population. During the past decade the number of youths attending college has risen around 50 per cent; during the decade

ahead it is expected to double, reaching perhaps seven million.
According to the U.S. Office of Education, 35 million to 40 million
adults are "interested" in after-hours study programs, and some
nine million are actually enrolled in organized courses.

Surely not far behind the formal educators as molders of taste
are the informal educators or tastemakers. They have always existed, but never in such quantity. In the past they consisted of a
tiny aristocracy, who so to speak administered a nation's culture;
today America probably supports the largest taste-conscious *haute
bourgeoisie* in history, expressing itself through an extraordinary
variety of communications. People who think they possess good
taste, like people who believe they possess the one true religion,
often harbor a missionary's urge to convert others; and the American people, for the good of their taste, are being subjected to a
constant drumfire of instruction, persuasion, and information. The
so-called shelter or home-service magazines, for example, play
an enormous role in creating the demand for houses and furnishings gratifying to behold. The mass magazines have made such
subjects as America's Arts and Skills and Adventures of the Mind
interesting to millions of people without talking down or unduly
oversimplifying.

WHAT PEOPLE DON'T KNOW HELPS THEM

And then there are the corporate managers and their designers,
who are extraordinarily powerful tastemakers. Most of the time,
some opinion notwithstanding, this business influence on taste is
for the good. Precisely because businessmen are so often at a loss to
know just how public taste is going to shift, they tend to let their
corporate and personal self-esteem line them up on the side of
good, or at least professional, design. And for their part, even the
most mercenary practitioners of the "We'll design you any damn
thing you want" school would rather turn out something they
regard as good than something pandering to bad taste. Most good
designers, indeed, take the view that the public's frequent uncertainty about its taste offers the opportunity of turning out some-

thing better than they might if the public knew exactly what it wanted.

The preference of corporate executives for "good" design is sometimes a matter of self-esteem; perhaps goaded by their wives, they feel sheepish about making stuff their friends regard as cheap or junky. Frequently their preference is more sophisticated: they want to create a high-class image of their company and its products. As David Ogilvy of Ogilvy, Benson & Mather puts it. "It pays to give a product a high-class image instead of a bargain-basement image. Also, you can get more for it." Or executives believe that taste is changing for the better and the wise policy is to anticipate it. "We try to design just ahead of the market," says Arthur BecVar, manager of General Electric's Industrial Design Operation in Louisville, "so that when public taste advances we are ready for it."

THE "ASPIRATION" DRIVE

The phenomenon that springs from these forces and at the same time strengthens them all, of course, is the old American urge for self-betterment and self-expression. The currently popular theory of how this urge works has been developed by what might be called the status-symbol school of sociologists, who hold that: (1) people constantly express their personalities not so much in words as in symbols (i.e., mannerisms, dress, ornaments, possessions); (2) most people are increasingly concerned about what other people think of them, and hence about their social status. Thus the taste of many Americans is expressed in symbols of various social positions.

Sociological classification into status groups—based chiefly on occupation and education—with more or less common traits and tastes, has been useful to advertising and marketing men trying to draw an accurate bead on their markets. But the group boundaries, the status-symbol sociologists hasten to add, are not necessarily the boundaries of people's aspirations. The urge for self-expression and self-betterment, shared by nearly all Americans, takes the form of aspiring to higher status. Thus people tend to buy things that symbolize their aspirations—a certain make of car, a certain style of house, a certain mode of dress. Their very status aspiration, in other words, drives them to emulate "better" taste and so upgrade their own.

But this does not yet mean, says Dr. Burleigh B. Gardner, founder of the motivation-research firm of Social Research, Inc. (which pioneered the status-symbol concept in advertising), that a workingman's wife wants to emulate the wealthy matron far above her, or that a steelworker wants to emulate the chairman of the board. A beer advertising campaign featuring a fox hunter in a pink coat flopped because the hunter symbolized nothing relevant to the ordinary people who drank the beer. The brewer aimed too high. As a rule, the sociologists point out, consumers emulate taste within reach.

THE SHIFTING SYMBOLS

Sometimes a product loses its efficacy as a status symbol; a good example, says Dr. Gardner, is the automobile. Because the U.S. motorcar industry has built its cars more and more alike, the old American custom of upgrading from one make to another has virtually disappeared. Many consumers took to foreign cars not so much because they were cheap to operate but because they were different. What has been happening, many status-symbol theorists agree, is that houses and furnishings are replacing motorcars as status symbols.

Nevertheless, the furniture industry has not yet enjoyed the fruits of this shift in status symbols. Kroehler, the largest U.S. furniture maker, hired Social Research to find out what the trouble was. The American housewife, Social Research reported, obviously does not choose furniture as she chooses can openers. She wants furniture she likes, but she also wants furniture in good taste—furniture that will proclaim her family status. The trouble is that she does not know for sure what good taste in furniture is, and the furniture industry has confounded her with a plethora of styles. Consequently she spends too much time just "looking around" at furniture instead of buying it. More and more stores are now hiring professional decorators to help customers with their frustration.

THE "HIGH MOBILES"

Who are the people who first adopt the tastes that others follow? The evidence is strong that these innovators are not necessarily the people with the most money. As a group, they are the "new suburbanites," a status with an obviously strong appeal. A Chicago *Tribune* survey recently gave respondents a choice of twenty-one characterizations of themselves and their lives. Most of them, even some tenement dwellers, identified themselves with the "new young suburbanites" and indicated that they aspired to their kind of life.

It would be foolish, of course, to say that all young suburbanites are pioneers in taste, but the group apparently does contain the important innovators. Opinion Research Corp. of Princeton, New Jersey, trying to identify the dynamic Americans, made a study of 105 suburban households. The "early adopters," it found, included about a quarter of the suburban families it interviewed. They are people who are moving upward in economic status, who are moving around geographically, who are active intellectually, who have acquired a good deal of education, and whose work and play throw them into contact with a wide variety of people. Opinion Research calls them "High Mobiles." The High Mobiles were the first to buy electric blankets, low-calorie beverages, dining credit cards, food freezers, colored sheets, wall-to-wall carpeting, and other things that later became popular. Opinion Research, naturally, argues that business can get a reliable indication of the future trend of consumer tastes by watching the preferences of the High Mobiles.

A "DIFFERENTIATION" TREND?

But even when emulating others, consumers do make innumerable choices in which status plays little or no part. Although the American urge for self-expression and self-betterment is as strong as ever, its manifestation in the form of status seeking actually may be declining. In *Housing Choices and Housing Constraints,* soon to be published by ACTION, sociologist Nelson Foote suggests that even occupational and educational differences in the future will carry less and less weight, and people will bother less with proclaiming status.*

Foote reasons that rising discretionary income will force people to "differentiate" as well as emulate. Just as the newly rich in time become prudent and discriminating buyers, so ordinary Americans who suddenly find themselves with more money to spend will become more discriminating about the way they spend it. They will tend to expand their individuality, says Foote, and will begin to regard life as "a pursuit of meaning." The theory seems fortified by group income trends: the disposable income of the lower income groups is rising faster than that of the upper income groups, and the lower income groups may be confronted with so many more opportunities for emulating the upper groups that emulation itself will become pointless.

At all events, Foote predicts that people will "differentiate" mainly in their leisure pursuits—in such activities as travel, theatregoing, gardening, crafts, participation in public affairs and voluntary associations. To put it another way, people will achieve status by being different—or by being themselves. Perhaps, as Dr. Ernest Dichter, president of the Institute for Motivational Research, has remarked, "social status is coming closer to self-realization."

Something of the sort, as a matter of fact, can be observed among Americans whose social position or self-esteem is so secure that the thought of striving for status amuses more than it worries them. Their tastes are diverse, and dominated by no authority, traditional or contemporary. They casually install a Victorian love seat and a Barcelona chair in the same room. They do not try to emulate or surpass their neighbors, but, if anything, go out of their way to be a little different from their neighbors. And they do not rush out to translate a salary rise into a status symbol.

---

* *The Status Seekers,* the best-seller by Vance Packard, gives the absurd impression that almost every human reaction in the U.S. is heavily, not to say totally, conditioned by status and status symbols. Packard comes to the sensational conclusion that class lines in the U.S. are growing more rigid, although much of the evidence he himself brings forward actually argues the other way.

THE LOWER MOBILES

But most of these people, so far, are probably the High Mobiles. Meantime, what is happening to the taste of the ordinary American consumer? Few designers of rank would be willing to argue that it is fine, but most would grant that it is improving measurably, if sporadically. To be sure, some designers and architects are depressed by the recent vogue for "Cinderella" or "Hansel and Gretel" houses—essentially simple dwellings decorated with atavistic gimcrackery like scallop-trimmed gables, "leaded" windows, and garages with artificial haylofts. But these confections seem to be prized most by people whose incomes have been rising faster than their taste standards; and anyhow they seem to be better to look at than the bleak bungalows of forty or fifty years ago. More important, the dwellings being built by the High Mobile taste setters usually meet the approval of the experts.

Automobiles, reflecting changing taste, seem headed for simpler, "cleaner" lines, with much less superfluous ornamentation. Appliances, despite such aberrations as clothes washers with instrument panels more dazzling than those on autos, are moving toward better design. "You can no longer design a thing so 'bad' it will sell," says Donald L. McFarland, head of General Electric's small-appliance design division, "or so 'good' it won't sell."

Furniture given to gross stylistic excesses seems actually to be growing scarce. "The broadening of consumer credit has helped a lot," says J. Chalmers O'Brien, vice president of Carson Pirie Scott & Co. in Chicago. "The only place many people could afford to buy a bedroom suite fifteen years ago was one of the borax houses. Now they can buy good furniture on time at the better stores."

"SHE MUST BE AMERICAN"

Improvements in Americans' taste show up strikingly in their choice of food and clothes. American food preferences are becoming astonishingly sophisticated. Dishes that could be found only in the *haute cuisine* of New York and a few other cities thirty years ago are now fairly common in millions of middle-class homes. Small-town hotel dining rooms and restaurants whose victuals were once an ordeal to even an undiscriminating drummer now turn out food that is not only edible but even appetizing. And the sale of dry table wine has increased no less than 64 per cent in the past decade.

And by the almost unanimous consent of all who pretend to know anything special about the subject, no women in the modern world have ever been so tastefully dressed as American women are today. "When you see a *really* well-dressed woman abroad today," says David Ogilvy, "you think, she must be an American." Precisely because women's clothes can be copied quickly and mass-produced cheaply, the general level of taste in clothing is high and still rising. What is more, all this mass production and style imitation, far from stifling individual expression, have actually encouraged and enabled the American woman to exercise it to a greater degree.

Here may lie a lesson for those who deplore the fact that so much of the advance in American taste amounts to imitation of others. To a considerable extent, of course, all taste must be learned. Even a genius must usually absorb a great deal of conventional knowledge before he can express himself with genuine originality. Yet American women and their clothes demonstrate that ordinary people can discriminate when they have learned enough.

FROM EXTREME TO EXTREME

The elevation of American taste, however, is surely not a gradual, even process. Business can look forward to frequent and extreme changes in style and fashion, probably to an endless and rapid series of fads. (Sociologists distinguish fad from fashion as something with a touch of the unexpected or irresponsible.) Such changes, of course, are an old story. Fashions in women's clothes have often been carried to faddish excess, whereupon they disappear quickly—as did the hoopskirt, the leg-of-mutton sleeve, the Empress Eugénie hat, the sack dress. Architectural and industrial fashion, which cannot be so quickly imitated as clothes fashion, does not change so rapidly, but even it tends to run from extreme to extreme. The two-story house gives way to the ranch house, the ranch house to the split-level; the long low look in motorcars to comfort, commodiousness, and perhaps even an upright look; the ornamented public building to the starkly simple one, the starkly simple one to the "subjective" style of Edward Stone. "American taste," says William Snaith, managing partner of Raymond Loewy Associates, "is probably now going into a vigorous kind of romanticism—an effort to escape from starkness."

Extremes of fashion, far from being reprehensible, are both natural and psychologically useful. They are the result of money and leisure, and the desire to express or achieve status, sometimes complicated by a yearning for notoriety. They enable people to revolt from custom discreetly, to participate in extremes of taste they would be embarrassed to indulge in all by themselves. "Fashion," sociologist Edward Sapir has written, "is custom in the guise of departure from custom."

The American people, with their rapidly rising discretionary income and leisure, seem likely to humor their "sideline" impulses more than ever, and so will intensify and accelerate the swings of fashion and fad. The lesson for business is clear. In an article in the *Harvard Business Review,* November-December, 1958, Dwight E. Robinson of the University of Washington wrote that "all of the fame and bulk of a leading textile, appliance, construction, or automobile company will not save it from fashion's dustbin. . . . She [fashion], and not the so-called fashion dictator . . . is the true autocrat; and only in a totalitarian state, where the consumer's taste is legislated by government edict, does she meet her match." She bids fair to be a power in the U.S. of the 1960's, and the designers who can intuitively divine what people want before they are fully aware of it themselves will come into their own.

KITSCH CULTURE

A good many intellectuals, as already noted, take a dim view of American taste. Consider *Mass Culture,* a recent anthology of essays on current American culture. Of its forty-nine articles, only seven were favorable to or optimistic about U.S. taste. Ernest van den Haag, professor at the New School for Social Research, for instance, argues that mass production, creating more leisure and wealth, is at the root of the trouble. Not that business aims at the lowest common denominator of taste, he says, but the trouble is that a mass-produced article or service, while reflecting everybody's taste to some extent, is unlikely to embody anybody's tastes fully. This matters particularly in education and entertainment, van den Haag goes on. Moreover, all culture is becoming homogenized by catering to the masses, and mass culture drives out high culture and folk culture because it tends to suck in the talents that might produce good things.

In the same volume Dwight Macdonald argues even more strongly that what the Germans call *Kitsch* or junk culture tends to drive out high culture. Because mass culture is so easy to produce, he says, it overwhelms by its very quantity, and people's taste sinks to that of the least sensitive and most ignorant: "There are just too many people." The future of high culture is dark, Macdonald concludes; the future of mass culture is even darker, and we will be lucky if it doesn't get worse.

THE AUDIENCE IS THERE

The main defect common to such talk is that it disregards social and economic forces such as those FORTUNE is describing and so underrates the nation's capacity both for self-criticism and for high culture. The U.S., indeed, probably gives ear to more criticism of its culture than any other nation in history. Although it does not automatically guarantee a large income to anyone who cries its shortcomings, it will endure and even reward name calling and invective provided that they contain some sense and are rendered in clear and vivid English.

And it is merely recording the obvious to say that high culture in the U.S. is not only very much alive but is growing fast. The American artistic output, as the whole world testifies, is both sizable and respectable. American writing, painting, sculpture, architecture, and music were once merely imitations and extensions of

European culture; today they influence the culture of the rest of the world as much as it influences them.

If, as Walt Whitman once observed, it takes great audiences to produce great art, the U.S. should very soon be launching a great new era of musical composition. There are today forty-two major American symphony orchestras, against six in 1905 and thirty-two in 1956. Counting those in colleges and smaller communities, the total is more than 1,100, and at least 275 of them were formed between 1951 and 1957.

A growing number of Americans are not put off by "difficult" listening. Alban Berg's atonal opera *Wozzeck,* which was expected to be a flop when introduced at the Metropolitan Opera last year, played to sold-out houses. When it was put on the air on a Saturday afternoon, several out-of-town newspapers assigned their music critics to review the broadcast. One reason for this broadening of U.S. musical taste is that the sale of serious music on records has been increasing at least as fast as the sale of all records. The fact is that many Americans with a record player today listen to more musical works in a year than even professional musicians once could in dozens of years.

THE RISING DEMAND FOR BOOKS

Although Americans may not read as many books per capita as the British, Scandinavians, and French, the astonishing fact, considering the competition of other diversions such as radio and television, is that they read as many as they do, and that many of them are as good as they are. Americans are buying some 630 million books a year (including paperbacks and juveniles but not textbooks), up from 330 million ten years ago. The success of the paperbacks, which are selling several hundred million copies a year, is enormously significant. A large percentage of the total is trash, but paperback versions of *The Iliad* and *The Odyssey* have together sold more than a million copies. So has J. D. Salinger's *The Catcher in the Rye* and George Orwell's *1984* (which argues, ironically, that the mass media of today will pave the way for the "double-think" of 1984). "The paperbacks," as Clifton Fadiman has noted, "are democratizing reading. They are conferring upon it the simple, healthy status of a normal habit."

What is also relevant, one of the most successful newspaper columns of recent origin is Mortimer Adler's feature dealing with philosophical questions suggested by readers. Inaugurated October 19, 1958 (in the Chicago *Sun-Times*), it has been syndicated in newspapers from one end of the country to the other.

Radio and television, which have received their share of criticism, cannot be excluded from any inventory of American cultural media. Although they thrive on mass production, they also cater to special audiences. One can sometimes see or hear on them works one might never have seen or heard in a country with an aristocratic high culture and no mass media, such as Britain and Germany fifty years ago.

All this, of course, does not mean that the masses, for the first time in history, are rushing to embrace high culture. What is significant is that millions of the kind of Americans who make the nation's tastes have clung to or taken up the values of high culture *voluntarily,* uncoerced by state or other cultural authority, in a tolerably free market, and in the face of powerful competition from a multitude of mundane leisure activities. What millions have thus found good, millions more, if past behavior means anything, will almost surely find good.

MORE QUALITY AND VARIETY

Taking everything together, then, it is reasonable to say that the forces changing American taste are changing it for the better. Thus business can look forward to a demand for "quality," for more choice and fashion, and for the uncommon or unusual. The large mass producers will probably have to provide more variety—as indeed the auto industry is doing today. And the small businessman with a product that isn't geared to the average will doubtless have a bright future.

Business will still be able to sell junk to a lot of Americans. But it surely will be able to make more money operating on the assumption that people want something "better," not only functionally but aesthetically.

CHAPTER EIGHT

The Coming Changes in Housing

THE biggest and the most important market in the U.S. centers around the American home. Last year Americans spent no less than $108 billion to build new houses and apartments and to operate, maintain, furnish, and equip homes already built. Housing in this broadest sense amounts to one-third of all consumer income after taxes and runs to more than the national product of Britain or West Germany. What happens to this gigantic market in the decade of the 1960's will obviously affect, directly or indirectly, the fortunes of a large proportion of the businesses in the U.S. It will also have a lot to do with what the American landscape looks like ten years hence and with the whole quality of American life.

The prospects for this vast market are in many ways bright. By 1970, on FORTUNE's projections, total expenditures on the American home may rise to $160 billion or more. Let us glance at the chief components. Of the $108 billion that Americans spent in 1959 on the home, about $22 billion was for construction of new houses and apartments and the alteration of old ones. And $47 billion went for the purchase of household goods and equipment and for household services including gas, electricity, telephones,

Total Expenditures for Housing and House Furnishings

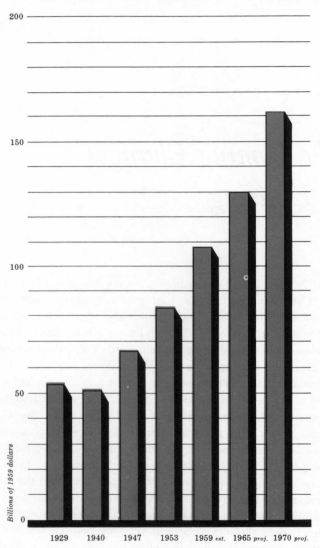

The statistical skyscrapers in the chart above represent total U.S. expenditures for building new houses and apartments and for maintaining, operating, and furnishing existing ones. Since 1947 these expenditures have expanded by 60 per cent. By 1970, outlays will be up to $160 billion, in 1959 prices, and may well exceed $165 billion.

and domestic service (see pg. 144-5). The remaining $39 billion was spent on the upkeep of homes now in being, taking the form of depreciation, repairs, and taxes on owner-occupied dwellings, and rents paid for tenant-occupied units.

In the Sixties all of these components will be growing, but their growth depends in no small measure on one component—new construction. And on the prospects for this, two widely divergent views are manifesting themselves within the building industry itself. One school expects an ever-normal housing boom in which consumers will spend a larger share of income on new housing than they did in the Fifties. I. J. Harvey Jr., board chairman of Flintkote, a manufacturer of building materials, agrees with the sociologists who think the house is replacing the car as the great American "status symbol." A small but highly articulate minority of executives, however, is afraid that bust is more likely than boom, largely because of the spiraling costs of construction labor and materials and of land. Thus, C. R. Mitchell, president of the U.S. Savings & Loan League, has called for a federal research program to halt the cost spiral. The alternative, he warns, is that "housing will become a declining industry."

Neither extreme is very likely, in FORTUNE's view. On the one hand, there are now firm grounds for believing that the upward curve of construction costs can at least be slowed down. On the other hand, the believers in a perpetual boom have certainly over-simplified the picture. To be sure, rising incomes will create a tremendous potential for the construction of new housing and improvement of old houses. But whereas total national product in the Sixties may rise by 50 per cent, new-household formation and replacement requirements point to only a 10 per cent rise in new housing units. At the same time, a number of factors may slow down the postwar tendency to build more expensive homes and hence hold the rise in dollar spending on housing to rather modest proportions. As a minimum, FORTUNE believes the market will expand from an average of $20 billion in the late Fifties to $23 billion a year in the first half of the decade and $25 billion in the second half. As a maximum, it might go as high as $25 billion a year in 1960-64 and $28 billion in 1965-69. On the minimum projection, housing would absorb somewhat less than the 6 per cent of disposable income that characterized the Fifties. On the maximum projection, the share would hold steady.

Whatever the exact percentage, housing construction will be a changing, exciting business. For example, the Sixties will see an upsurge in rental construction reminiscent of the apartment-house boom of the 1920's. It will see a spreading cleavage within the market for single houses, with demand increasing both for small "retirement houses" and vacation cottages and for large houses for large families. The organization of the home-building industry will take on a new shape, with large land-development companies like Webb & Knapp and Arvida taking over much more of the purchasing, planning, and developing of land, and with giant and highly mobile builders like Levitt, Centex, and Woodrow, and prefabricators like National Homes, taking over a steadily rising share of the actual construction. Most important of all, the technology will be changing rapidly and radically, with much greater use of factory-made components that minimize on-site labor. There is even a real possibility that the long-heralded "industrialized house" will become a reality before the Sixties are over, opening up vast new possibilities for the markets of the Seventies.

THE BOUNDARIES OF DEMAND

Underlying all these changes in consumer choice and in technology, certain familiar and basic factors will be shaping the market —i.e., household formation and replacement. The stimulus from the first will not be so large as many builders expect. During the late Fifties household formation outstripped most forecasts because both young and old single persons decided to live alone in unprecedented numbers. Now, however, this stimulus is about played out; only 3 per cent of all single women over the age of twenty-five, for example, are still living with their families. The most probable forecast, therefore, is for a rise in net household formation from the 900,000 annual rate of the last five years to a rate of 1,020,000 in 1960-64 and 1,080,000 in 1965-69. The rate will pick

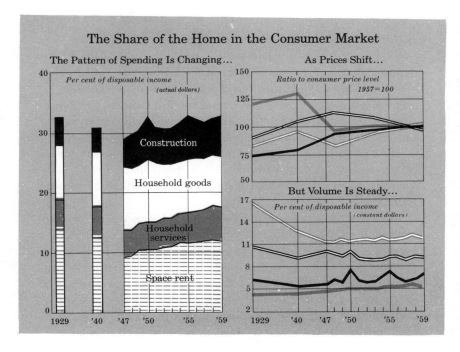

The Share of the Home in the Consumer Market

The Pattern of Spending Is Changing...

Per cent of disposable income (actual dollars)

Construction

Household goods

Household services

Space rent

1929 '40 '47 '50 '55 '59

As Prices Shift...

Ratio to consumer price level 1957=100

1929 '40 '47 '50 '55 '59

But Volume Is Steady...

Per cent of disposable income (constant dollars)

1929 '40 '47 '50 '55 '59

Americans have sharply increased their dollar expenditures on the home and its appurtenances over the years, but the percentage of disposable income (shown in chart at left) has changed much less. The percentage peaked in 1929 and then fell off. Since World War II it has risen again, with a sharp rise in rent and housing construction and a sharp decline in the portion spent on goods. But these latter changes have mainly been the effect of price changes. For construction costs and rents have risen faster than all consumer prices (chart top right) and prices of goods have risen more slowly. Eliminating these price changes (chart bottom right), the volume of construction outlays has fluctuated but has maintained a stable trend. Rent purchases relative to income have risen slightly, and the volume of goods purchased has declined very little.

During the Sixties, construction as a percentage of disposable income may decline somewhat, or at best hold about even. But the share of income spent on household goods and services may rise somewhat (pp. 144-45). The total of all expenditures for the home will probably take about the same proportion of the consumer dollar as in 1957. It should be noted in considering all of the above percentages that FORTUNE has departed from normal national income accounting by treating home construction as a consumer outlay, rather than as an investment expenditure.

up more sharply in the early Seventies, however, to 1,280,000.

Replacement demand, meanwhile, may not provide the lift to housing that it gave in the late Fifties, when new construction plus units created by conversion exceeded household formation by 625,000 units per year. This rate of replacement was unprecedented, and together with $4.5 billion a year spent on improving old houses, resulted in a vast upgrading of the existing housing stock. The number of substandard houses was cut in half, from 37 per cent of the total to 19 per cent today. Indeed, by the early 1970's, three houses and apartments out of five will be of postwar vintage.

In view of this, it seems unlikely that replacements will exceed the recent level—barring a major technological revolution. Actual physical scrappage of houses and apartments will come to about 300,000 units a year, according to Professor Sherman Maisel of the University of California, who has analyzed the probable effects of urban renewal, slum clearance, and highway programs. More than 200,000 units a year will be removed from the supply in an economic rather than a physical sense, as a backwash of population shifts from farm to city, from slums to decent sections. Meanwhile vacancies will have to rise if the growing population is to have the mobility it needs. This could call for building an additional 100,-000-odd units per year.

Household formation plus replacement needs therefore add up to a total sustainable demand of 1,650,000 units a year in the early Sixties and 1,700,000 in the second half of the decade. New construction won't be that high, for part of the demand—roughly 200,000 units a year—will be satisfied by converting old homes and apartments into multiple units, and through production of trailers and seasonal bungalows. Taking everything together, production of houses and apartments probably will average about 1,450,000 a year in 1960-64 and 1,500,000 in 1965-69, compared to 1,370,000 in 1956-59. In terms of the more familiar Bureau of Labor Statistics figures of nonfarm housing starts, this works out to a rate of 1,315,000 units a year in 1960-64 and 1,375,000 a year in 1965-69.

HOW MUCH HOUSE PER HOUSE?

How much the market grows in dollar terms, of course, will depend not just on how many homes are built but on what kinds of homes are sold. Since 1947 the average value per new house or apartment has increased by more than 20 per cent, in 1959 dollars, thanks to an 18 per cent expansion in floor area, a 10 per cent increase in the number of rooms, a one-third rise in the number of bathrooms, and use of better insulation, heating systems, etc. Some builders seem confident that the trend of "more house per house" will accelerate in the 1960's as incomes rise. "My customers are more interested in homes than anything else," says Robert F. Schmitt, a highly successful and imaginative young Cleveland builder. "They will do without a car, TV, country club, boat, anything to have a home for their kids in a good neighborhood. They strap themselves, sacrificing almost everything else to get a home."

This should be welcome news to many critics of U.S. life who have long argued that Americans were spending too little of their income to improve their housing, and too much on less important things, especially cars. But Mr. Schmitt's customers aren't necessarily typical. There are other students of the American consumer —Nelson Foote of General Electric, for instance—who think that Americans will spend their increased incomes on travel, recreation, and services rather than on better homes. Since 1957, at least, the tendency toward more house per house has in fact been reversed —perhaps temporarily, perhaps not. In an economy as big as the U.S., there's plenty of room for speculation about consumer psychology and the way rising income will affect popular choice.

But quite aside from this large question, dollar expenditures on housing will depend to no small degree on whether families want to own their homes or to rent. This decision is highly important for the housing market because the average apartment costs less to build than the average new house. And here the trend seems unmistakable. According to Dr. Louis Winnick of the New York City Planning Commission, author of a recent ACTION study on rental housing, the strength of the demand for apartments will be as distinguishing a feature of the housing market of the 1960's as the trend to home ownership was of the market of the 1950's. Over the 1960's, Dr. Winnick believes, rental construction probably will average at least 400,000 units a year, or considerably better than 25 per cent of all new building, as against 125,000 units in the Fifties.

THE APARTMENT BOOM

Indeed, the boom is already under way; apartment-house construction in 1959 was close to 250,000 units (18 per cent of total units)—three times the postwar low of 82,000 in 1956. In Los Angeles County, for example, construction of apartment units exceeded single-home output in April, 1957, for the first time since construction statistics have been collected; since then new apartment units have been outnumbering new single houses about three to two. In far-out suburban Orange County, which bears roughly the same relationship to Los Angeles as Suffolk County does to New York City, rental units were running nearly 50 per cent of the total home building last year, and in Long Island's Nassau County the office of the county executive felt constrained, last summer, to to put out a special bulletin calling attention to the apartment boom.

Since many of the new rental units are going up in the suburbs, the growth in demand for apartments obviously does not depend on any mass disenchantment with suburbia, nor does it necessarily imply any reversal of the long-term trend toward home ownership. Owning and renting primarily appeal to two quite disparate groups: owning to families with young and teen-age children, and renting to one- and two-person households—i.e., bachelors (male and female), young couples whose children haven't arrived yet, older couples whose children have left home, and widows and widowers. And these demographic factors are working powerfully in favor of renting. By 1970, for example, there will be six million more people between the ages of twenty and twenty-four than there are today (a larger increase than occurred in all of the

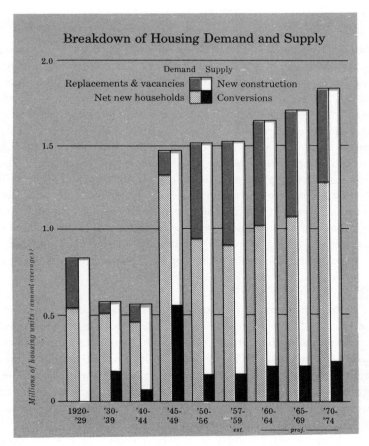

Breakdown of Housing Demand and Supply

Demand   Supply

Replacements & vacancies — New construction

Net new households — Conversions

Millions of housing units (annual averages)

2.0

1.5

1.0

0.5

0

| 1920-'29 | '30-'39 | '40-'44 | '45-'49 | '50-'56 | '57-'59 *est.* | '60-'64 | '65-'69 *proj.* | '70-'74 |

The housing market is changing shape as a result of a new pattern of demand and supply. In the Fifties, household formation declined but as families upgraded their housing standards the rate of replacements rose. During the Sixties, household formation will rise moderately but replacements will hold about even with the recent unprecedented rate of 625,000 units a year. Actual demolitions will run to perhaps half that. Units not demolished but virtually taken out of the market, plus vacancies in the usual sense of that word, account for the other half.

Most of the new housing demand in the 1960's probably will be met by the construction of entirely new year-round units. Conversions, which contributed three-eighths of the total additional housing supply in the late 1940's, will take only 10 per cent of the market over the current decade; this conversion total, moreover, includes construction of new seasonal cottages and semi-permanent trailers.

past eighty years). This will result in the formation of 2,650,000
new households with a head under twenty-five years old. According to the 1950 Housing Census, 85 per cent of the households
in this age group are renters rather than home owners. The preference for renting is also strong in the twenty-five-to-twenty-nine-
year-old age group, which will be expanding in the Sixties, compared to an actual decline in the Fifties. Finally, renting will
receive a boost owing to the lengthening of life expectancy. The
over-sixty-five population will be expanding by nearly four million; and the growth in social-security, pension-fund, and life-
insurance benefits will enable a rapidly increasing proportion to
live alone rather than double up with children or other relatives.
During the 1960's, therefore, the number of single-person households over sixty-five years of age will increase by about 2,300,000.

NEW LOOK IN APARTMENTS

If this new demand for apartments is to be satisfied, however,
builders will have to provide accommodations suited to the special
needs of each of these groups rather than the uniform and tasteless
(and expensive) barracks now being built in most cities. There are
signs of a change already. Most new apartment houses, for example,
are fully air conditioned, and a rapidly growing number are built
around a swimming pool, yacht basin, or club of some kind for
the exclusive use of the tenants.

At least one giant builder, moreover—Webb & Knapp—is showing what can be done with imagination anchored to technical
competence. Webb & Knapp has been working recently on apartment projects in Philadelphia, Los Angeles, New York City, Chicago, and Washington, D.C. In its Philadelphia City Line project,
for example—one of four in that city—Webb & Knapp designed
for families with young children two buildings that contain play
areas on each floor and space for a nursery school. It has planned
two other buildings specifically designed to lure disenchanted
commuters, with large rooms, gadget-filled kitchens, ample storage
space, and other appurtenances of a house in the suburbs.

Over the course of the 1960's a continued high rate of apartment building will change the face of metropolitan America, just as the apartment boom of the 1920's fixed the appearance of New York City and most other big cities for the next thirty years. A good bit of new construction, for example, will consist of garden apartments built in the inner rings of the suburbs, where land is cheaper than in the cities proper but, increasingly, too expensive for single-home development. And new construction in cities proper will not be confined to tall elevator buildings. In some of its most exciting city projects—e.g., in Washington, D.C., Chicago, Philadelphia—Webb & Knapp is combining high-rise apartment towers and low-rise garden apartments with attached "town" or "patio" houses designed for sale rather than rent.

While rental builders will be enjoying their greatest boom since the 1920's, house builders will do well to maintain their volume of the 1950's; the chances are that their market will shrink even though total housing starts (including apartments) are rising. Certainly it will change shape and direction. The most important change is that the builder of moderate-priced homes for families embarking on home ownership for the first time will face as severe a shortage of customers as plagued the apartment builder of the 1950's. The median age of new-home buyers, according to one study, is thirty-six, and 43 per cent of all buyers are in the thirty to forty age bracket. The sobering fact for home builders is that the number of such households will decrease by 295,000 during the 1960's (from 10,909,000 to 10,614,000), although the total number of families in this age bracket needing housing will not shrink as much, owing to a high degree of mobility and some shifts from renting to home ownership. If they are to sell houses in any large quantity, builders will have to look in two quite different directions—toward large families who already own a house and want a better one, and toward childless couples who typically rent but may be persuaded to buy.

The second-time buyers should provide a particularly lucrative market. Families whose head is between forty and fifty-four overwhelmingly prefer owning to renting, and their number will rise by 1,600,000 during the 1960's. Equally important, families in this

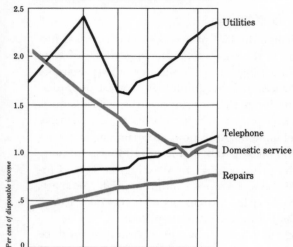

Breakdown of Household Services

Per cent of disposable income

Utilities
Telephone
Domestic service
Repairs

2.5 / 2.0 / 1.5 / 1.0 / .5 / 0

1929 / '40 / '47 / '50 / '55 / '57

Housing's Other Half:

It takes a heap of goods and services to make an American house a home—no less than $47 billion worth last year. Over the years Americans have devoted a remarkably stable proportion of their disposable incomes to household goods and services—14.3 per cent in 1957 vs. 14.2 per cent in 1929. Since 1957, however, the share has been rising, and by 1970 it may be up to 15 per cent or better. This would bring the market for household goods to $48 billion by 1970 (vs. $29 billion in 1959) and that for household services to $29 billion (vs. $18 billion in 1959).

What makes this past stability so remarkable is the fact that it reflects such widely disparate trends in the markets for individual goods and services. The chart above, for example, shows rather dramatically the effects of the much advertised "servant problem" on consumer budgets. Since 1929, consumers have halved the proportion of income allocated to domestic service, from 2.1 per cent in 1929 ($1.7 billion) to 1.1 per cent ($3.5 billion) in 1958, the latest year for which detailed consumer-expenditure data are available.

Expenditures for servants began to rise slightly in the mid-Fifties. But in contrast with the 1920's, when a good deal of domestic employment was accounted for by the families that kept two or three in help, the new market consists of a vastly larger number of families with a part-time maid or cleaning woman. The supply of servants has been swollen in recent years by a substantial exodus of Negroes from the South. As the economy continues to expand, however, they will be attracted to better-paying and otherwise more desirable jobs in industry, as was the case during World War II. The combination of short supply and low productivity, moreover, will again push the cost of domestic service into the luxury bracket. And a number of new appliances due to be marketed on a mass scale during the Sixties—e.g., electrostatic air cleaners—will ease the burden on housewives.

While they were cutting the share of income going for domestic servants, consumers have been raising the proportion allocated to telephones, to electric, gas, and water utility service, and to home repairs. The telephone, for example, is taking almost twice as large a share of the consumer dollar now as it did in 1929—i.e., 1.2 per cent ($3.8 billion) in 1958 vs. 0.7 per cent ($570 million) in 1929. Part of the growth came from increasing market penetration, part from greater use of the phone by those who already had one. Now that 79 per cent of all homes have telephones, vs. 42 per cent in 1929, it's unlikely telephone expenditures will increase much faster than disposable income.

Electric, gas, and water utilities expanded their share of the market from 1.7 per cent in 1929 to 2.5 per cent in 1958 and the share will continue to rise somewhat. This is less of a rise than the usually startling figures on kilowatts of electricity and cubic feet of gas consumed would suggest, because utilities held their rates steady over the period while other prices were rising. Rates have been moving up in recent years, but the uptrend will be restrained by the battle that is now being waged between electric and gas utilities for the home-heating (and to a lesser extent, the home-appliance) market.

As to appliances, the outlook is reasonably favorable, despite some fairly rough going in recent years. The industry lost ground after the initial postwar boom, its share of disposable income dropping from 1.9 per cent in 1950 to 1.6 per cent in 1957 ($4.8 billion). The market for the old standbys—refrigerators, washing machines, ranges, vacuum cleaners, etc.—had become saturated, and none of the newer appliances like dishwashers, freezers, clothes dryers, or even air conditioners took up the slack. (Radio and TV hit their peak in 1950; since then, the market has been shifting toward less expensive portable sets.) Now, however, the appliance industry should be able to increase its share of consumer income, for several of the newer appliances—air conditioners, dishwashing machines—are coming up fast, and replacement requirements are rising sharply for the older ones. General Electric, for one, feels confident that it can accelerate replacement through something it calls "fragmentation"—breaking up the standard kitchen package of refrigerator, range, etc., into small and sometimes portable components, e.g., a heating-and-cooling "refreshment center" that can be wheeled out to the patio, or a three-piece refrigerator placed around the kitchen for maximum convenience. And there are a number of Buck Rogersish appliances that will be ready for the market within the decade, e.g., the electrostatic air cleaner built into the heating and air-conditioning system, which removes most of the dust from a house by setting up static-electricity charges.

Manufacturers of carpets, draperies, china, and other such house furnishings (see top line of chart right (have been a prime victim of the informal living style that has developed in the suburbs. After climbing to 3.4 per cent of disposable income in 1950 ($7.2 billion), the share dropped steadily, to 2.6 per cent ($8.1 billion) in 1958. Furniture manufacturers, on the other hand, have been able to keep their share of the market (1.4 per cent—$4.5 billion in 1958) in the face of the same pressures, by developing new products, e.g., aluminum lawn furniture, and by redesigning traditional indoor furniture along much lighter, more casual, and less expensive lines. The share should rise somewhat, because of rising replacement demand from the older, better-heeled, second-time house buyers.

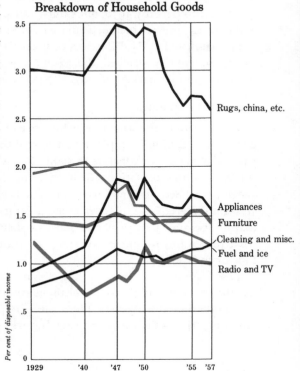

Breakdown of Household Goods

Rugs, china, etc.

Appliances

Furniture

Cleaning and misc.

Fuel and ice

Radio and TV

Per cent of disposable income

1929   '40   '47   '50   '55 '57

group will be in the market for larger houses. The demand for space depends partly on the number of children a family has and even more on their age. During the 1960's the number of children under eighteen will be growing faster than the number of households, and teen-age population—housed mainly in families in the forty to fifty-five age group—will grow faster still. Of the 14,200,-000 increase expected in the number of children under eighteen, 8,300,000 will be in the ten to seventeen group.

What gives this market its rich potential is the fact that families in the forty-five to fifty-five age group are at or near the peak of their earning power. They are also, of course, at the peak of their expenditures for food, clothing, cars, and other "essentials." In the past, large families have met their demand for more space by buying old (and frequently substandard) houses. But the steady rise—50 per cent—expected in real income over the 1960's should make it possible for them to come into the new-house market in growing numbers. By 1970, one family in three in this age bracket will have an after-tax income of more than $10,000 a year, according to estimates by Dr. Paul Boschan of Guardian Life Insurance Co., vs. one in five now. Indeed, the second-time buyers are beginning to dominate the market already.

DISCRIMINATING BUYERS

The growth of the second-time buyers will also make the market a lot more exacting for builders, for second-time buyers are usually particular about such factors as room size, number of bathrooms, thickness of the insulation, adequacy of the heating and hot-water system, etc. "Second-time buyers are much more discriminating," Jess Bollinger of Bollinger-Martin, a large Louisville firm, explains, "because they're not in need of shelter." To find exactly what they want, Bollinger says, they are quite willing to look for four or five years.

The biggest obstacle to selling second-time buyers, however, may be the difficulty that some of them are likely to find in selling the houses they already own. The decline in the thirty to forty-year-old population—the usual first-time buyers—could put a crimp in the market for second-time buyers. (In such a case, expenditure for additions and alterations might skyrocket; FORTUNE has projected a rise from $4.5 billion in recent years to $7 billion by the late 1960's.) But this might be offset by a much higher rate of home ownership among Negroes, Puerto Ricans, and other minority groups as rising incomes permit them to leave their slums. Since World War II, for example, there has been a steady exodus from New York City's Harlem and Bedford-Stuyvesant Negro ghettos to settled, middle-class, single-house neighborhoods on the outer ring of the city.

LURING THE RENTER

If builders are to come close to the volume of the 1950's, however, they will also have to lure both very young and elderly couples from the apartment to the house market. This can be done if the right product is offered at the right price. According to Professor Burnham Kelly of M.I.T., young couples are not necessarily wedded to renting. What they want, he says, is "minimum-involvement housing." But so far builders have not shown much ingenuity in designing small, inexpensive houses for the younger generation.

They have, however, been quite successful in attracting buyers at the other end of the age scale. The building boom now under way in Florida, for example, makes it clear that there is a very large potential demand for small, relatively inexpensive "retirement houses." The Mackle Co. of Miami put up some 5,000 houses last year, mostly in the $7,000-to-$14,000 range, and Mackle's parent, General Development Corp., has sold over 75,000 lots in the past two years. The phenomenal growth of permanent trailer developments in Florida, Arizona, and southern California suggests that a radical innovation in house design can attract people normally thought of as renters.

THE ADVANCE OF TECHNOLOGY

On balance, therefore, the housing market of the Sixties will provide plenty of opportunities for the builder, but the going will be harder than in the Fifties. Despite rising incomes and the importance of the "second-time buyer," demographic factors put a premium on rentals and small houses and so tend to hold down total dollar expenditures. In large measure, however, how much Americans spend on housing will depend on perhaps the most critical factor of all—technological change, which will determine the costs and appearance of all housing, hence its comparative value in the market place.

There is no encouragement for builders, certainly, in the trends of the last thirty years. Since 1929, the cost of home-building labor and materials has gone up 135 per cent, vs. a 75 per cent rise for consumer prices as a whole, and while national attention was being focused on the steel-industry negotiations in the spring of 1959, the building-trades unions quietly won increases averaging 4 per cent. Land costs, moreover, have sharply reversed the forty-year downtrend that had been cushioning the labor-and-material cost spiral, roughly doubling since 1951.

This rise in labor and land costs, however, has been partially offset by other factors, and these hold promise for the future. Since 1949, according to the Roy Wenzlick Co. of St. Louis, the selling price of a standard one-family house has risen 27 per cent, or about one-fourth less than the cost of the labor and materials. A number of builders have been even more successful in offsetting cost increases through higher productivity. In his new development of 16,000 houses in Levittown, New Jersey, for example, William Levitt was selling a 1,400-square-foot house for $13,240 in 1959— no more than the cost per square foot of the original Levittown, Long Island, houses in 1946. Levitt has raised his productivity through changes in construction techniques, e.g., spacing trusses twenty-four inches apart instead of sixteen inches; by designing new products, e.g., a one-coat paint; and by very close control of costs through time-motion studies, and the like.

And Levitt is no longer a maverick. There are several builders whose volume in some years equals or surpasses Levitt's, e.g., Centex (1958 sales: $40 million); General Development, which estimated its 1959 sales at $70 million. And there is a growing number of somewhat smaller-scale builders with an impressive record of increasing productivity. Joseph Eichler of Palo Alto, for example (1958 sales: $14 million), had been able to hold his costs per square foot constant from 1950 until the wage boost in the spring of 1959.

There are even some indications that the building trades may drop their make-work technique. Because of the inroad of sheet-rock and other forms of "dry wall" construction, for example, the plasterers' union now permits use of machinery that enables a plasterer to lay a wall in half the time needed with a hand trowel. And with union approval, a bricklayer can now receive on the site a full day's supply of bricks strapped together at the factory.

THE NEW COMPETITION

But the most solid reason for believing that the cost spiral will be slowed is the tremendous intensification of technological competition among manufacturers of building materials. As is so often the case, the stimulus came from outside; the housing market became rich and varied enough to attract research-based firms from other industries. "Competition from aluminum and chemical companies," according to Walter Hoadley, treasurer of Armstrong Cork, one of the most aggressive of the old-line companies, "will be an exhilarating experience for both manufacturers and builders." The exhilaration has already started, and the once rather stodgy and slow-moving building-supplies industry has taken on a new tone and pace. "The moment of decision is on us right now," said F. E. Dutcher, vice president of Johns-Manville, in 1959. His company recently established a new research division to work on prefabricated components.

The result of this new competition is that every aspect of home building is undergoing change. The most rapid progress is being made in industrializing the basic house enclosure itself through the use of large wall, floor, and ceiling panels that contain the structural member, exterior and interior surface, and insulation in a single piece. The National Association of Home Builders has erected two "research houses," one, in Knoxville, Tennessee, using a panel manufactured by Masonite Corp. of Chicago, the other, in South Bend, a polystyrene sandwich panel produced by Koppers. National Homes, the largest U.S. prefabricator, is experimenting with load-bearing aluminum wall panels for future production. Simpson Timber, which entered the home-building field less than three years ago, is now turning out a plywood panel. The LuReCo system of panels and trusses developed by the Lumber Dealers Research Council is being widely used, and the Douglas Fir Plywood Association announced a system of its own not long ago.

MODERN PLUMBING

And innovation isn't stopping with the frame itself. The mechanical equipment that goes into the house—heating system, plumbing, kitchen appliances, etc.—now usually costs as much as the basic structure, and change is coming from a number of sources. American Radiator & Standard Sanitary Corp., for example, is studying ways to reduce the installed cost of bathrooms and kitchens through greater prefabrication. General Motors, which makes oil burners, refrigerators, air conditioners, etc., is known to have given some thought to developing a whole mechanical package for the home builder, and General Electric is working on the idea, too.

There is even progress in cutting what so far has been the most stubborn cost of all, that of tying the house to its environment. Carl Boester, a consultant in home-building technology, has designed a system of concrete blocks that makes it possible to lay a foundation in a matter of hours instead of days. The N.A.H.B.'s research house in Knoxville included a sewerless toilet developed by Boester and a Purdue University professor named Don Bloodgood, which eliminates the need for cesspool or sewer connection, and Boester has designed a self-contained recirculating water system.

THE INDUSTRIALIZED HOUSE

All these changes in the design and production of individual components will force a larger and more fundamental change in the design and production of the house itself. "So far," the well-known architect Carl Koch has written in the ACTION study, *Design and Production of Houses,* edited by Professor Burnham Kelly of M.I.T., "there has been no fully industrialized house. Our houses are full of well-designed modern products but they do not add up. The sum of all the parts does not begin to make a whole."

The parts are beginning to add up now, for manufacturers of building materials are being forced to take over a larger and larger share of house design to find an outlet for their products. So far, the effects are largely to raise aesthetic standards, since national manufacturers can afford to use top-ranking architects. More fundamental changes in design are coming that will radically alter the whole pattern of production. "I honestly believe that the home builder is destined to become nothing more or less than a connector of utilities and a developer of land," says Andrew Place, a South Bend builder and member of the N.A.H.B. research committee, who put up the N.A.H.B. "research house" using Koppers' new polystyrene-foam wall panels. By the late 1960's, in other words, the long-awaited "industrialized house" with all its cost savings may be a reality.

There are also some solid reasons for believing that the "land problem" will not be so great a handicap to building in the Sixties as had seemed likely. To be sure, industrialization can't cut land costs or increase its availability—but proper development and organization can. One way is to develop whole new communities in virgin territory. Webb & Knapp is doing this with its Godchaux Sugars holdings between Baton Rouge and New Orleans; so are Arvida and General Development with their huge acreages in Florida. Even in such thickly settled areas as Los Angeles and New York's Westchester County, there is actually more land available than is generally realized. The problem, according to land developers like David Slipher of Webb & Knapp and Willard Woodrow of Woodrow Construction Co., is that the big undeveloped tracts belong to families and estates that face a terrible capital-gains tax if they sell. These families, moreover, are generally reluctant to sell, unless they feel that the new buyers will enhance the value of other property in the area. But big land companies with large financial resources may be able to overcome some of this resistance. They can even offer the reluctant seller shares of stock instead of cash and so remove some of his tax problem. In any case, new and imaginative land acquisition is going ahead. Webb & Knapp is in the process of building up an inventory of land sufficient to carry it through the 1960's. Woodrow Construction is negotiating for big tracts in the New York and Chicago areas and General Development and Arvida have enough land in Florida to keep them going for quite some time.

HOW MUCH MONEY?

One critical factor remains to be considered—namely, whether building activity at the levels projected here can be financed. There are some builders, for example Bill Levitt, who talk darkly of imminent collapse because of a shortage of money. (Levitt also warned of collapse in 1957, when building activity was running more than one-quarter lower than last year.) All things considered, however, the outlook is favorable. True, builders won't receive the stimulus from easy credit that boosted sales in the 1940's and 1950's. It's doubtful that lenders will extend repayment terms much beyond thirty years even with FHA insurance. Then, too, there will be less stimulus from lowering down payments, which are about as low as they can get in the government-insured sector. But this stimulus won't be so necessary as in the past, for there will be a doubling in the number of families with over $7,500 a year. Below about $7,500 a year, families hold very small liquid assets; above the mark, average holdings increase very rapidly.

What builders worry about most, of course, is the diversion of funds that occurs whenever money gets tight. But this will be much less of a problem in the Sixties. The reason for the diversion is the interest ceiling on FHA and VA mortgages, and the ceiling has already been raised. More important, more and more homes are being built without government insurance. The growth in the number of high-income families, along with the revival in apartment building, has already increased the volume of conventional mortgages from 50 per cent of all mortgages in 1955 to over 65 per cent in 1959.

Over a ten-year period, moreover—whatever the year-to-year fluctuations—there is not likely to be any serious shortage of funds. In the aggregate, savings will grow as fast as the economy. There are, of course, some serious obstacles to be overcome if builders are to receive their share. For example, the conventional mortgage will have to be made a more flexible instrument—perhaps through private insurance or guarantee of the sort started in the last few years. And builders will have to tap the huge resources of pension funds and other institutions not now in the mortgage market. The problem is less the pension funds' inherent unwillingness to invest in mortgages than the absence of the sort of financial instrument that would make it easy for them to do so. It seems likely that such an instrument will be developed.

THE GREAT DISCRETION

Taking everything together, it is abundantly clear that builders will not lack for opportunity and excitement over the decade ahead. As a minimum, the market (including alterations and additions) shapes up to at least $23 billion a year in the first half of the decade and $25 billion in the second, and it is well to emphasize in conclusion that this is a minimum. For, obviously, in the new age of the discretionary dollar, spending on housing could go a lot higher—especially in view of the discrepancy that now exists between personal incomes and housing standards. Since 1929, real income per household in America has risen by some 30 per cent, but the value of the average house and apartment, measured in constant dollars, has actually declined, in line with family size. One reason is that building activity was abnormally low in the depression and during World War II; another is that rising building costs tended to discourage investment in better housing. Whatever the reason, Americans today are living in homes worth roughly one-third less than families of the same income occupied in 1929 —and this despite the enormous upgrading that occurred during the 1950's.

NARROWING THE GAP

During the Sixties this gap might well be narrowed. FORTUNE's minimum projections assume continued heavy replacements and further upgrading. And as consumer incomes after taxes rise by another 50 per cent, there could be an explosive widening of the whole housing market. Indeed, if Americans were to lay out the same proportion of income on housing as they did in the late Fifties, expenditures for new construction would rise to $38 billion in the late Sixties. And even this could be surpassed. For despite demographic factors tending to restrict housing, it is not hard to see where more dollars might go. If, for example, the "industrialized house" were to become a reality by the late 1960's, it would open up a whole new range of possibilities at costs that could alter the consumers' scale of preferences. They might trade in their old houses at a much faster clip; they might stuff their new houses full of industrialized electronic gadgets or include a swimming pool as standard equipment; or they might buy vacation cottages, or rent in-town apartments in quantities not now envisaged.

Whatever the precise amount that's spent on new construction, the rest of the housing market will also be expanding. New construction will raise the amount spent on the maintenance and upkeep of homes ("space rent") from $39 billion in 1959 to at least $58 billion in 1970. Meanwhile, expenditures for household goods are likely to rise from $29 billion in 1959 to $48 billion in 1970, and those for household services from $18 billion to $29 billion. This would bring the total expenditures on housing to at least $160 billion by 1970 and quite possibly to $165 billion or more. In the 1960's, in short, as in the 1950's, the business of the home will be big business indeed.

CHAPTER NINE

The "Ordinary" $125 Billion Market

THE desire of food," Adam Smith pointed out, "is limited in every man by the narrow capacity of the human stomach." But the capacity of the American stomach might well have impressed the father of economics. In 1959, Americans spent about $70 billion for the plain and fancy things they ate. In addition they spent $54.5 billion for other "ordinary" personal items: an estimated $28 billion for clothes, $9.6 billion for alcoholic beverages, $6.8 billion for tobacco products, and a little more than $10 billion for miscellaneous services and goods ranging from cosmetics to watches. By the year 1970 the total of all these expenditures may well rise to the extraordinary total of more than $175 billion.

These enormous consumer outlays augur well for the future— the more so because they tend to go on in good times and bad and are highly resilient to economic recession. At the same time such outlays are not apt to grow so rapidly as some other sectors of the economy. Expenditures for food, clothing, and other personal necessities and indulgences, considered in the charts on page 158, are apt to follow established norms. These expenditures will rise with rising personal incomes, but not so fast as out-

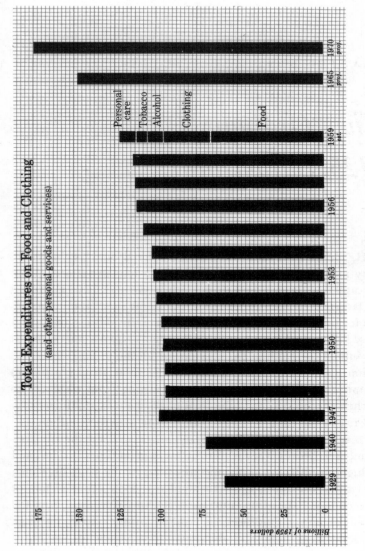

Total Expenditures on Food and Clothing

(and other personal goods and services)

Billions of 1959 dollars

Personal care
Tobacco
Alcohol
Clothing
Food

1929 1940 1947 1950 1953 1956 1959 est. 1965 proj. 1970 proj.

175 150 125 100 75 50 25 0

Consumer expenditures on personal "necessities" are shown in the above chart in constant (1959) dollars, giving actual volume. They rose from $100 billion in 1950 to $125 billion in 1959, a gain of 25 per cent. In the faster-growing economy of the Sixties they may well rise by over 40 per cent.

lays on other goods. Indeed, in 1970, these outlays may be only 35 per cent of total disposable income as against 37 per cent in 1959 and 40 per cent back in 1950 (measured in constant dollars).

This is a natural tendency resulting from at least three reasons. The first is that in the case of food, at least, Adam Smith was basically right; there are definite physical limits as to how much can be consumed. The second reason is that food, clothing, and all other personal consumer goods are subject to some competition from more glamorous types of expenditures for cars, appliances, new housing, and travel. Finally, it should be noted that there has been a price drop in food and clothing, in particular, relative to other products. This tends to reduce the share of disposable income going into these markets. The decline is also, of course, good news to the housewife and means that Americans are better fed and clothed than ever before.

FOOD: PLAIN AND FANCY

In the decade of the Sixties demand for food will, of course, go on expanding as the result of population growth and the rapid upgrading of taste and diets. At the same time, food tends to obey the law formulated by Ernst Engel, the German statistician, which holds that as incomes rise, the percentage spent on food declines. When FORTUNE surveyed the food market in 1954, it looked as though Americans had repealed this law, since the share of income spent on food in the early Fifties remained at least as high as it had been in the Twenties. It turned out, however, that the Department of Commerce had overstated food expenditures; the department's error has since been corrected.

Food is also undergoing important price changes as the result of increasing farm productivity and plain U.S. business competition as manifested in the supermarket and grocery trade. This competition is especially important in knocking down the prices of the so-called convenience foods—cake mixes, frozen foods, precooked foods. When these enter the market, they usually command a premium price over regular unprepared foods. But the low-cost chain stores tend to eliminate these differentials and press

The Pattern of Spending

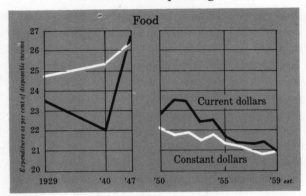

Food

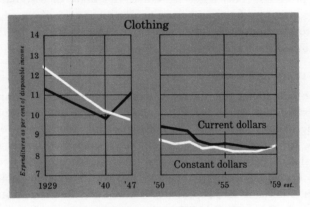

Clothing

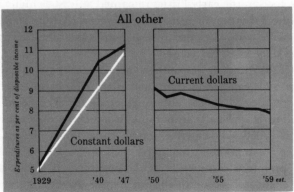

All other

down prices as in the well-known case of frozen orange juice. Indeed, a recent study by the Department of Agriculture suggests that the over-all difference in price between fifty-two prepared foods and their old-fashioned equivalents is a mere 1 per cent. Food manufacturers are constantly pushing out new products such as "boil-in-bag" foods, which are frozen prepared dishes in polyethylene bags, and are ready to serve after being heated in boiling water. Such products and many more to come will certainly broaden and widen the general food market and raise food standards, even though the share of income going to food continues to decline.

The market for clothing is also in flux. The dominating factor during the past twelve years has been the trend toward casual living, or what one man in the men's clothing industry has called "the backyard way of life." The net effect of this was to make people want simpler and less expensive clothing and to cut down the clothing industry's share of disposable income. Now some interesting new trends are at work. There was a long, steep decline in women's suits (a drop of about a third in units from 1953 to 1958), but in 1959 sales took a sharp upturn. Output of more expensive dresses, however, has been generally rising. Sales of house dresses have been declining, giving way to what the garment industry describes as "house-dress-type negligees," defined by one observer as "something women can work around the house in, but still wear to answer the doorbell." Women's play clothes

---

Despite the rise in expenditures for food, clothing, etc., the shares of disposable income going for these items have been shrinking, as shown in the charts opposite. The black lines indicate these shares in current dollars; the white lines, which are in constant dollars, indicate actual physical volume. The decline expressed in current dollars is steeper than the decline in volume because the prices of food and clothing have declined relative to all other consumer prices—i.e., they rose less sharply in the inflation of the 1950's than other prices. However, among the miscellany of "all other" necessities—tobacco, personal care—prices in the 1950's moved almost exactly with the average of other prices. Hence, the single line in the chart (lower right) stands for the share of the market of these goods as expressed both in current dollars and in volume.

have had a steady rise, but output of slacks has risen phenomenally, doubling in four years. In all this can be discerned a tendency for women to fancy up the casual clothes they wear during the day.

In men's clothes the trends are pretty much what they have

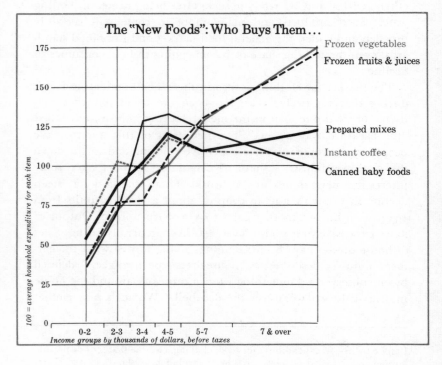

The new convenience foods are now an accepted part of the American budget. This chart gives a view of how families at various income levels purchase them, based on the 1956 *Life* Study of Consumer Expenditures. All families above $3,000 or $4,000 pretax income spent about the same sums for instant coffee and prepared mixes. Upper-income families actually spent less on canned baby food (partly because such families were older, had fewer children). Frozen fruits, juices, and vegetables, however, took a relatively large share of the extra income of the more affluent groups. This is normal. The upper groups always have bought more fruits and vegetables than the lower—fresh or frozen.

been for the past decade. The sales in units of summer and light-weight suits continue to rise; yet despite all the excitement about new synthetic mixes, the increase in lightweight suits has not been fast enough to counter the continued decline in sales of winter-

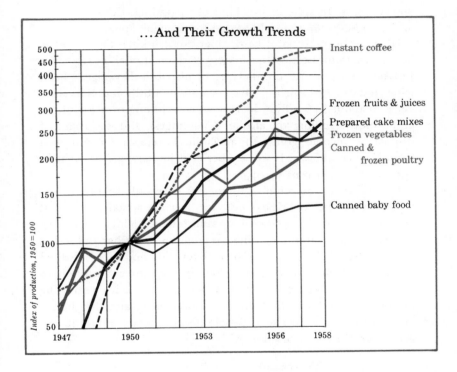

... And Their Growth Trends

Instant coffee

Frozen fruits & juices

Prepared cake mixes
Frozen vegetables
Canned &
    frozen poultry

Canned baby food

Index of production, 1950=100

Now that the new foods have gained such widespread acceptance, their rate of growth has been slowing down in many cases. In the chart above, this is noticeable in the flattening of the lines for instant coffee and baby foods, which have achieved the widest markets. And there has even been a slowdown in the growth curves for cake mixes, frozen vegetables, and frozen fruits and juices (the 1958 dip in fruits and juices was largely due to a poor Florida citrus crop). Only poultry seems to have maintained its former growth, at least among the major items for which reliable statistics are available from the Department of Agriculture.

weight suits. Hence, the total number of men's suits produced declined from 21,665,000 in 1953 to an estimated 20,500,000 in 1959. The output of odd jackets meanwhile rose 37 per cent, to about 9,500,000 units in 1959, while slacks rose about 40 per cent, to about 80 million pairs; sales of dungarees and overalls are down. "Teamsters are wearing slacks to work nowadays," one observer says. In spite of this kind of upgrading, the market for men's clothes is not so bright as that for women's apparel.

Despite the tradition of hard American drinking, there is little in the figures to increase the anxiety of the National Temperance League. Expenditures on all types of alcoholic beverages—beer, wine, and distilled spirits—have risen about a billion dollars since 1953, to about $9.6 billion in 1959 (not including over $1 billion of business spending on alcoholic beverages). But the share of disposable income going to alcoholic beverages has dropped steadily since the war. It was 5.1 per cent in 1947, 3.4 per cent in 1953, and 2.9 per cent in 1959.

Per capita consumption of liquor has risen only slightly in the past decade. The American's taste for beer has actually slackened and total production has stayed the same (about 2.6 billion gallons). Per capita consumption of wine has gone up somewhat and so has that of hard liquor. Drinking of whiskey, gin, and other distilled spirits rose from 194,700,000 gallons in 1953 to 215 million in 1958, and ran about 227 million gallons the following year. The liquor industry hopes that this is a new plateau and that liquor sales will continue to rise as people do more entertaining in the age of the "discretionary dollar."

CIGARETTES—WHO'S AFRAID?

The great lung-cancer scare about five years ago had a profound effect on cigarette sales, which account for some 87 per cent of the entire market for tobacco products. In 1954, cigarette smoking dipped 6 per cent below the 1952 high of 394 billion, and did not pass the old mark again until 1957. But by 1958 consumption was up to 436 billion, and in 1959 it went up another 4 per cent. In part this is due to population gains, particularly to the big in-

The Shares for Clothing, Drinking, Smoking, etc.

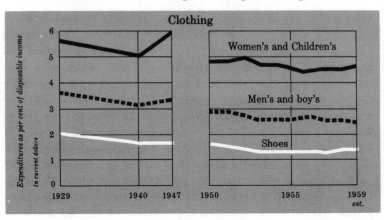

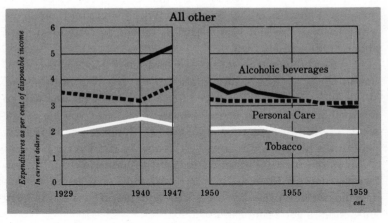

The breakdown for the shares of income going to clothing and all other "ordinary" expenditures is shown in the charts above. It should be noted that there has been a slowdown in the rate at which these items have been losing their share of disposable income. Since 1956, women's and children's clothes have done well and there has even been some increase in the share of income going to shoes. Similarly, tobacco's share of the dollar has gone up (despite lung-cancer scares), and alcohol, which was dropping the most in the 1950's (from 4 to less than 3 per cent of income), has also begun to hold its own in the last year or two. Personal care has always been a fairly steady performer over all, but within the group, beauty preparations and the like have been growing considerably, while laundry and cleaning services have taken a declining share of income.

crease in the number of teen-agers, who appear to be smoking more furiously than ever before. Ironically, another big factor is the filter-tip cigarette, which now accounts for about 50 per cent of all cigarettes; people switch to filter-tip cigarettes because they fear lung cancer, but they end by smoking more of them than they did of the old straight cigarettes. The net effect is that consumption per person (over fifteen years of age) is now up to 180 packs a year—above the old pre-cancer-scare peak of 175.

The trends in the personal goods and services industries, which collectively accounted for about $10 billion of consumer spending in 1959, are mixed. Laundering (about $900 million) and dry cleaning (about $1.9 billion) will continue to get an increasingly smaller share of disposable income because of all the home washers and dryers and the drip-dry suits that don't need cleaning or pressing. Toiletries (about $2.5 billion) are increasing their share, while barbershops and beauty parlors (about $2 billion) are just about holding their own.

In general the outlook for sales of "ordinary" goods and services, including food, clothes, liquor, and all the rest, is a healthy one. While it is true that their share of total consumer income will go down, there will be an actual growth in physical volume as the result of rising population and incomes. Indeed, per capita expenditures in this whole area will probably rise by 1.5 per cent a year in the 1960's as against 1 per cent in the 1950's. And manufacturers serving these markets have the additional assurance that demand for the everyday necessities and luxuries remains huge and stable in good times and bad.

CHAPTER TEN

Detroit's Next Decade

ONCE again, after several vexatious and baffling years, the U.S. automobile industry is setting its sights high. There is a good prospect that the Big Three's new "compacts" will generate more excitement about automobiles than anything that has happened since Henry Ford brought out his first Model A in 1927. Many auto men, indeed, believe the Big Three will sell more than a million compacts during the 1960 model year. As for the independents, Studebaker aims to sell up to 150,000 Larks, and George Romney of American Motors, who has been using big advertisements to warn people against "untried" compacts produced in "crash programs," plans to hold first place in the field by selling more than 500,000 of his restyled but undeniably well-tried Ramblers.

Meanwhile foreign cars, most of them *small* (not to be confused with "compact"), will continue to hold an important place in the U.S. market; paced by Volkswagen, which has been running six months behind on orders, imports ran up an estimated volume of 600,000 in 1959. But of course the great bulk of the U.S. automobile market is still the big "conventional" car, and here, too, the prospects are good. The big cars did astonishingly well in 1959, and

By 1970 There Will Probably Be 80 Million Cars on the Road

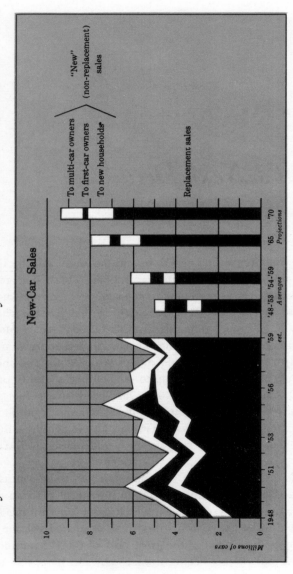

The U.S. passenger-car industry may be selling eight million cars a year by 1965, and 9,400,000 by 1970. Here car demand since 1948 is broken down into its basic components and projected to 1970: (1) replacements as measured by scrappage, plainly enough the most important of the components, which will probably come to 5,700,000 a year by 1965 and 6,900,000 by 1970; (2) new households buying cars, the result of population growth, whose purchases will come to as many as 900,000 a year by 1965 and 1,100,000 by 1970; (3) other households buying cars for the first time, which may number 450,000 a year by 1965 but will probably fall to 300,000 by 1970; (4) people buying a second (or third or fourth) car for the first time, who may add up to about 950,000 a year by 1965 and 1,100,000 by 1970.

Car Ownership by Households

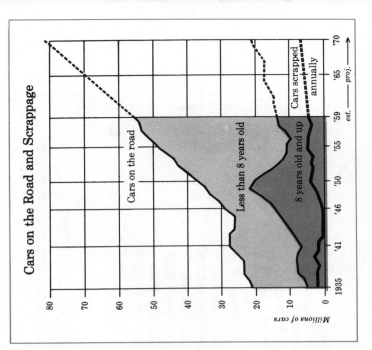

The number of households owning cars will grow by 1,330,000 a year during the 1960's. Nearly 80 per cent of all households already own cars, and perhaps 85 to 90 per cent will own cars by 1970. More important, there will be a high rate of household formation in the 1960's owing to the high birth rate of the 1940's. The unpredictable factor will be the extent of demand for second (or third or fourth) cars.

Cars on the Road and Scrappage

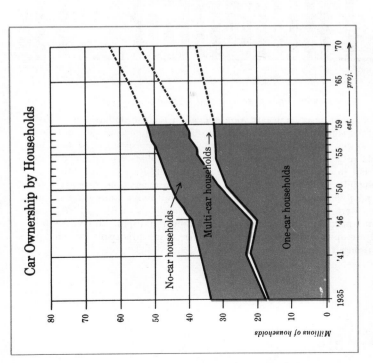

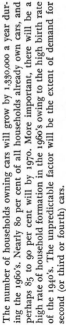

As the car population increases from 55 million to 70 million in 1965 and perhaps to 80 million or more in 1970, the number of cars eight years old or more—the age of heavy scrappage—will increase from 13,500,000 now to about 17 million in 1965 and perhaps 21,500,000 in 1970. Thus scrappage can be expected to rise from 4,400,000 units in 1959 to perhaps 5,500,000 in 1965 and nearly seven million in 1970.

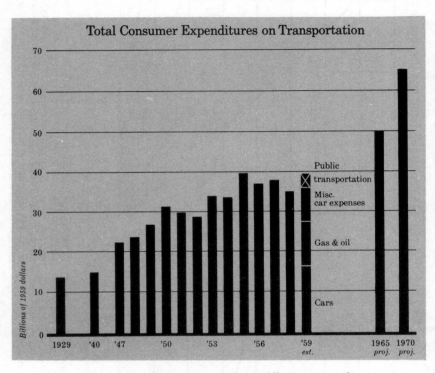

Total Consumer Expenditures on Transportation

Billions of 1959 dollars

Public transportation
Misc. car expenses
Gas & oil
Cars

1929 '40 '47 '50 '53 '56 '59 *est.* 1965 *proj.* 1970 *proj.*

The Car Continues to Crowd Out Public Transportation

Consumer spending on transportation, measured in 1959 dollars, has tripled since 1929, rising from $13 billion to $39 billion. By 1970 it will probably increase to $65 billion. As chart top right shows, transportation's share of consumers' disposable income, measured in current dollars, has increased from 9.2 per cent in 1929 to 11.7 per cent in 1959. Chart lower right shows how the automobile has dominated the rise. In 1929 consumers spent 7 per cent of their disposable income on cars and 2 per cent on public transportation; in 1959 they were spending 11 per cent on cars and less than 1 per cent on public transportation. Nine-tenths of all consumer transport outlays are for cars and car operation; three and a half times as much is spent just on gas and oil as on all forms of public transport.

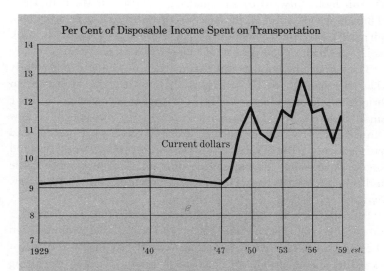

Per Cent of Disposable Income Spent on Transportation

Current dollars

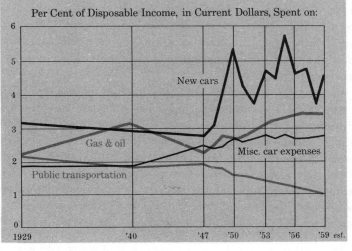

Per Cent of Disposable Income, in Current Dollars, Spent on:

New cars

Gas & oil

Misc. car expenses

Public transportation

Detroit looks forward to an equally good year for them in 1960. Thus total U.S. automobile sales for 1959 came close to 6,500,000, surpassed only by 7,400,000 in 1955. And it now begins to look as if 1960 had a good chance of being the best year ever.

The important point about this market, however, is not merely that cars happen to be selling well, but that the vistas are so bright for the decade ahead. The compact cars, together with the small imports, are the dramatic, immediate evidence of a new "functional" market characterized by a variety of needs, and satisfied only with a variety of prices and models, both big and small. Addressing its talents to this market, the automobile industry is diversifying its output and providing itself with a new dynamic.

Familiar as it is, the American people's affection for passenger cars—when they get the kind they want—must give pause to even the most sophisticated observer. American consumers today, for example, spend eleven times as much on buying and operating cars as they do on all forms of public transportation, local and long distance—buses, planes, subways, taxis, trains. Thus "consumer expenditures for transportation," an economic and historical concept of some importance, today boils down chiefly to cars.

During 1959 Americans spent an estimated total of $36 billion on cars—nearly $16 billion for new ones and some $20 billion for maintaining and running their cars. In addition, business and government spent several billions on the cars they own.* FORTUNE suggests that the auto industry will enjoy eight-million-car years by the middle 1960's and close to ten-million-car years by 1970—which means that the U.S. car population will increase by perhaps 2,500,-000 a year, or by almost as much as the U.S. human population is increasing. By 1970 consumers probably will be spending over $60

* The Commerce Department credits 18 per cent of all new-car sales to government and business, including professional men and other individuals in business for themselves. How many of the 55 million cars on the road are actually business cars is unknown. The Automobile Manufacturers' Association estimate for 1957 was 8,250,000.

billion on passenger cars—perhaps $26 billion buying them and $34 billion operating them.

This spacious prospect, like many such prospects in a free society, is not the outcome of an orderly sequence of predictable events. In the late 1950's no big business had a more uneven time of it than the auto industry, and never in its own erratic history had its fortune been so inconstant. The beginnings of the trouble go back, of course, to the early 1950's, more precisely to 1953, when the industry finally seemed to have satisfied the postwar "shortage" of cars, prolonged as it was by the Korean war. In 1953 people had a lot of money to spend, but their demand for cars in terms of units was slowing down. As FORTUNE suggested that year, the industry probably would offset this slowdown in unit demand by selling *more car per car*—not merely larger and heavier cars, but cars equipped with improvements like automatic transmissions, power steering, power brakes, and other innovations.

And this is precisely what the industry did. It gave people more car and they paid more per car than ever before. To encourage obsolescence, the industry also went in for striking and frequent style changes. So despite the recession of 1954, dollar sales stayed comfortably high. And then in 1955, when the industry introduced a variety of mechanical and style innovations, and when lenders simultaneously made credit terms extravagantly easy, unit sales reached an all-time high of 7,400,000. For these 7,400,000 cars, Americans paid $15.8 billion—5.75 per cent of their disposable income, the highest share ever. The industry's success made it exceedingly optimistic about its future, and it placed large bets on that future in the form of heavy outlays for new capacity.

But then, in 1956, unit sales fell off to 5,900,000. This was a disappointing figure, but auto men conveniently ascribed it to the "overbuying" of the year before. But things did not improve in 1957. Displaying an almost insolent indifference to such wonders as the new middle-price Edsel, the American people bought only six million units. And in the recession year of 1958 sales thudded down to 4,700,000, or 800,000 fewer than in the recession year of 1954.

What had happened, of course, was that the industry had built up car per car too rapidly. All through the 1950's realization per unit (in constant dollars) rose steeply, and so gradually limited the number of potential buyers. In 1953, FORTUNE estimates, the industry got 25 per cent more real dollars per car than it got before the war. Between 1953 and 1957 it got another 10 to 12 per cent. In the same years, however, unit sales rose only 4.5 per cent. Value per car, in other words, rose faster than consumer income. At the same time, the motor industry made its cars too much alike, in appearance and price as well as size and power. By 1957 it took an expert to distinguish a fully equipped "low price range" car from a "middle price range" or even a "high price range" car, either in cost or in appearance. Alfred Sloan used to say that it should be General Motors' aim to provide a car for every purse and purpose. But by 1957-58 most of the industry found itself providing a more or less uniform car for a limited number of purses.

As people's incomes rose, paradoxically, they were less inclined to put a lot of money into a single big car. For one thing, the industry, by making cars so much alike, had all but ruined the value of any specific car as a status symbol. More important, most families in the $4,000-and-over income groups were now suburbanites, who found they needed not only special-purpose cars, but often more than one car.

Into this vacuum of needs rolled the European imports and George Romney's new compact Rambler. Offering variety as well as less car per car, they were (as now seems perfectly logical) extraordinarily successful. In an otherwise weak and declining car market, sales of these vehicles rose from 100,000 in 1956 to 500,000 in 1958. "The car today," George Romney began to argue, "is primarily a means of personal, individual mobility. The big all-purpose car is not."

LESS CAR PER CAR

Detroit's official line during the recession of 1957-58, however, was still to argue that its own surveys showed that people wanted all-purpose cars and to describe small and compact cars as a short-lived fad. But the industry privately had begun to question some of its assumptions about Americans as car owners. Were people still able and willing to spend more and more on a single automobile? Why should people pay a premium for a car as a status symbol when cars looked so much alike? Did the industry's policy of "dynamic obsolescence" through radical styling changes make as much sales sense as it once did? In this doubting mood, Detroit also lowered its sights. It publicly forecast only some 5,500,000 sales for 1959 and changed what once had been rosy estimates for the 1960's.

Detroit also went ahead and made one of the most important policy decisions it has ever made. Half fearing that their so-called conventional cars were all wrong, the Big Three not only tooled up for their own compact cars to compete with the independent compacts, but also planned compact versions of the Buick, Dodge, etc. Early in 1959, ironically, after everybody knew the compacts were coming, sales of conventional cars began to surge. By year's end such sales had come to some 5,400,000 units, compared to 5,900,000 in 1956. People obviously needed and wanted the big cars, too.

But the distinguishing characteristic of the year's sales was the variety of cars Americans were buying—it was even possible for small boys (and their nostalgic fathers) once again to identify different makes of cars as they rolled past. More than a million of 1959 calendar year sales were compacts and small cars—600,000 imports, 500,000 Ramblers and Studebaker Larks, and an estimated 100,000 of the Big Three compacts. Conventional cars, too, were becoming more various. A full 15 per cent of these sales in 1959 were accounted for by station wagons, against 10 per cent in 1956. A higher percentage of convertibles and expensive Cadillacs and Thunderbirds was sold than ever before. Thus, as we enter the 1960's, for the first time since the 1920's Detroit is offering a car for every purpose and purse. The passwords around town are no longer "more car per car" but "specialization" and "the functional market."

Despite a further increase in the size and weight of conventional cars, enough small and compact cars are being sold now to reduce slightly the average sale price per car. On the average, in other words, people are buying less car per car. Both unit and dollar sales have come into a sounder relationship with consumers' disposable income. Even though people will probably buy more than seven million units in 1960, spending per car may drop further. The Big Three may sell more than 800,000 compact cars, and total sales of small and compact cars may exceed two million, or between 25 and 30 per cent of total sales. Thus they will offset all the increase in the still rising cost of conventional cars.

THE HEART OF THE MARKET

In such fashion the auto industry has gone through a kind of massive correction. Like the stock market when it comes out of its own kind of correction, the industry has emerged stronger and in better balance, ready to climb to new highs. The change toward variety and specialization is made to order for the changes now taking place in the consumer market. By 1970, families with more than $7,500 in disposable income will comprise two-fifths of all families, against 23 per cent today; their number will increase from 12 million to nearly 25 million. One characteristic of the new families in this income bracket is that for the most part they buy new rather than used cars (hence these families account for the majority of new car sales). Since so many are suburbanites, they want various kinds of cars, depending on their needs and circumstances—station wagons, stripped sedans, sports cars, compact cars, small cars. And since about 40 per cent already own more than one auto, they are in the market for millions of new second cars of all kinds.

Their preference for new machines has already had an interesting effect on the market. As more and more people have moved into the $7,500-and-up bracket, more and more people have been able to pass up a used car, which was once all they could afford, in favor of a new car. Thus the price of used cars has tended to decline relative to new ones, which of course has made for lower trade-in allowances. Lower allowances have caused the $7,500-

and-over people to hang on to their cars longer, and have also helped make them less vulnerable to style and status-symbol appeals.

Obviously enough, only an auto industry with a wide variety of cars in a wide variety of price ranges will be able to meet the needs of the $7,500-and-over bracket. People in this group, indeed, are the heart of the "functional" car market of the 1960's. Instead of buying hand-me-downs, they will buy new cars for specific uses. Instead of trading in big cars every two years or so, they will tend to own more cars per family, and hold on to their cars longer. Instead of trying to emulate the big all-purpose sedans of the top income groups, they will tend to be less influenced by style and "status symbol" appeals.

RISING REPLACEMENT NEEDS

And now let us see how all this might work out, in fairly specific unit and dollar terms, during the interesting decade ahead. Estimating unit volume is unusually hard today because small and compact cars may do much better (or conceivably worse) than now appears likely. Yet the unit market has its inherent limits, and the forces that influence and determine unit sales can be appraised with tolerable accuracy over the long term, given basic assumptions about the course and level of the economy as a whole. FORTUNE assumes that the economy will grow at 4.2 per cent a year during the 1960's.

Now, every car sold either (1) adds to the number of autos in use, or (2) replaces a car being scrapped. A new auto, of course, is not bought every time another one is scrapped; but ultimately and inevitably replacement sales are measured by scrappage figures, and total new sales in any year can be regarded as equal to the scrappage figure plus the growth in the number of cars on the road. Ever since the 1920's, as the number of cars on the road grew, the replacement of worn-out cars has naturally constituted a larger part of total sales than the growth in the number of cars. Growth sales since World War II have averaged a little more than two million cars a year, but scrappage rose from 2,800,000 in 1948-53 to four million in 1954-59.

Prior to World War II, half the cars produced in any given year were scrapped by the time they were a little more than ten years old; recently the figure has declined to nine and a half years. If this rate holds, scrappage will come to 5,700,000 by 1965 and to nearly seven million by 1970. Will the recent rate prevail?

INNOVATION MEANS SALES

Despite gabble to the contrary, the auto industry has never made more durable cars than today, at least in the sense that their parts wear better than ever. Yet there are many forces working to accelerate obsolescence and to keep the scrappage rate at least as high as it is now.

People are driving their autos a few more miles every year. Despite the growth of multiple-car ownership, the trend toward more intensive use has continued and probably will continue. Although cars are more durable than they used to be, they are also more complex. Removing a spark plug is a project for an expert armed with a special tool. Late models are fitted with a whole array of intricate and delicate accessories like power steering and automatic transmission, which are both costly to repair and often need repairing when they have only a few years behind them. To cap it all, the price of automobile repairs is going up faster than other prices. For while the wages of automobile repairmen, like those of plumbers and carpenters, are rising at least as fast as other wages, the productivity or hourly output of auto repairmen is rising very little, if at all.

Not so long ago a man could buy a plain five-year-old car for less than $500 and run it 10,000 miles a year without spending an inordinate amount on repairs. Today he may pay a little more for a used car, complete with automatic transmission, power steering, and a host of other accessories. But one day he may be assailed by strange noises and growls, as well as a distressing front-end shimmy. He discovers that his automatic transmission and power steering need overhauling, and the job will set him back $250 or more. The obvious solution is to trade his car in for whatever he can get, and so accelerate its passage to the scrap heap.

As in the past, the industry will continue to spur scrappage by improvement and innovation. Style cannot yet be written off as a factor in obsolescence, but mechanical and operating improvements and innovations will probably be more important. The much-publicized gas-turbine engine is not likely to go into passenger cars during this decade, though it may be installed in trucks soon. By 1970, however, some passenger cars may boast the free piston engine, which employs pistons to compress gases that power a turbine. Air-conditioning systems will certainly be simplified and reduced in price. Steering-gear joints will be improved with oilless bearings that require little attention. The steering wheel may be replaced by a steering stick. Suspension systems will be improved and may be adjustable at will. In short, there are a lot of changes in store. If no single change is likely to be sensational, there will be enough of them to give each year's cars demonstrable points of superiority over the previous year's.

THREE "GROWTH" FACTORS

So much for replacements. Now look at the number of cars that will be bought because of basic growth in the market. "Growth" customers fall into three groups: (1) new households, the result of population growth; (2) established households buying their first cars; (3) and households adding a second (or third or fourth) car.

(1) New households will come close to being the single biggest factor in the growth of the market. Owing to the low birth rate of the 1930's, households are now being "formed" at a rate of 900,000 a year. But owing to the high birth rate of the 1940's, household formation will average 1,050,000 in the 1960's (with the figure being somewhat higher in the second half of the decade) and climb to about 1,200,000 by 1970. At the end of 1959 there were 52 million households, but there will be 58 million by 1965, and nearly 64 million by 1970. A larger proportion of the new households will be very young or very old than is the case now, but even so, the new households can be expected to account for 900,000 new-

car sales a year by 1965 and 1,100,000 by 1970. (Even if only 80 per cent of new households were to buy cars, the sales figures would be reduced by only 100,000 a year or so.)

(2) Established households buying their first car will be a relatively small factor in the growth of the market of the Sixties. Some 78 per cent of all households now own cars, against only 50 per cent in 1947, and the other 20 per cent is concentrated in congested cities or in poverty pockets in the Deep South and elsewhere. The proportion of households owning cars has recently been rising very slowly, and of course will never reach 100 per cent. If it rises perhaps to 85 or 87 per cent during the decade, established households might account for 450,000 new-car sales a year in the mid-Sixties, then taper off to about 300,000 by 1970.

(3) Households adding a second (or third or fourth) car will be an important factor in the growth of the market, though perhaps less important than some industry estimates have suggested. Today some 20 per cent of all car-owning households own two or more cars—up from a little more than 10 per cent in 1951. General Motors and Ford think the figure will hit 25 per cent by 1965, while American Motors' George Romney says 33 per cent would be more like it. Theoretically, indeed, the low cost of compact and small cars should boost multiple-car ownership.

But the fact is that the multiple-car market has *already* enjoyed sharp growth, and it is not clear how the rate of increase in multi-car families can rise much beyond the present rate. Multiple-car ownership has recently been rising by nearly 750,000 a year. A third of this gain is probably attributable to the increase in families with more than $7,500 a year. Forty per cent of them own two cars, against only 12 per cent for those with lower incomes. This group will grow faster in the Sixties than it did in the Fifties. However, most of the increase in two-car ownership up till now has been the result of the flight to the suburbs by nearly all income groups. The suburban population will not grow as much in this decade as it did in the Fifties—owing in part to the increase in the number of young and old couples.

An unknown factor is the growth of three or four car families.

Teen-agers will multiply in the 1960's—but their car ownership may do no more than preserve the life of cars that otherwise would be scrapped. Obviously the increase in multiple-car ownership is difficult to gauge. But it is reasonable to expect the percentage of households owning two or more cars to rise by 50 per cent. If so, total growth will approach a million units a year by 1965 and come to about 1,100,000 by 1970.

Total growth in new-car sales, then, adds up to 2,300,000 a year by 1965 and to 2,500,000 by 1970. Total unit sales—growth plus replacement—would thus come to eight million by 1965 and 9,500,000 by 1970.

DOLLARS ARE WHAT COUNT

But if, as many argue, the "low-priced" small and compact cars together will eventually claim as much as half of all sales, what will happen to dollar volume? Won't the industry be forced to take a smaller share of consumer income than it has been getting?

Let us assume for the moment that small and compact cars will account for a third of all sales, and that relatively expensive station wagons, convertibles, and luxury sedans will claim a rising share of the other two-thirds. During the early 1960's the rising prices of the latter cars, which will come equipped with more refinements and accessories than ever, would probably more than offset the lower prices of the smaller cars. Thus average realization per car would rise 2 or 3 per cent. With unit sales of eight million by 1965, the industry's total dollar sales would increase a little faster than consumer income, or from $16 billion in 1959 to a little more than $20 billion.

By 1970, however, total dollar sales would have to hit $26 billion to claim the same rising share of consumer income they will probably claim in 1960-65. And to realize $26 billion from 9,500,000 cars, the industry would have to get 12 per cent more money per car by 1970 than it did in 1965. What will make this unusually hard is that Detroit is in the throes of a production revolution that may end up with the industry turning out not only authentically small cars but compact versions of nearly every make and style, including what are now the biggest and most expensive. Can the industry still go on increasing its take per unit?

MORE COMPACT PER COMPACT

There are good reasons why it can. To begin with, the compact versions of the expensive cars doubtless will not be low-priced compacts—any more than the imported Jaguar sedan, though it is a compact auto, is a low-priced one. What is more, it is doubtful that the *sole* appeal of the compact and small car ever was economy. As consumer incomes rise (and remember they will be rising fast), the industry doubtless will apply the more-car-per-car formula to smaller cars as well as to larger ones. The lesson of the past three or four years, after all, is not that people don't want and aren't willing to pay for a well-equipped car, but that prices must not increase *too* fast, and that many people don't want big cars. Thus many devices may make compact cars more expensive than the 1960 models—such as air conditioning, automatic transmission, and station-wagon versions of the compacts. Although 80 per cent of all new cars are now equipped with automatic transmissions, only 20 per cent have air conditioning.

Other accessories may well be loaded on even the most austere cars. As anyone who has read all through a passenger-car manual is aware, taking care of a modern car according to the book could be almost a full-time job for a hard-working man. Anything the industry can do to reduce the bother and expense of maintenance would be a boon to car owners, and it surely could be sold, at a good price, as both a time and money saver. So the auto industry may be tempted to install devices that will bring dollars to the manufacturers at the ultimate expense of the garage and service man. Among them is the semi-automatic, one-shot lubrication system, which eliminates most of the bother of greasing.

It is conceivable, to be sure, that Americans will buy many more cars, and spend much less per car, than the estimates here suggest. But the fact remains that the nation can only use so many cars, and so long as people are able and willing to spend more and more on personal transportation, they will doubtless buy more expensive cars.

Americans, as we have noted, have been spending more maintaining and operating cars than buying them. Although the ratio of operating costs to new-car outlays has fluctuated widely with the fortunes of the auto industry, consumers over the years have spent about $1.35 operating and maintaining cars for every dollar they spent on new ones. They laid out a little over $21 billion on maintenance and operation in 1959; and if these expenditures keep pace with new-car purchases, they will amount to about $28 billion by 1965 and $35 billion by 1970.

"IT'S THE UPKEEP"

Following is a breakdown of the average of automobile operating costs in 1957-58:

	Millions of dollars
Gas and oil	$10,450
Repairs, washing, greasing, storage, parking, rental	4,200
Tires, tubes, parts	2,500
Auto-insurance premiums (less claims paid)	1,400
Bridge, tunnel, ferry, and toll roads	230
	$18,780

During the past decade, the number of cars on the road has been rising 63 per cent, but gas and oil outlays have been rising 83 per cent. Reasons: gasoline prices rose faster than other prices until 1957; people drove more miles per car; and gas consumption per car-mile rose too. Motor-oil sales, incidentally, contributed nothing to the trend. Because the average motorist changes his oil every 3,100 miles (against 1,900 miles, for example, in 1952), oil sales have actually declined 5 per cent since 1955.

In the decade ahead the number of cars on the road will increase by less than 50 per cent. If these automobiles were all large gas eaters, total outlays for gasoline would again leap by considerably more than 50 per cent—perhaps by more than 70 per cent. But by 1970 at least 25 per cent of the cars on the road will be compacts. If these compacts burn 20 per cent less gas than the "conventional" cars, the national consumption of gas would be 5 per cent less than if all cars were conventional. Thus total spending on gas and oil during this decade might increase by about 65 per cent, or as much as all consumer spending for transportation.

Other consumer outlays for car operation should rise proportionately with car sales. Although the relative price of tires is declining somewhat, that of parts is not. The relative price of repairs and other service jobs, as already noted, is in a secular rise because these services employ a lot of labor whose productivity is not going up as fast as the productivity of labor as a whole. But this rise may well be offset by the tendency to build cars that need less servicing, and by the inevitable tendency of cars that need a lot of repairs to reach the scrap yard sooner than they might otherwise.

Outlays for bridge, tunnel, ferry, and road tolls will probably continue to increase as more people drive more miles—but not so fast as miles driven. For superhighways will presumably be augmented by the national freeways, which are scheduled eventually to absorb all toll roads. Thus toll payments, in relation to total miles traveled, will probably go down.

For years consumer outlays on auto insurance did not rise as fast as car expenditures in general. Owing to the increasing cost of accidents, however, they have recently been going up at an abnormal rate. What is more, the rates for unmarried drivers aged eighteen to twenty-five, whose numbers—and accidents—are increasing sharply, are rising to levels almost twice as high as those for other drivers. For a while, insurance charges may increase more rapidly than other operating costs, but even so will not bulk large enough to make a great difference in total operating costs.

All in all, it is reasonable to expect consumers' car maintenance and operating costs to continue to add up to about a third more than their purchases of new cars. There seems, indeed, a kind of "normal" relationship between spending on cars and spending on operating them.

BIAS FOR CARS

The dynamic sector of the whole consumer-transport market, plainly enough, is the new-car market. Now that the auto industry is giving people the variety they need and want, they should go on displaying their bias for the passenger automobile during the Sixties at least. They may buy a few more units than the projections here suggest, or they may spend more per car. But it looks as if they were still willing, in this sweet land of personal transportation, to go on spending a growing percentage of their income on the passenger automobile.

CHAPTER ELEVEN

The Long Decline
of Public Transportation

AMONG all the changes wrought by the automobile, none is more striking than what it has done to the once great business of moving people around by train, streetcar, subway, and bus. As long ago as 1929, the auto had already captured three-quarters of American consumer spending on personal transportation. Even during the depression, popular spending on public transportation barely held its one-quarter share of the transport market, and only in the gas-rationed, car-short war years did it gain a little. Since World War II, consumer outlays for public transport have been shrinking both relatively and absolutely. In 1959 they amounted to less than a twelfth of all consumer outlays for transportation. Specifically, people spent a grand total of $39.3 billion on transportation, and of this $39.3 billion only a trifle more than $3 billion was spent on all forms of public transport—buses, trains, subways, airplanes, and taxis. The remaining $36-plus billion went into automobiles.* Motorists are spending almost as much just for bridge and road tolls as all Americans spend on intercity bus fares.

* This does not include government and business spending on personal transportation, for which no figures exist.

Despite the inherent efficiency of mass transportation, Americans have steadily forsaken it. The process has been accelerated by tax and other government policies that do not give a fair break to public transportation. But beyond this, most Americans have a stubborn preference for moving about in their own cars, even when they know that true costs are often more than the price of taking a bus or train. Most motorists of course forget the amortization, insurance, etc., and count the cost of using their car simply in terms of gas and oil. And a very heavy cost that very few consumers count is that of their own time as drivers. Even when they find driving a vexing and time-consuming routine, they seem to prefer the convenience of going when they want to go. For the motorcar gives them the sensation—or perhaps the illusion—of being liberated from the confines of time, space, and arbitrary man-made restrictions like timetables and queues.

Since all this is a well-established part of the American character, there is little prospect of any real comeback in public transportation. Of the $3.2 billion consumers spent on it in 1958, $1.9 billion went for local and $1.3 billion for intercity transport. Unless great and as yet unheralded changes are forthcoming in civic transport programs, spending on local transportation may decline a little by 1970. On the other hand, consumer spending on intercity travel, thanks to the booming airline business, may increase to $2 billion or more. By 1970, therefore, consumers may be spending between $3.5 billion and $4 billion on public transport, or around a half billion more than they are now. But suppose for the sake of argument they will be spending $1 billion more: the increase is still relatively insignificant. By 1970, as noted earlier, Americans will be devoting more than $60 billion a year to buying and operating their motorcars, or about $25 billion more than they are now.

TOO FEW HOURS, TOO FEW DAYS

Consumer spending on local transportation—travel on streetcars, local buses, subways, commutation trains, and taxis—has been more or less static since World War II, while about every other kind of spending in the U.S. was soaring. The dollar total

actually dropped a little, from $2.1 billion in 1949 to $1.9 billion
in 1958. But fares have risen considerably, and thus total physical
volume of local transport has declined steeply. All local public
transport is saddled with a desperately difficult, perhaps insoluble,
basic problem. Public transportation is still crucially important
during rush hours five days a week, but thanks to the private car,
it is increasingly ill patronized at other times. As volume drops
and overhead costs mount, rates must rise while service must be
curtailed. So volume declines still more, and the whole sad cycle
repeats itself.

Nearly two-thirds of all local public transport is accounted for
by bus and rapid transit, including subways. Passenger revenues
of the nation's six subway and elevated systems—New York City,
Boston, Chicago, Philadelphia, Cleveland, Hudson & Manhattan
—have risen 23 per cent since 1949. But this rise is the result of
fare increases; the number of passengers carried dropped 35 per
cent. Local bus service in small and middle-sized cities is fighting
for survival; total bus passenger revenue has increased by only
13.5 per cent since 1949, while the number of passengers carried
has declined 38 per cent. Streetcars, of course, are disappearing.
Even taxicabs have suffered at the hands—or wheels—of the private car. In 1949 consumers spent $583 million on taxicabs; in
1958, despite much higher fares, they spent only $593 million.
Some officials of the American Taxicab Association, however,
believe that the decline in public transport will benefit taxicabs,
and their business will increase somewhat.

Rail commutation, though it often affords commuters a cheaper
and less strenuous way of getting to their offices than any other
form of transport, is languishing. Rail commuter volume rose
to seven billion passenger-miles in the late 1920's. It fell off sharply
during the depression, and never returned to its old high, even
during World War II. Now it is down to fewer than 4.8 billion
passenger-miles. Owing almost entirely to fare increases, dollar
volume rose from $79 million in 1949 to $121 million in 1958,
but actual volume is slowly shrinking.

Certainly there appears to be no future for private rail commutation operated for profit, even if it could regain the volume it enjoyed years ago. More than other local transport, it is afflicted with the handicaps of being a rush-hour, five-day-a-week operation. Equipment cost has soared to the point where even full trains, running relatively few miles a day as they do, cannot earn the interest on the investment in them. Worse, commutation services suffer from exorbitant labor costs. Train crews must usually be put on an overtime basis because they are paid from the time they begin to work in the morning until they return in the evening, regardless of what they do all day long. So practically all rail commutation services, if they are to survive, will be taken over or otherwise subsidized by municipalities, which may ease their road traffic problems by keeping down commutation fares. Given such a boost, rail commutation may increase somewhat.

Helicopters may conceivably play a role in local transportation during the 1960's. A few years ago some enthusiasts saw helicopters taking over much commuter traffic, both rail and bus, and estimates ranged up to 25 million passengers a year by 1970. But recently less starry-eyed authorities pointed out that the physical problem of accommodating helicopters "on any old rooftop" is insurmountable, and will prevent them from replacing many existing services, to say nothing of contributing much to the growth of public transport.

TOO LITTLE TOO LATE?

The larger cities, it is true, are growing more and more concerned about traffic congestion. Traffic engineers point out that if everybody now coming into Manhattan below Fifty-second Street were to enter by private car, the whole of the island below that street would have to be given over to multiple-level parking buildings. They also calculate that if automobile population continues its increase, and if the proportion driven into the large cities remains the same, all land areas in those cities, by 1980 or so, will be needed for parking. Such projections, however, dramatize rather than illustrate the problem. Cities like New York would be impossible without public transportation; it is bound to survive there. On the other hand, decentralization is a fact; the number of people entering and leaving big city centers apparently will not grow so fast as the number of cars.

But the time is doubtless coming soon when larger cities must integrate public and private transportation so that people can drive their cars to peripheral stations and be picked up there by rapid transit. Only one or two cities, notably Cleveland, have done so. The New York Metropolitan Transit Commission's plan for combining New Jersey commuting lines with New York transit systems is all but dead. The much-publicized scheme for a San Francisco Transit District, however, is not. No less than $115 million in auto tolls from the San Francisco-Oakland bridge will be used to finance a rapid-transit tube between San Francisco and Oakland. And in November, 1960, citizens of five Bay area counties will vote on a $500-million bond issue to finance the first stage of a $1.5-billion system, designed to cover the whole area.

Whether enough such schemes can be got under way in time to stay the decline of local transportation during this decade, much less increase it, is dubious. Municipalities and metropolitan areas seem more inclined to discuss and argue than to do anything, and while they argue the number of cars on the road goes on increasing by some 2,500,000 a year. Providing them with highways and freeways seems to have the national priority.

ONLY PLANES ARE SOARING

Consumer spending on intercity travel rose from $1 billion in 1949 to $1.3 billion in 1958. But this increase is wholly accounted for by the airline business, which went from $151 million in 1949 to $612 million in 1958. Consumer outlays for intercity rail transportation, by contrast, declined from $515 million to $361 million, and those for bus transportation from $324 million to $291 million. Passenger-miles, of course, dropped much more.

So the trend may go in the future. Total consumer spending on intercity travel during the 1960's should rise from $1.3 billion to perhaps $2 billion—but only because the outlays for airline travel will doubtless double again by 1965, and rise steeply between

1965 and 1970. This increase will probably be partly offset by a decline in intercity rail travel, and possibly by a decline in intercity bus travel.

In certain areas, intercity rail travel, unfortunately for the many railroads that lose a lot of money on it, has years left ahead of it. Between some large cities such as New York-Philadelphia-Washington it will probably hold its own and perhaps even increase somewhat. But intercity rail service, on the whole, is being steadily curtailed or discontinued, and total consumer outlays for it seem bound to drop steadily and measurably.

COMPACT BUSES YET

A few bus men are still relatively optimistic about their future. One official figures that buses will capture many people now riding the rails. He also points to the age groups of the Sixties—large numbers of young people who cannot afford to drive cars, and older people who value speed less than sightseeing and convenience. Booming vacation travel, too, he says, should help; and he also envisions fast super-turnpike buses fed by smaller compact buses.

But long-distance bus travel has a hard time competing with air coach, and short-haul bus service cannot very well compete with the private car. Buses and railroads now vie for the 200-to-500-mile intermediate-haul business, and buses may benefit as more rail service is abandoned. Even here, however, buses might continue to lose "business" to the private car. A network of free superhighways will make a 300-mile journey by car a routine event. Small and compact cars will also make it an inexpensive one. A trip in a small car such as the Volkswagen is almost as cheap, all costs counted, as a bus fare; on an out-of-pocket basis, it is much cheaper. A compact car probably can carry the driver and one passenger as cheaply, all costs counted, as a bus can. For the bus business, as for all other kinds of public transportation, the private car remains the deadliest competitor.

CHAPTER TWELVE

The Money Left Over for the Good Life

I T IS a cliché of our time that Americans have become a nation of *nouveaux riches*, pouring more and more of their rising incomes into big-fin Cadillacs, pleasure boats, swimming pools, and other frivolities. According to some critics, indeed, the "conspicuous waste" with which Thorstein Veblen taxed the captains of industry in the 1890's became in the 1950's the offense of all Americans. By 1970, it must sometimes seem, life in the U.S. will be one long ball.

This picture is familiar; it also happens to be badly overdrawn. For all their wealth, Americans spend their money in remarkably sober fashion. In 1959 their after-tax income ran to $336 billion. As previous chapters have shown, three-quarters of this $336 billion were spent on food, clothing, housing, and transportation. This leaves $84 billion to be accounted for. Here again the figures on where the money goes are rather surprising, in view of all the talk about spending on gewgaws and fun. Some $24 billion, for example, is put aside in the form of savings—a somewhat larger share of income than the long-term average. Nearly $19 billion goes to pay the costs of medical care. Of the remainder, $4 billion goes for the upkeep of religious and welfare institutions, $4 billion for private education, and $17 billion for what the Commerce Department statisticians call "personal business"—i.e., bank service charges, brokerage charges, interest on personal loans, and the like. In the Commerce Department accounts, that leaves only $16 billion for fun—for admissions to movies and spectator sports, for sporting goods and participant athletics, and for books, magazines, gardening, and foreign pleasure travel.

This figure, of course, understates the full amount that Americans actually lay out for recreation and leisure. A good deal of spending for the operation of automobiles and for other forms of transportation and much that goes for housing and home goods and even food (e.g., liquor) must also count as fun. If we track down all the pleasurable spending Americans do, the "fun market" comes to $41 billion (see box on page 194). The significant fact that emerges, however, is that spending for recreation has grown no faster than consumer income in the postwar, whichever definition is used.

According to economic theory, as their incomes rise, consumers will spend a rising share on "luxuries" like recreation, just as they spend a declining share on necessities like food. But on the lower Commerce Department estimate, the percentage of disposable income that goes for fun has remained at about 4.8 per cent. Using the broader definition, which produces the $41-billion figure, spending for pleasure went down from 14.2 per cent of disposable income in 1947 to 12.3 per cent in 1953. (The proportion has been stable since 1953.) Outlays for medical care, education, and "personal business," on the other hand, have been taking a steadily rising share of the consumer's dollar (see chart on page 193), and personal savings have been running at a consistently high rate.

Over the next decade, of course, the pattern of consumer spending *could* change very radically. On FORTUNE's projection, consumer after-tax income will rise by 50 per cent and its disposal will depend even more than now on discretion and taste. This could well push up the proportion of income spent on recreation and leisure. But food, clothing, housing, and transportation are

The Mostly Serious Uses of $84 Billion

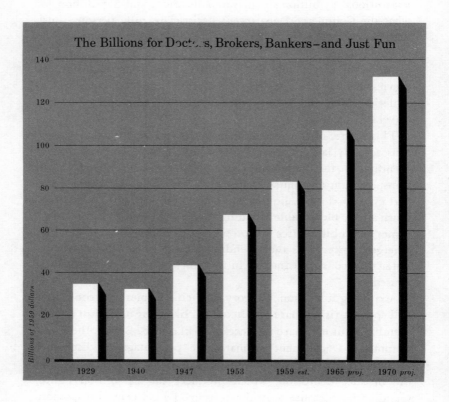

The Billions for Doctors, Brokers, Bankers—and Just Fun

Billions of 1959 dollars

1929 1940 1947 1953 1959 *est.* 1965 *proj.* 1970 *proj.*

The statistical skyscrapers in the chart above show how much consumers spend after meeting the costs of housing, transportation, food, and clothing. In dollars of 1959 purchasing power, this residual spending has doubled since 1947, from $43 billion to approximately $84 billion in 1959, and is likely to go to $130 billion in 1970.

The chart opposite shows where these "extra dollars" go. They go for personal savings, for recreation, and for a miscellany of rather sober expenditures like medical care, education, religion, bank service charges, brokerage charges, insurance, interest on personal debt, and the like.

The "extra dollars" represent a slightly larger share of income now than in 1929—25.4 per cent vs. 22.3 per cent—and an even sharper rise since 1947, when the proportion was only 17.6 per cent. But outlays for recreation,

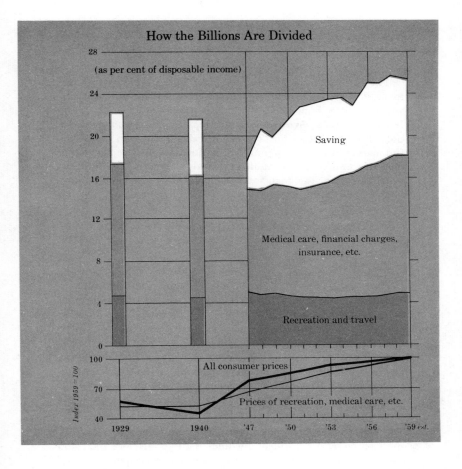

How the Billions Are Divided

(as per cent of disposable income)

Saving

Medical care, financial charges, insurance, etc.

Recreation and travel

All consumer prices

Prices of recreation, medical care, etc.

Index 1959 = 100

1929   1940   '47   '50   '53   '56   '59 *est.*

narrowly defined, are taking only 4.8 per cent of after-tax income vs. 4.9 per cent in 1947 and 4.7 per cent in 1929. The share of income going for medical care, education, religion, and what the Commerce Department calls "personal business" has risen very sharply, however—from 9.9 per cent to 13.2 per cent. This is only slightly more than the 12.6 per cent of income allocated in 1929, when the composition of the spending was very different (see charts on page 200). Part of the rise since 1947 is due to price increases— 16 per cent greater than for consumer prices as a whole (see lower panel).

The share going to personal savings—7.2 per cent—is well above the abnormally low figure of 2.8 per cent in 1947; it is also slightly above the long-term average. (Savings were abnormally low in 1929 because people drew down their cash and savings to cover their stock margin calls.)

The size of any market is, to some degree, what statisticians make it. This is particularly true of the so-called "fun market," which, as already noted in the text, is subject to at least two different definitions. According to the Department of Commerce figures on expenditures for "recreation" and for foreign travel, the fun market in 1959 ran to only $16 billion. But if we include other types of consumer spending that certainly are indirectly connected with recreation, the 1959 total is much larger—i.e., $41 billion. Here's how the larger fun marke broke down in 1958, the last year for which detailed figures are available:

The largest component of the $39-billion total was $15 billion identified by the Commerce Department for recreation and foreign travel.

Spending for domestic vacations and pleasure travel (including weekends) —scattered in the government accounts under transportation, housing, food, and clothing—came to $10.5 billion, or twice as much as in 1947. FORTUNE put together its estimate of annual domestic spending from a variety of sources—e.g., intermittent surveys by Curtis Publishing and annual Commerce Department data on spending for hotels and motels, intercity travel, gasoline, etc. The 1958 vacation budget was allocated roughly as follows: $5.4 billion for lodging and meals, $1.2 billion for plane, train, and bus fares, $2 billion for auto expenses, and about the same for vacation homes and incidental purchases.

U.S. consumers in 1958 paid out $9.2 billion for alcohol, which the Commerce Department includes in its totals for "food and tobacco." This is only 7 per cent more than was spent in 1947. And on FORTUNE's estimate, based on industry sources, the bill for pleasure dining came to roughly $1.1 billion in 1958—a 30 per cent rise since 1947.

Consumer expenditures for the purchase and repair of TV, radios, phonographs and records, and musical instruments according to the Commerce Department accounts, came to $3.8 billion in 1958, vs. $3 billion in 1953 and $1.6 billion in 1947. Although the Commerce Department includes these expenditures in its total for recreation, as recreation, FORTUNE has counted them as part of the cost of furnishing and operating a home, which is the way most consumers seem to regard their radios and TV sets.

likely to take almost as large a share of the consumer's dollar in the Sixties as they did in the Fifties. And, as we shall see, there are good reasons for believing a stable or even rising proportion of income will be going into private education, medical care, stocks, mutual funds, life insurance, and other forms of "serious" spending and capital accumulation. It is obviously impossible to predict now just what choices consumers will make in a decade that will see profound changes in the level and distribution of incomes and in the occupations by which those incomes are earned. But it is clear that spending for recreation and leisure, whether broadly or narrowly defined, will be under substantial pressure from a long list of very sober items in the consumer budget.

DO-IT-YOURSELF SPORTS

When we analyze the leisure market itself, moreover, it develops that Americans are using their spare time, energies, and income in responsible ways. For instance, total American expenditures for alcohol in the postwar period have risen only about 7 per cent as against an 85 per cent rise in disposable income, and expenditures for dining out, despite the servant shortage, has risen by only 30 per cent. Vacation outlays have about doubled, but this is scarcely proof of undue self-indulgence. The most impressive change has been a shift from passive to active forms of recreation in the more conventional use of that term. Since 1947 U.S. consumers have reduced their spending for "spectator amusements" —motion pictures, ball games, prize fights, etc.—from $2.3 billion to $2.2 billion. The drop has been most pronounced in motion-picture box-office receipts, and is, of course, partly accounted for by the early postwar rise in TV. But since 1953 expenditures on TV sets have shown relatively little growth, and the same has been true of most of the spectator amusements. Expenditures for theatres, operas, and concerts, however, have shown a steady rise since 1947—from $188 million to $313 million, which is one-fourth more than total admissions paid to sporting events.

Outlays for "active" forms of recreation, meanwhile, have been growing rapidly. Since 1947, consumers have more than doubled their expenditures (from $2.3 billion to $5 billion) for sporting goods, golf lessons, green fees, bowling-alley fees, and the like. According to the National Recreation Association, there are about 7,500,000 active softball players. Some seven million Americans own their own boats, compared to about two million in 1947. And judging by the number of hunting and fishing licenses issued, roughly 30 million Americans went fishing and 20 million went hunting in 1959. Indeed, the national park and forest systems and other outdoor facilities are being taxed to capacity. The search for more participant and satisfying leisure activities is even more noticeable in the non-athletic sphere. Consumers have doubled their purchases of books, newspapers, and magazines, from $1.8 billion to $3.5 billion. The biggest book-sales gains, interestingly enough, have not been in detective stories and Westerns, but in religious and business books and the more expensive "hard-cover" paperbound treatises on sociology, politics, and philosophy.

What has been happening to hobbies, as Eric Larrabee has written, "should refute the prophets of spectatoritis, the disease which was going to reduce the mass media audience to an imbecility of non-participation." Thus, some 2,500,000 camera owners are classified by *Photo Dealer Magazine* as "advanced amateurs"; as many as half of them operate their own darkrooms, and most belong to one of 12,000-odd photography clubs. (No one sounds more outraged than a serious amateur photographer commenting on commercial work that doesn't measure up to his purist standards.) There is an indeterminate number of hi-fi addicts; six specialized hi-fi magazines have been started just since 1951. Sales of art supplies have been booming; according to a recent *Time* study of leisure habits, more than one million American families are paying for private art lessons, four million are paying for music lessons for one or more members of the family. And while the amateur community orchestras springing up throughout the country may not sound like the Boston Symphony, they do represent a democratization of "high culture" that has no equal anywhere in the world.

This growing seriousness and ardor represent one of the dramatic cultural changes of our time. Indeed, there are some students of American life who occasionally wonder whether Americans are pushing their pursuit of excellence too far. If present trends continue, they fear, there may be no room left for the dilettante in the classical sense—the man who cultivates a moderate interest in almost everything. "If a thing is worth doing," Professor David Riesman likes to say in defense of dabbling, "it's worth doing badly."

WHO WANTS TO LOAF?

In the long run, however, the amateurs' search for excellence will be a good thing for American culture—and will certainly increase the aggregate amount of recreation spending; the more seriously a person takes his leisure, the more he spends. No matter how much equipment he has, for example, the serious devotee of high fidelity is always in desperate need of some new electronic marvel. And owning a boat, as millions of Americans who defied the elder Morgan's famous injunction have discovered, can be almost a bottomless drain on income.

Leisure spending may also be increased by the growth of a new leisure class—retired men and women living on the proceeds of social security, private pensions, life insurance, as well as dividends and property income. Not working, as noted earlier, is the fastest growing of all major "occupations" in the U.S. today. By 1970 there will be about eight million men and eleven million women over sixty-five, and for the first time this age group will represent a major spending force. How much of their incomes will go for recreation, however, remains to be seen; a steadily rising proportion of the elderly are setting up their own households, which means higher spending for household goods and the like.

It's doubtful, moreover, that those who remain in the labor force will take as large a part of the gains of higher productivity in leisure as they have in the past. Originally, the demand for shorter hours stemmed from the need to ease the physical burdens of work; in the 1930's and early postwar, the demand reflected a desire to relieve or prevent unemployment by spreading the work. But there has been no significant reduction in the standard work week for over a decade. Nor is there any evidence of any great demand for shorter daily or weekly hours, although there is tremendous interest in longer vacations and more frequent paid holidays. On the contrary, as George Brooks of the paper workers' union reported three years ago to an A.F.L.-C.I.O. Conference on Shorter Hours, "The evidence is all on the other side. Hundreds of local and international officials have testified that the most numerous and persistent grievances are disputes over the sharing of overtime work. The issue usually is not that someone has been made to work, but that he has been deprived of a chance to make overtime pay." Workers, Brooks concluded, "are eager to increase their income, not work shorter hours." Some 3,500,000 workers, in fact, hold down two jobs, and one-third of West Coast residents queried about their attitudes toward a four-day week indicated that they would use the third day off to get another job.

And this orientation toward work rather than leisure will increase, as work itself becomes more satisfying. It is a commonplace to point out how ironical it is that the "workers," not the bosses, constitute the American leisured class; professional and managerial groups hardly know the forty-hour week, in large part because for them the break between work and play does not exist. In a ranking of goals in order of priority, for example, Harvard Business School graduates put "leisure" last and "satisfaction in my work" first. One-third of the 1,700 top executives recently surveyed by FORTUNE work better than fifty-five hours a week. But the number of people for whom this is true is mounting rapidly; the number of men in managerial and professional and technical occupations, for example, will rise nearly 40 per cent over the decade ahead, vs. a 20 per cent expansion in the male labor force as a whole, and a larger and larger proportion of blue-collar work is becoming almost professional in character. By 1970, in fact, more than half of the male labor force will have jobs that offer a real measure of creative fulfillment and provide a sense of individual worth. This is bound to influence Americans' judgment on the relative value of leisure and work.

MORE MONEY FOR THE DOCTOR

Taking everything together, it seems doubtful that recreational spending will grow any faster than disposable income during the 1960's. There are just too many other expenses with a higher claim on consumer income. To be sure, "discretionary income" will be rising. But people frequently commit their discretionary income for years ahead (just as they commit their leisure time) by the big choices they make about how to live—e.g., deciding to get married, having children, buying a house, educating children privately, etc. The luxuries of one generation, moreover, become the necessities of the next; this is why the rate of savings has not risen with consumer incomes. Whether thought of as luxuries or necessities, most of the nonrecreational expenditures—medical care, private education, insurance, financial charges—as well as recreational spending grow very rapidly once a person passes the $7,500 or $10,000-a-year mark. And these are the income groups that will be expanding most rapidly in the 1960's.

A steadily rising share of consumer income has been going into medical care, for example, all through the postwar. Private expenditures jumped from $7.7 billion in 1947 (4.5 per cent of consumer income) to $17.8 billion in 1958 (5.6 per cent). The sharpest rise has been in payments to hospitals, which have tripled, from $1.4 billion to $4.3 billion. Outlays for drugs have gone up one and one-half times, from $1.3 billion to $3.3 billion, while payments to doctors and dentists have gone from $2.8 billion to $5.6 billion. The rest of the $18-billion outlay in 1958 went for medical and hospital insurance ($1.4 billion), funeral and burial expenses ($1.4 billion), ophthalmic and orthopedic products ($1.1 billion), and payments to nurses, osteopaths, chiropractors, etc. ($800 million).

Obviously this increase is not due to the fact that Americans are in worse health than they used to be. The rise in medical expenditures has financed an improvement in the national health that has been one of the unsung achievements of the postwar. Some of the spending rise, to be sure, reflects the increased costs of medical and hospital care, which have risen twice as fast as consumer prices

Per cent of disposable income used for:

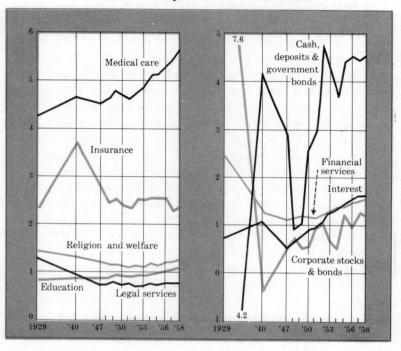

These two charts show the changes in the more "serious" uses of the "extra dollars" of disposable income. The share going to medical care jumped from 4.3 per cent in 1929 to 5.6 per cent in 1958, that for education from 0.8 per cent to 1.1 per cent. But a smaller share of income is going for the upkeep of religious and welfare institutions, and the same is true of expenditures for financial services and for purchases of stocks and bonds (including brokerage charges and interest on brokers' loans). There has, however, been a sharp rise in the proportion of income paid out in interest on consumer debt. The share going to life insurance has been remarkably stable.

as a whole. But the index takes no account of the enormous rise in the productivity of medical services as a result of the new wonder drugs, new diagnostic techniques and treatment, reduced hospitalization time per confinement, greater specialization among physicians, etc.

Since 1950, in fact, the U.S. has made good more than half of the deficiency in medical care that the Twentieth Century Fund calculated existed at that date, and there are no signs of any abatement in the rise in medical standards; on the contrary, higher standards seem to generate a demand for even better care. So do higher income and broader medical-insurance coverage. And there are no signs of a slowdown in the rise of medical costs relative to other prices. The chances are, therefore, that by 1970 consumers will be laying out roughly twice as much on medical care as they are now, in the neighborhood of $33 billion. This would increase the share of after-tax income from 5.6 to about 6.5 per cent.

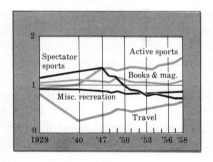

This chart shows the great substitution of participant for passive forms of recreation. Thus, the share of income going to "commercial spectator amusements" like the movies, ball games, and horse races dropped from 1.1 per cent in 1929 to 0.7 per cent in 1958, while the share going to athletic activities, boats, sporting goods, etc., climbed from slightly under 1 per cent to 1.6 per cent. The share for foreign travel is up sharply over 1947, though still below 1929, when far fewer people went abroad but traveled in much grander style. Books, magazines, and newspapers now claim a slightly larger share—i.e., 1.1 per cent—of income.

WELFARE AND EDUCATION

In addition to health, Americans are, of course, meeting many other claims on their incomes. The $4 billion expended in 1959 on religious and welfare institutions was about double the figure for 1947. Spending for charitable activities has grown very slowly —owing in part to the fact that social security and other forms of government relief take care of many of the needs once met by private donations, and perhaps more importantly to the fact that the economy has been at full or nearly full employment all through the postwar years. But expenditures for religious activities—i.e., the upkeep of churches, salaries of ministers, etc.—have been growing 50 per cent faster than personal income (though maybe not so fast as they should). Church building has been going forward at a rapid pace. And since 1946, church membership has risen twice as fast as the population as a whole.

Meanwhile, expenditures for private education—secular as well as religious—have been advancing dramatically. Consumer outlays for schools, colleges, music lessons, and the like are two and one-half times as large as in 1947—i.e., $3.4 billion vs. $1.4 billion —and the share of disposable income has gone from 0.8 to 1.1 per cent. Outlays for private elementary and secondary schooling alone have gone from $420 million in 1947 to $1.1 billion now, largely because of mushrooming attendance at Catholic parochial schools. There are no signs of any slowdown. Nor are there signs of any easing of the drive toward self-improvement, which since 1947 has nearly tripled spending for business, trade, and correspondence-school courses, as well as for music, art, dancing lessons, and the like.

What will really push up private spending on education during the 1960's, however, will be the big bulge in attendance at the college level. (Colleges now account for 40 per cent of private education spending.) The population of college age (i.e., eighteen to twenty-one) will increase 50 per cent over the next decade, and the proportion in that age group attending college will also rise. It has already gone from 14 per cent in 1950 to about 21 per cent today;

by 1970 the rate will certainly be very much higher. Indeed, a recent Ford Foundation survey revealed that more than two-thirds of American parents expect to send their children to college. Including students of all ages, college attendance will nearly double over the current decade, compared to a 50 per cent rise in the past decade.

Judging by the Ford Foundation survey, attendance could go as high as ten million. Not all the parents who would like to send their children to college will be able to, of course; those polled by the Ford Foundation underestimated the *present* cost of college education by one-third. And only two in five have started saving for college. But cost will be less of a barrier in the Sixties than it has been up to now, for financial institutions are developing a variety of long-term loan arrangements to meet just this need. Banks across the country, for example, are now offering loans covering tuition and all other expenses with repayment spread evenly over a six-year period. A number of educators have been urging much longer-term loans. Since college is a capital investment that "pays off" in higher earnings, they argue, loans could be repaid by the student, rather than his parents, out of the increment in his earnings after graduation.

WHO PAYS CASH?

After paying for medical care, religion, education, and recreation, as well as for food, clothing, housing, and transportation, consumers still have some $42 billion, or 12.5 per cent, of after-tax income remaining. This money goes in the main for equally sober purposes: $5 billion for interest on personal debt incurred in order to finance purchase of cars and other durables, to repair and modernize homes, pay medical bills and college tuition, and so on; $13 billion for service payments to bankers, brokers, and insurance companies, and to lawyers, unions, professional associations, and employment agencies; and $24 billion for purchase of stocks and bonds, deposits in banks and savings and loan associations, and other forms of personal savings.

What is most interesting about this welter of financial dealings by consumers is that they are no longer the exclusive preoccupation of the well-to-do. Millions of Americans are now concerned with such matters as choosing between various insurance policies, joining investment clubs or mutual-fund plans, reducing their tax liability, refinancing mortgages, or taking out installment loans to finance college tuition or personal speculations or auto purchases. And financial dealings take a growing bite of disposable income. According to the Federal Reserve's Survey of Consumer Finances, for example, 55 per cent of all spending units now have their own checking accounts, compared to 34 per cent in 1946. Bank service charges have been climbing steadily—from $1.8 billion, or 1 per cent of income, in 1947, to $4.7 billion, or 1.5 per cent of income, in 1958. And consumers last year paid out $760 million in brokerage charges and interest on broker loans and $1.4 billion for legal services.

THE UNPROFLIGATE DEBTORS

They are also shelling out over $5 billion in interest on consumer installment debt—five times as much as in 1947. But the rise in consumer credit does not mean that Americans have become a bunch of wastrels. On the contrary, their astounding record of repayment suggests that they have been responsible in their use of credit too. When debt began to expand too rapidly in 1955, for example, consumers quickly began to police themselves; the debt expansion since then has been relatively modest.

Some of the increase in borrowing has, of course, been due to a relaxation of traditional taboos against debt. But most of it reflects much more fundamental changes in consumer spending patterns. Consumers use more credit now than they used to simply because they buy far more durable goods—goods that provide services they formerly purchased from business firms. Instead of traveling by train or bus, as noted earlier, consumers increasingly drive their own cars (auto paper accounts for roughly 40 per cent of all consumer installment credit). Instead of patronizing laundries or employing servants, they own their own washing machines, dryers, vacuum cleaners, and the like. And instead of spending their free time in the local saloon or movie theatre, they own their own TV set or their own boat.

What is most important from the standpoint of the growth of the economy, however, is that the consumers' penchant for debt has not reduced their willingness to put money aside for the future. On the contrary, three-quarters of all installment borrowers have liquid assets as well—i.e., savings accounts, savings bonds, stocks.

$24 BILLION FOR THE FUTURE

The plain fact is that consumers have been saving a slightly higher proportion of their disposable incomes in recent years than they have over the long term—i.e., between 7.2 and 7.9 per cent, vs. a long-term average of 7 per cent. And there is every reason to expect that consumers will continue to save during the 1960's at something close to the current 7.2 per cent rate, which would mean a rise from $24 billion in 1959 to perhaps $37 billion in 1970.

Some economists and bankers have expressed fears of a savings shortage over the next decade, because of changes in the age distribution of the population, which may tend to reduce the propensity to save. The heaviest savers, for example, are people between the ages of thirty-five and fifty-five, and their number will increase by only 3 per cent over the next decade, while the population under thirty and over sixty-five years of age, which tends to save very little, will be expanding very rapidly. But the effects of these changes in the population mix will be offset by the changes in the level and distribution of income, which will greatly increase the number and proportion of families in the income brackets that account for the bulk of personal savings. Indeed, these changes might well push the savings rate above the level of recent years.

Savings per family increase very sharply at about the $7,500-a-year mark and take an even bigger jump at $10,000—and the number of families earning over $7,500 a year will double over the next decade, with an even sharper rise in the over-$10,000 group. The relation between age and savings is likely to be changed as a result: young people will be able to save more than they do now because their income will be much higher.

The principal reason for expecting no radical change in the proportion of income going into savings, however, is the uncanny stability that the ratio has averaged over the past sixty years or more. Despite the most profound changes in the social-economic structure of the country—the shift from a rural, agrarian to an urban, industrialized society, the tremendous growth in real income, and the radical changes in income distribution, educational level, life expectancy, etc.—Americans since the turn of the century have been saving an average of 7 per cent of their disposable incomes. And FORTUNE's analysis of the specific factors governing savings indicates that this same balancing of forces will continue during the 1960's.

THE NEW COMPETITION

Meanwhile the financial institutions through which the bulk of personal savings are channeled are not just sitting back waiting for the money to come in. On the contrary, they are actively bidding in the market place for the consumer's dollar. A substantial part of all savings—$14 billion in 1958—is accumulated in the form of cash, savings deposits, savings and loan shares, and government bonds. The once gentlemanly rivalry among commercial banks, mutual savings banks, and savings and loan associations has given way to extreme competition. And the reputedly staid and stodgy life-insurance companies are learning to go after consumer dollars with all the covetousness and agility of a soap manufacturer. One large life-insurance company, for instance, hired a soap-company market researcher as head of its market-development department. "It used to be that we tried to sell whatever policies the actuaries decided to build," a vice president of another company observes. "Now we're using market research to find out what kinds of policies people want or are likely to buy, and we're telling the actuaries to build them."

In the process life-insurance companies will have to readjust to changing population trends if they are to grow as rapidly as they have in the past decade. Since the number of people in the age group between thirty and forty-four will be declining, the insurance companies will seek to persuade them to carry more insurance. And they will have to cultivate the younger age groups much more intensively; the population aged twenty to twenty-nine will jump by nearly nine million. Insurance companies have already begun this cultivating. The "family policy" introduced by Prudential just three years ago (and aimed at young couples) has already captured 25 per cent of the ordinary life-insurance market and Prudential is promoting a straight life policy "for the man whose pocketbook has not yet caught up with his ability."

In addition, insurance companies are making a determined effort to cope with changes that are occurring in the savings pattern. Sales of straight life insurance (where the purchaser builds up cash values through his premium payments) have not been growing as fast as have much cheaper "term insurance" (which has no savings feature attached). One reason for this is the rise of group insurance. But another major reason is simply the growing preference of many people for forms of savings and investment that offer faster growth than insurance and also give some protection from the declining value of the dollar. It is to meet this competition that Prudential is promoting the "variable annuity." "For God's sake, don't quote me," says an official of one large company, "but I don't see how we can expand our business by selling a product that pays in fixed dollars."

TWELVE MILLION CAPITALISTS

In any case, partly as the result of inflation and partly for other causes, interest in stock and equity ownership is rapidly growing. "Any time I ask a cab driver to take me to the Mutual of New York Building," an executive of that giant life company grumbles, "we get into a discussion of the pros and cons of mutual funds vs. common stocks." And a lot more people than just New York cabbies are now concerned with the market. In 1952, according to the New York Stock Exchange, there were only 6,500,000 individual owners of equities in the U.S. By early 1959 the number had grown to 12,500,000—nearly double the 1952 total, and perhaps 50 per cent more than the number who held stock back in 1929. One adult in eight, in other words, now owns stock in his own name. And millions more own stocks indirectly through their equity in pension-fund reserves.

The broadening of stock ownership is due to much more fundamental factors than just a speculative fever induced by the bull market. Indeed, there is no evidence that the bear market of 1957-58 slowed down the rate of growth at all; mutual funds actually grew faster than ever in 1958. One index of the seriousness with which Americans are taking their investments is the growth in the number of investment clubs, in which a small group of people pool their resources and meet regularly (usually weekly) to discuss investment strategy. According to the Stock Exchange, there are roughly 15,000 such clubs in existence today—a 50 per cent increase just in the last three years.

In addition, more than one-quarter of the shareholders added since 1956 first bought their stock through employee stock-purchase plans run by the companies they work for; 1,340,000 people now invest regularly through such plans. Perhaps another million shareholders were added through the sales efforts of mutual funds. There are, all told, approximately 2,500,000 mutual-fund shareholders, and a growing proportion of them—32 per cent—invest monthly or quarterly through either a voluntary or a contractual accumulation plan.

The spreading popularity of stock ownership has sometimes been interpreted to mean that the U.S. has discovered a new form of "people's capitalism." Actually, stock ownership in and of itself scarcely warrants such a generalization. There are risks of loss as well as potential rewards in owning equities. Nor would our society necessarily be better off if every man were an entrepreneur by reason of holding shares in his strong box. What makes capitalism the handmaid of democracy is not just the widespread diffusion of property rights of all kinds. It is equally important that under the market system of economy, production is uniquely geared to consumer demand and taste.

THE NEW SOCIETY

But if the consumer is king, it matters tremendously for society what kind of taste he has. The encouraging thing about American capitalism is that the American consumer is, after all, a responsible person, despite all the gibes and criticisms leveled against him. This growing responsibility and discernment are evident from the manner in which consumers are using their disposable income on needed consumer goods, on education and health, and on savings and investment. If, as seems likely, the trends continue rising, consumer incomes will bring Americans an improvement not just in material standards, but in the whole quality of American life.

Appendix

CHAPTER ONE

THE MILLIONS ARE ARRIVING FASTER

	U.S. population
1857	30,000,000
1886	59,800,000
1907	89,900,000
1925	119,700,000
1947	148,900,000
1958	179,800,000
1970 *proj.*	210,000,000

Sources: Back data from Bureau of the Census increased by 3.3 per cent to adjust for underenumeration. Projection for 1970 adapted from Pascal K. Whelpton and Arthur A. Campbell, *Family Planning, Sterility and Population Growth*, McGraw-Hill, 1959.

Children by order of birth
(in thousands)

	First	Second	Third or higher	Total
1940	940	639	980	2,559
1941	1,045	672	986	2,703
1942	1,225	749	1,015	2,989
1943	1,143	840	1,121	3,104
1944	1,001	788	1,150	2,939
1945	961	763	1,134	2,858
1946	1,291	935	1,185	3,411
1947	1,574	1,019	1,224	3,817
1948	1,343	1,047	1,247	3,637
1949	1,235	1,093	1,321	3,649
1950	1,140	1,097	1,395	3,632
1951	1,195	1,116	1.512	3,823
1952	1,169	1,122	1,622	3,913
1953	1,150	1,120	1,695	3,965
1954	1,160	1,119	1,799	4,078
1955	1,138	1,104	1,862	4,104
1956	1,166	1,109	1,943	4,218
1957	1,180	1,111	2,017	4,308
1958	1,156	1,075	2,019	4,250

	Projections	
	Medium	*High*
1960	3,920	4,506
1965	3,867	4,883
1970	4,323	5,449

Sources: Back data from National Office of Vital Statistics. Projections from *Family Planning, Sterility and Population Growth.*

THE ACTUAL AND THE IDEAL

	Actual family size of women born in:				"Ideal" family size of women born in:		
	1876-1880	1896-1900	1906-1920	1911-1925	1907-1919	1911-1924	1926-1937
					Queried in 1941	Queried in 1945	Queried in 1955
Average number of children	3.63	2.68	2.38	2.56	2.38	2.79	3.03
Number of children	Per Cent Distribution by Numbers of Children						
0	8.4	12.6	13.8	10.9	—	—	—
1	16.9	21.6	21.6	18.4	(1)	(1)	—
2	15.2	20.9	25.1	25.4	40	25	19
3	12.5	14.6	16.3	19.3	32	33	32
4	10.6	9.8	9.4	11.6	21	31	41
5 and more	36.3	20.4	13.8	14.5	6	10	8

Sources: Data on actual family size from Pascal K. Whelpton and Arthur A. Campbell *Cohort Fertility, Part I*, National Office of Vital Statistics. "Ideal" family size for 1941 and 1945 from Gallup Polls; for 1955 from *Family Planning, Sterility and Population Growth*.

EDUCATION AND INCOME MAKE LESS DIFFERENCE
... AND RELIGION MAKES MORE

Number of children
expected by women
born in:

............By wife's education

	Grade School	High School (1-3 yrs)	High School (4 yrs.)	College
1916-20	3.7	2.7	2.6	2.7
1921-25	3.6	2.9	3.0	2.6
1926-30	3.5	3.0	2.9	3.0
1931-37	3.3	3.1	3.1	3.5

............By husband's income

	Under $3,000	$3,000-$6,000	Over $6,000
1916-20	3.2	2.8	2.9
1921-25	3.1	2.9	3.0
1926-30	3.3	3.1	3.2
1931-37	3.2	3.1	—

............By wife's religion

	Catholic	Protestant	All groups
1916-20	3.1	2.8	2.9
1921-25	3.3	2.9	3.0
1926-30	3.5	3.0	3.1
1931-37	3.8	2.9	3.2

Source: *Family Planning, Sterility and Population Growth.*

The Babies of the 1940's and the Households of the 1960's

Net population change by age groups
(in millions)

	1950-60	1960-70 *proj.*
Under 10 years	8.8	2.9
10-19	8.6	8.4
20-29	−2.0	8.6
30-39	1.6	−2.1
40-49	3.1	1.6
50-59	2.5	2.9
60 and over	5.1	5.2

Average Annual Increase in Households
(in thousands)

	1940-1950	1950-1958	1958-1970 *proj.*	
			High	*Low*
Husband-Wife	750	487	692	499
Individual	126	280	269	101
Other	0	89	102	84

Sources: Population data from *Family Planning, Sterility and Population Growth;* household data and projections from Bureau of the Census.

	U.S. population (in millions)
1900	78.6
1905	86.1
1910	95.5
1915	103.9
1920	110.0
1925	119.7
1930	127.3
1935	131.6
1940	136.5
1945	144.5
1950	156.7
1955	170.7
1958	179.8

	Projection		
	Low	*Medium*	*High*
1960	183.4	184.6	186.0
1965	190.6	195.6	201.4
1970	197.4	208.0	219.3
1975	205.4	222.5	239.3
1980	214.7	239.0	262.1
1985	224.0	256.0	288.0
1990	232.0	273.3	315.0
1995	239.0	291.7	346.0
2000	246.0	312.0	381.0
2010	252.0	353.0	457.0
2020	259.0	398.0	549.0
2030	266.0	450.0	660.0
2040	273.0	509.0	792.0
2050	280.0	575.0	952.0

Sources: Back data from Bureau of the Census increased by 3.3 per cent to adjust for underenumeration. Projections from *Family Planning, Sterility and Population Growth.*

CHAPTER THREE

Almost as much controversy surrounds the measurements of productivity as the interpretation of the final figures. FORTUNE prefers the simplest definition of productivity: output per man-hour (though labor obviously is not the only factor of production nor the principal source of productivity gains).

FORTUNE's estimates of postwar productivity changes by industry are based on unofficial indexes of output and man-hours for the period 1947 to 1955 developed by Jack Alterman and Eva Jacobs of the Bureau of Labor Statistics. They have been adjusted and up-dated, and converted into productivity figures. The figures on long-term productivity trends (see table p. 223) use the statistics of output per man-hour for the period 1889 to 1957 developed by Professor John Kendrick of the National Bureau of Economic Research. Dr. Kendrick's series has been updated for 1958, and linked to earlier FORTUNE estimates of output per man-hour for the period 1850 to 1890, based on Twentieth Century Fund data. (It should be noted that Dr. Kendrick does not entirely share the conclusions FORTUNE has drawn from the post-1889 figures.)

In analyzing occupational changes, FORTUNE has used the decennial population censuses plus unpublished data for the post-war from the Census Bureau's Current Population Survey.

CURRENT PRODUCTIVITY TRENDS

Year	Quarter	Manufacturing productivity	Private non-farm productivity
1947	1	98.8	98.4
	2	100.2	100.1
	3	100.0	101.0
	4	101.0	100.6
1948	1	102.2	99.6
	2	104.6	101.0
	3	104.6	101.3
	4	104.6	102.5
1949	1	106.1	102.8
	2	107.8	104.0
	3	109.2	106.6
	4	108.9	103.3
1950	I	111.8	108.4
	2	116.3	108.7
	3	118.0	110.7
	4	115.9	112.7
1951	1	115.6	112.6
	2	115.1	113.6
	3	112.7	115.2
	4	112.8	115.9
1952	1	114.4	117.2
	2	115.0	116.1
	3	116.7	117.3
	4	118.3	118.6
1953	1	119.0	120.4
	2	120.4	121.9
	3	121.8	120.9
	4	119.4	118.9

Year	Quarter	Manufacturing productivity	Private non-farm productivity
1954	1	120.9	121.7
	2	123.4	122.1
	3	124.2	123.6
	4	125.3	124.8
1955	1	127.6	128.3
	2	128.8	129.8
	3	130.1	129.6
	4	129.0	128.8
1956	1	130.0	129.1
	2	130.8	127.2
	3	130.8	127.4
	4	131.0	130.3
1957	1	133.5	131.4
	2	133.8	131.6
	3	135.1	131.6
	4	133.8	131.4
1958	1	134.7	129.7
	2	137.2	129.8
	3	140.3	131.7
	4	141.4	134.1
1959	1	144.1	138.0
	2	145.7	139.0

Source: Manufacturing productivity calculated by FORTUNE from Federal Reserve production indexes and Bureau of Labor Statistics data on man-hours. Private nonfarm productivity calculated from Department of Commerce figures on output and Bureau of the Census data on man-hours.

Postwar Productivity Trends by Industry
(output per man-hour 1947 = 100)

	Utilities	Transp.	Mfg.	Agric.	Trade	Services
1947	100.0	100.0	100.0	100.0	100.0	100.0
1948	102.6	102.9	103.2	124.0	99.5	102.5
1949	110.9	105.0	107.5	117.8	100.6	105.6
1950	121.1	120.3	114.2	133.0	110.6	105.2
1951	130.8	125.0	116.2	131.5	110.8	105.3
1952	138.5	125.5	118.6	141.4	114.7	107.7
1953	143.9	128.4	122.2	155.8	117.2	108.8
1954	153.0	132.2	125.2	169.0	116.0	110.1
1955	166.3	140.6	131.9	170.8	121.8	108.7
1956	173.9	148.2	131.1	170.8	120.9	111.3
1957	185.2	149.1	134.8	184.0	124.2	114.5
1958	198.7	151.6	138.3	210.2	123.6	116.5

Source: See introductory text.

	Sources of G.N.P. (per cent of total)		G.N.P. per man-hour (in 1958 dollars)		Distribution of man-hours by industry (per cent of total)	
	1947	1957	1947	1957	1947	1957
Miscellaneous	12.8	13.1	—	—	7.5	9.0
Utilities	3.1	5.0	3.68	6.75	1.9	2.3
Mining	3.2	2.8	4.33	6.51	1.7	1.4
Manufacturing	31.3	31.6	2.69	3.63	26.5	27.3
Transportation	6.5	5.8	2.43	3.63	6.1	5.1
Trade	20.4	20.1	2.22	2.76	20.9	22.7
Construction	4.1	4.8	1.85	2.34	5.1	6.3
Agriculture	9.8	8.4	1.22	2.28	18.2	11.7
Services	8.8	8.4	1.65	1.85	12.1	14.2

Source: See introductory text.
Note: Totals do not necessarily add to 100 due to rounding.

Long-Term Productivity Growth in the U.S. Economy
(output per man-hour 1947 = 100)

Year	Value	Year	Value
1850	17.7	1923	58.0
		1924	60.5
1870	22.4	1925	60.4
		1926	62.1
1889	28.8	1927	63.2
1890	30.1	1928	63.2
1891	30.8	1929	66.0
1892	32.6	1930	64.3
1893	31.3	1931	65.0
1894	31.5	1932	62.7
1895	33.5	1933	61.7
1896	32.7	1934	69.0
1897	34.9	1935	71.3
1898	35.4	1936	74.8
1899	36.1	1937	75.2
1900	36.7	1938	77.8
1901	39.2	1939	80.7
1902	37.8	1940	81.8
1903	38.6	1941	88.8
1904	38.5	1942	90.2
1905	39.5	1943	93.4
1906	42.5	1944	100.7
1907	42.4	1945	105.0
1908	40.3	1946	99.6
1909	43.3	1947	100.0
1910	42.5	1948	102.4
1911	43.4	1949	107.4
1912	44.2	1950	115.8
1913	45.7	1951	118.6
1914	42.7	1952	121.1
1915	44.4	1953	126.0
1916	47.7	1954	129.3
1917	45.3	1955	133.7
1918	48.9	1956	133.7
1919	52.1	1957	138.0
1920	51.7	1958	140.6
1921	55.3		
1922	54.8	1970 *proj.*	198.8

Source: See introductory text.

Two Influences on Productivity

	Capital per worker	Index of Skills
1910	100.0	100
1911	101.9	
1912	104.6	
1913	107.8	
1914	110.3	
1915	111.8	
1916	114.8	
1917	117.1	
1918	118.2	
1919	122.1	
1920	123.5	111.7
1921	123.8	
1922	124.9	
1923	127.7	
1924	129.7	
1925	132.8	
1926	134.6	
1927	136.0	
1928	137.4	
1929	141.3	
1930	142.9	119.5
1931	142.2	
1932	139.4	
1933	136.5	
1934	133.9	

	Capital per worker	Index of Skills
1935	132.1	
1936	131.8	
1937	132.3	
1938	130.9	
1939	130.1	
1940	130.6	123.7
1941	130.2	
1942	124.0	
1943	115.3	
1944	112.8	
1945	115.7	
1946	129.2	
1947	133.9	
1948	137.9	
1949	141.5	
1950	145.6	138.9
1951	149.3	
1952	154.3	
1953	158.9	
1954	162.8	
1955	165.9	
1956	168.6	
1957	173.6	145.4

Source: Capital per worker calculated from FORTUNE's estimates of capital stock and Bureau of the Census labor force figures. Index of Skills calculated by FORTUNE from Bureau of the Census occupation data weighted by Bureau of the Census figures on income differences between occupations.

The Changing Occupational Structure of the Labor Force
(per cent)

	Manufacturing 1940	Manufacturing 1957	Trade 1940	Trade 1957	Services 1940	Services 1957	All Other 1940	All Other 1957
Proprietors, managers, and professional	7.4	12.7	28.7	26.3	24.4	28.9	8.8	14.7
Clerical	10.6	12.4	10.2	13.1	13.0	18.0	12.9	16.1
Sales	3.5	3.2	27.3	23.5	4.7	4.3	.5	.5
Skilled workers	19.5	20.3	5.0	6.8	7.1	5.5	30.7	35.7
Semiskilled workers	43.7	42.2	13.5	14.0	7.4	6.1	29.9	17.2
Unskilled and service workers	15.2	9.3	15.3	16.3	43.5	37.2	17.2	15.8

Source: See introductory text.
Note: Totals do not necessarily add to 100 due to rounding.

CHAPTER FOUR

THE RISING TEMPO OF AMERICAN ECONOMIC GROWTH

	G.N.P. (billions of 1959 dollars)	Output per man-hour (1947 = 100)	Man-hours (1947 = 100)
1910	118	42	75
1913	129	46	80
1915	123	44	78
1918	148	49	84
1920	140	52	83
1921	128	55	74
1923	165	58	86
1926	189	62	90
1929	202	66	92
1931	170	65	79
1933	141	62	69
1935	170	71	72
1937	204	75	82
1938	194	78	75
1940	229	82	82
1942	296	90	99
1944	353	101	102
1945	349	105	96
1946	314	100	97
1947	314	100	100
1948	326	103	101
1949	325	108	98
1950	353	116	99
1951	380	119	102
1952	393	121	103
1953	410	126	103
1954	403	129	99
1955	436	134	104
1956	447	134	107
1957	453	138	106
1958	437	141	102
1959	480	146	106
1960 *est.*	500	150	109
1965 *proj.*	615	—	116
1970 *proj.*	750	199	124

Source: Gross National Product for 1910-1958 calculated from Commerce Department figures. Output per man-hour is calculated as described in Appendix to Chapter Three. Historical data on man-hours from various sources including Bureau of Labor Statistics and Bureau of the Census.

Breakdown of Total G.N.P. Calculated in Constant Dollars
(per cent of total G.N.P.)

	Defense	"Investment"	Consumption	Total government
1929	1.8	33.3	64.9	11.0
1948	7.0	29.8	63.2	14.8
1953	14.7	27.4	57.9	24.1
1957	11.3	28.0	60.7	19.5
1960 *est.*	10.2	28.8	61.0	20.1
1965 *proj.*	10.8	30.1	59.1	21.3
1970 *proj.*	9.7	30.1	60.2	21.0

Source: For definitions and sources of data, see note on page 229. Conversion into constant dollars by FORTUNE on basis of Department of Commerce and Bureau of Labor Statistics detailed price data.

Conflicting Price Trends

	Investment goods and services	Consumption goods and services
	(Index: 1957 = 100)	
1929	79	111
1948	93	104
1953	95	104
1957	100	100
1960 *est*	101	99
1965 *proj.*	103	98
1970 *proj.*	105	97

Note: These indexes show the movements of the prices of both groups of goods and services relative to the total price level.

Source: Calculated from Department of Commerce and Bureau of Labor Statistics data.

Breakdown of G.N.P. Calculated in Actual Prices
(per cent of total G.N.P.)

	1929	1948	1953	1957	1960 est.	1965 proj.	1970 proj.
"Investment" and Defense							
Defense	1.4	6.8	13.5	11.3	10.2	10.9	10.0
Inventories	1.7	2.2	1.1	0.5	1.0	0.9	0.9
Capital goods	9.9	10.4	9.4	10.3	9.6	11.5	11.3
Education	2.5	2.4	2.6	3.1	3.1	3.2	3.3
Health	3.9	4.1	4.3	4.8	5.0	5.4	5.7
General government	1.7	2.3	2.2	2.3	2.4	2.5	2.6
Housing	3.6	4.2	4.1	4.0	4.3	4.0	4.0
Other construction	2.5	1.8	2.3	3.0	3.4	3.8	4.1
Consumption							
Food	20.3	23.8	19.3	18.2	18.2	16.5	15.7
Clothing	11.8	10.3	8.1	7.9	7.7	7.0	6.6
Rent	10.9	6.9	7.5	8.0	8.3	7.7	7.6
Cars	2.5	2.2	3.2	3.3	3.3	3.4	3.5
Other transportation	5.7	5.1	5.5	5.5	5.5	5.5	5.7
Household and Recreation goods	7.4	7.8	7.1	7.2	7.1	6.8	7.1
Other services	14.0	9.6	9.7	10.6	10.8	10.9	11.9

Source: Most of the historical figures calculated from National Income Accounts published by the National Income Division of the Department of Commerce. Defense figures include both government and private net exports. Inventories include farm and CCC purchases. Government expenditures also included in Health, Education and Other Transportation categories. Government expenditures for 1953 and 1957 calculated from National Income Division breakdowns; earlier figures based on Bureau of the Census data.

Note: Totals do not necessarily add to 100 due to rounding.

DOLLAR PROJECTIONS OF "INVESTMENT" AND DEFENSE
(billions of dollars)

	1957	1960 est.	1965 proj.	1970 proj.
Defense	51.3	51.5	67.1	75.0
Inventories	2.3	5.1	5.5	6.8
Capital goods	46.7	48.5	70.7	84.8
Education	14.0	15.7	19.7	24.8
Health	21.7	25.3	33.2	42.8
General government	10.4	12.1	15.4	19.5
Housing	18.1	21.7	24.6	30.0
Other construction	13.6	17.2	23.4	30.8

DOLLAR PROJECTIONS OF CONSUMPTION
(billions of dollars)

	1957	1960 est.	1965 proj.	1970 proj.
Food	82.4	91.0	101	117
Clothing	35.8	39.0	43	50
Rent	36.2	40.5	47	57
Cars	14.9	17.7	21	26
Other Transportation	24.9	27.7	34	44
Household and recreation goods	32.6	35.2	42	53
Other services	48.0	54.0	67	89

Note: Projections include the effects of relative price movements but not general price changes.
Source: See note page 229.

CHAPTER FIVE

FORTUNE's figures on distribution of family personal income are in constant 1959 dollars and after federal income taxes. The figures for 1929 to 1953 represent Commerce Department pretax income distribution data converted to 1959 dollars; those for 1959 are estimated, and those for 1970 are based on FORTUNE's own projections of the size and composition of output. (These projections were made before the July, 1959, revision of national income figures by the Commerce Department; however, its effects on this calculation would be minor. The same projections, with FORTUNE's detailed estimates of industry productivity trends, were also used to forecast the 1970 occupational distribution on page 233.)

The income distributions here are not exactly comparable to those FORTUNE presented in *The Changing American Market,* which appeared before Commerce began to publish its own income distribution figures. FORTUNE's earlier figures were given in 1953 prices (the 1959 prices are 10 per cent higher), and they were for cash incomes only, while those here include certain types of "imputed" income. Also, the figures used in *The Changing American Market* excluded all direct taxes, while only federal taxes are excluded here.

The effect of all these differences is to make the income figures used in the distributions about one-fifth larger than they would have been if the prices and definitions used in *The Changing American Market* had been used again. On either basis, however, the growth of over $7,500 family units in the 1960's becomes rapid. The number of these units would show a 150 per cent rise (to 18 million) by 1970 on *The Changing American Market* basis, vs. the 100 per cent rise (to nearly 25 million) reported here.

THE HIGH INCOME MASSES
25 MILLION FAMILIES WILL HAVE OVER $7,500 . . .

Income classes (in 1959 dollars)	Family Units (in millions)				
	1929	1947	1953	1959	1970 *proj.*
Over $7,500	3.3	5.7	8.6	12.3	24.6
$15,000 and over					5.7
$10,000-15,000					9.9
$ 7,500-10,000					9.0
$4,000-7,500	7.1	16.9	20.8	22.0	24.8
$2,000-4,000	13.8	14.0	13.1	13.4	11.4
Under $2,000	11.9	8.2	8.0	7.5	5.6
$1,000-2,000	6.7				
$0-1,000	5.2				

. . . AND OVER 60 PER CENT OF THE INCOME

Income classes (in 1959 dollars)	Family personal income after taxes (in billions of 1959 dollars)				
	1929	1947	1953	1959	1970 *proj.*
Over $7,500	55.0	69.7	102.7	148.9	313.4
$15,000 and over					116.1
$10,000-15,000					119.8
$ 7,500-10,000					77.4
$4,000-7,500	36.9	92.9	114.6	121.6	139.9
$2,000-4,000	40.4	41.6	39.6	40.9	35.4
Under $2,000	12.9	9.5	9.6	8.7	6.5
$1,000-2,000	10.1				
$0-1,000	2.8				

The New Labor Force: How Far Can the Upgrading Go?
(millions of people)

	Men					Women				
	1900	1920	1940	1957	1970 *proj.*	1900	1920	1940	1957	1970 *proj.*
White Collar Jobs										
Total	2.4	3.9	5.7	9.7	13.3	.5	1.2	2.0	3.4	5.0
Professional	.8	1.3	2.3	4.1	6.5	.4	1.0	1.6	2.3	3.6
Managerial	1.6	2.6	3.4	5.6	6.0	.1	.2	.4	1.1	1.4
Total	1.7	3.3	4.8	5.6	6.6	.4	2.1	3.6	7.8	11.7
Sales	1.1	1.5	2.5	2.6	3.4	.2	.5	.9	1.6	2.4
Clerical	.6	1.8	2.3	3.0	3.2	.2	1.6	2.7	6.2	9.3
Blue Collar Jobs										
Total	5.5	10.2	13.2	17.2	20.8	1.4	1.8	2.6	3.6	4.4
Skilled	3.0	5.4	6.1	8.5	10.3	.1	.1	.1	.2	.5
Semi-skilled	2.5	4.8	7.1	8.7	10.5	1.3	1.7	2.5	3.4	3.9
Total	4.2	5.9	7.1	6.4	7.6	2.0	2.3	3.8	4.9	6.2
Service	.7	1.2	2.4	2.9	3.6	1.9	2.1	3.7	4.8	6.1
Laborers	3.5	4.7	4.7	3.5	4.0	.1	.2	.1	.1	.1
Farm Jobs										
Total	9.9	10.3	8.5	4.8	4.3	1.0	1.2	.6	.8	.7
Farm workers	4.4	4.1	3.3	1.6	1.4	.7	.9	.4	.7	.6
Farmers	5.5	6.2	5.2	3.2	2.9	.3	.3	.2	.1	.1

Sources: Back data from Bureau of the Census (as of April of each year).

CHAPTER EIGHT

TOTAL EXPENDITURES FOR HOUSING AND HOUSE FURNISHINGS
(billions of 1959 dollars)

1929	53.5
1940	51.0
1947	66.9
1953	83.8
1959 *est.*	108.0
1965 *proj.*	130.0
1970 *proj.*	162.0

Source: See following table for breakdown of expenditures and sources for data. Conversion of actual dollar figures into 1959 dollars by FORTUNE using detailed price indexes from the Department of Commerce and Bureau of Labor Statistics.

THE PATTERN OF CONSUMER SPENDING FOR THE HOME IS CHANGING AS PRICES SHIFT, BUT VOLUME IS STEADY.

Actual dollars spent as per cent of actual dollars of disposable income

	1929	1940	1947	1948	1949	1950	1951	1952	1953	1954	1955	1956	1957	1958	1959 est.
Construction	4.5	4.1	4.8	5.7	5.5	7.2	5.9	5.8	5.8	6.3	7.1	6.3	5.8	5.9	6.8
Household goods	9.3	9.1	10.6	10.4	10.0	10.7	10.0	9.4	9.2	9.1	9.4	9.2	8.9	8.7	8.8
Household services	4.9	5.3	4.4	4.3	4.5	4.6	4.6	4.7	4.8	4.9	5.1	5.3	5.3	5.6	5.3
Space rent	13.8	12.3	9.2	9.3	10.2	10.2	10.2	10.6	10.9	11.3	11.3	11.2	11.5	12.0	12.0

Source: See note page 236.

HOUSING PRICES RELATIVE TO ALL CONSUMER PRICES
(Index: 1957 = 100)

	1929	1940	1948	1953	1957	1959
Construction	75	79	95	98	100	100
Household goods	90	103	110	108	100	97
Household services	122	131	96	100	100	102
Space rent	84	96	84	97	100	101

Constant dollars spent as per cent of constant dollars of disposable income

	1929	1940	1947	1948	1949	1950	1951	1952	1953	1954	1955	1956	1957	1958	1959 *est.*
Construction	6.1	5.2	5.5	6.1	5.9	7.4	6.1	5.9	5.9	6.6	7.2	6.2	5.8	5.9	6.8
Household goods	10.3	8.9	9.8	9.5	9.2	9.8	8.9	8.7	8.6	8.7	9.1	9.1	8.9	8.7	9.0
Household services	4.0	4.1	4.5	4.5	4.6	4.7	4.9	4.8	4.8	4.9	5.1	5.3	5.3	5.6	5.2
Space rent	16.4	12.7	11.2	11.1	11.3	11.1	11.2	11.3	11.2	11.6	11.4	11.3	11.4	12.0	11.9

Source: Actual dollar figures from National Income accounts. FORTUNE has departed from normal national income accounting by treating home construction as a consumer outlay, rather than as an investment expenditure. Price indexes (except rent) calculated from data published by Department of Commerce and Bureau of Labor Statistics. The space rent index is calculated from Department of Commerce actual dollar figures and from FORTUNE's estimate of the constant-dollar value of space rent (i.e., constant-dollar value of housing stock).

BREAKDOWN OF HOUSING DEMAND AND SUPPLY

(millions of housing units; annual averages)

	1920-29	1930-39	1940-44	1945-49	1950-56	1957-59	1960-64	1965-69	1970-74
Demand						*est.*	*proj.*	*proj.*	*proj.*
Replacements & vacancies	280	75	105	150	570	625	625	625	550
Net new households	550	505	465	1325	940	900	1020	1080	1280
Total	830	580	570	1475	1510	1525	1645	1705	1830
Supply									
New construction	830	400	500	915	1355	1370	1445	1505	1605
Net conversions	—	180	70	560	155	155	200	200	225
Total	830	580	570	1475	1510	1525	1645	1705	1830

Source: New construction data based on a reconciliation by FORTUNE of Bureau of the Census and Bureau of Labor Statistics data. Other figures from Bureau of the Census.

BREAKDOWN OF HOUSEHOLD SERVICES
(per cent of disposable income)

	1929	1940	1947	1948	1949	1950	1951	1952	1953	1954	1955	1956	1957	1958
Utilities	1.72	2.42	1.61	1.59	1.74	1.78	1.81	1.92	1.99	2.16	2.23	2.30	2.35	2.48
Telephone	0.68	0.81	0.81	0.83	0.92	0.94	0.95	1.00	1.04	1.05	1.08	1.11	1.15	1.20
Domestic service	2.06	1.60	1.38	1.25	1.24	1.24	1.17	1.10	1.07	0.98	1.07	1.09	1.07	1.10
Repair service	0.41	0.51	0.61	0.62	0.64	0.66	0.67	0.69	0.70	0.72	0.74	0.76	0.77	0.79

BREAKDOWN OF HOUSEHOLD GOODS
(per cent of disposable income)

	1929	1940	1947	1948	1949	1950	1951	1952	1953	1954	1955	1956	1957	1958
Rugs, china, etc.	3.00	2.95	3.49	3.44	3.35	3.45	3.40	3.00	2.80	2.62	2.73	2.69	2.61	2.55
Appliances	0.92	1.16	1.87	1.83	1.65	1.90	1.70	1.60	1.58	1.57	1.71	1.67	1.50	1.39
Furniture	1.44	1.39	1.50	1.47	1.42	1.48	1.40	1.42	1.42	1.42	1.52	1.51	1.45	1.41
Cleaning & misc.	0.75	0.93	1.16	1.11	1.10	1.08	1.09	1.03	1.07	1.11	1.14	1.15	1.19	1.23
Fuel and ice	1.93	2.04	1.73	1.81	1.59	1.59	1.49	1.39	1.30	1.30	1.27	1.21	1.17	1.14
Radio and TV	1.22	0.65	0.84	0.78	0.90	1.18	1.00	0.99	1.03	1.07	1.02	0.98	0.97	0.98

Source: National Income accounts.

CHAPTER NINE

TOTAL EXPENDITURES ON FOOD AND CLOTHING
AND OTHER PERSONAL GOODS AND SERVICES

	Billions of 1959 dollars		
1929	61.0		
1940	73.1		
1947	101.5		
1948	98.4		
1949	97.9		
1950	99.3		
1951	99.9		
1952	102.9		
1953	105.0		
1954	106.1		
1955	111.1		
1956	115.2		
1957	116.6	Food	69.9
1958	117.0	Clothing	28.0
1959 *est.*	124.4	Alcohol	9.6
		Tobacco	6.8
		Personal care	10.1
1965 *proj.*	150		
1970 *proj.*	177		

Source: Back data from Department of Commerce. Converted into 1959 dollars by FORTUNE.

THE PATTERN OF SPENDING
EXPENDITURES AS PER CENT OF DISPOSABLE INCOME

	Food		Clothing		All other[1]	
	In 1959 dollars	In current dollars	In 1959 dollars	In current dollars	In 1959 dollars	In current dollars
1929	24.6	23.5	12.2	11.3	5.1	5.3
1940	25.2	22.0	10.0	9.8	9.1	10.4
1947	26.4	26.9	9.6	11.0	10.8	11.1
1950	22.0	22.9	8.6	9.4	9.2	9.1
1951	21.7	23.5	8.4	9.3	8.9	8.7
1952	21.8	23.4	8.5	9.2	8.8	8.8
1953	21.4	22.4	8.2	8.7	8.6	8.6
1954	21.7	22.5	8.2	8.5	8.5	8.4
1955	21.2	21.6	8.1	8.5	8.2	8.2
1956	21.1	21.3	8.0	8.4	8.1	8.1
1957	20.9	21.2	8.0	8.3	8.0	8.0
1958	20.7	21.3	8.1	8.3	8.0	8.0
1959 *est.*	20.8	20.8	8.3	8.3	7.9	7.9

[1] Includes alcohol, tobacco and miscellaneous.
Source: Same as previous table.

The "New Foods": Who Buys Them . . .
(Average household expenditure for each item = 100)

Income groups (before taxes):	Frozen fruits & juices	Frozen vegetables	Prepared mixes	Instant coffee	Canned baby food
0-$2,000	41	41	54	64	38
$2,000-$3,000	77	70	88	102	70
$3,000-$4,000	78	90	102	98	128
$4,000-$5,000	106	101	120	117	138
$5,000-$7,000	130	129	110	110	123
$7,000 & over	173	174	122	107	98

. . . And Their Growth Trends
(Indexes of production, 1950 = 100)

	Frozen fruits & juices	Frozen vegetables	Canned & frozen poultry	Canned baby food	Prepared cake mixes	Instant coffee
1947	24	59	58	67	17	67
1948	25	76	96	96	49	75
1949	67	96	84	93	84	81
1950	100	100	100	100	100	100
1951	130	131	112	92	102	126
1952	188	154	127	103	123	173
1953	208	184	122	122	164	236
1954	228	162	157	125	185	283
1955	268	191	160	122	211	321
1956	271	256	172	125	233	446
1957	293	228	199	132	228	476
1958	245	240	229	134	256	496

Sources: Household expenditures from *Life* "Study of Consumer Markets"; production trends from Department of Agriculture.

The Shares for Clothing, Drinking, Smoking, etc.
Expenditures as Per Cent of Disposable Income
(in current dollars)

| | Clothing | | | Alcohol | Tobacco | Miscel-laneous[1] |
	Women's & children's	Men's & boys'	Shoes			
1929	5.6	3.6	2.0	—	2.0	3.5
1940	5.0	3.1	1.7	4.7	2.5	3.2
1947	5.9	3.3	1.7	5.1	2.3	3.8
1950	4.8	2.9	1.6	3.8	2.1	3.2
1951	4.8	2.9	1.5	3.5	2.1	3.1
1952	4.9	2.8	1.4	3.6	2.1	3.1
1953	4.7	2.6	1.3	3.4	2.1	3.1
1954	4.7	2.6	1.3	3.3	2.0	3.1
1955	4.6	2.6	1.3	3.2	2.0	3.1
1956	4.4	2.7	1.3	3.1	1.9	3.1
1957	4.5	2.5	1.2	3.0	2.0	3.0
1958	4.5	2.5	1.3	2.9	2.0	3.0
1959 *est.*	4.6	2.4	1.3	2.9	2.0	3.0

[1] Miscellaneous includes expenditures for shoe cleaning and repair; cleaning, dyeing, pressing, alteration, storage and repair of garments; laundering; jewelry and watches; toilet articles and beauty preparations; barbershops, beauty parlors and baths; watch and jewelry repairs and miscellaneous clothing services.

Source: Department of Commerce.

CHAPTER TEN

NEW-CAR SALES
(in millions)

| | Replacement sales | "New" (non-replacement) sales: | | | Total sales |
		to new households	to first car owners	to multi-car owners	
1948	1.30	.90	1.10	.30	3.60
1949	2.32	.62	1.50	.36	4.80
1950	3.72	.76	1.25	.60	6.33
1951	3.22	.60	.82	.50	5.14
1952	2.54	.55	.71	.43	4.23
1953	3.52	.57	.88	.80	5.77
1954	3.23	.59	.92	.75	5.49
1955	4.00	.77	1.54	1.10	7.41
1956	4.31	.62	.24	.78	5.95
1957	4.33	.65	.10	1.01	6.09
1958	3.62	.63	.10	.37	4.72
1959 *est.*	4.40	.65	.60	.85	6.50
1948-53 average	2.77	.67	1.04	.50	4.98
1954-59 average	3.98	.52	.62	.91	6.03
1965 *proj.*	5.70	.90	.45	.95	8.0
1970 *proj.*	6.90	1.10	.30	1.10	9.4

Sources: Total sales from Ward's Automotive Reports. Breakdown of non-replacement sales by FORTUNE, based on surveys of ownership made by Federal Reserve Board and by Crowell-Collier. Replacement sales (scrappage) estimated by FORTUNE.

CAR OWNERSHIP BY HOUSEHOLDS
(in millions)

	One-car households	Multi-car households	No-car households	Total households
1935	16.2	.7	16.1	33.0
1941	21.6	1.1	13.6	36.3
1946	19.3	1.7	17.8	38.8
1947	21.1	1.9	17.2	40.2
1948	23.1	2.0	16.6	41.7
1949	25.0	2.3	15.9	43.2
1950	26.6	2.7	15.1	44.4
1951	27.8	3.0	14.5	45.3
1952	28.8	3.3	14.0	46.1
1953	29.7	3.9	13.2	46.8
1954	30.7	4.5	12.4	47.6
1955	31.7	5.3	11.6	48.6
1956	31.8	6.1	11.5	49.4
1957	31.9	7.2	11.2	50.3
1958	32.0	7.2	11.9	51.1
1959 *est.*	32.4	8.1	11.4	51.9
1965 *proj.*	—	—	—	58.0
1970 *proj.*	38.0	17.0	8.5	63.5

Sources: Total number of households from Bureau of the Census April data converted to end-of-year estimates. Breakdown of car ownership among households by FORTUNE, based on surveys of ownership made by Federal Reserve Board and by Crowell-Collier.

	Cars scrapped annually	Number of cars on the road: 8 years old and up[1]	Total[2]
1935	1.90	4.5	20.59
1936	2.22	5.5	21.89
1937	2.18	7.1	23.21
1938	1.75	7.3	23.42
1939	2.23	7.5	23.91
1940	1.61	7.1	25.76
1941	1.94	6.7	27.58
1942	.51	—	27.36
1943	.51	—	25.40
1944	.51	—	24.96
1945	.51	—	25.18
1946	.48	13.8	27.62
1947	.86	15.6	29.86
1948	1.30	17.9	32.03
1949	2.32	20.9	33.97
1950	3.72	19.8	36.48
1951	3.22	16.5	39.31
1952	2.54	13.4	41.11
1953	3.52	11.1	42.77
1954	3.23	10.1	45.07
1955	4.00	10.0	47.37
1956	4.32	9.5	49.81
1957	4.32	10.7	51.57
1958	3.62	13.0	52.78
1959 *est.*	4.40	13.5	55.40
1960 *proj.*	4.84	14.0	—
1961 "	4.92	15.0	—
1962 "	5.11	15.0	—
1963 "	5.35	16.5	—
1964 "	5.50	17.2	—
1965 "	5.72	17.5	—
1966 "	5.92	17.5	—
1967 "	6.14	17.5	—
1968 "	6.34	19.1	—
1969 "	6.65	20.3	—
1970 "	6.98	21.5	81.50

[1] These data are as of July 1 whereas the total number of cars on the road are for December 31. Nevertheless, a rough idea of the number of cars on the road less than eight years old may be calculated by subtracting these from the total.

[2] This total includes cars owned by business, institutions and government, as well as by households (which are detailed in the preceding table).

Sources: Scrappage, 1935-1945, from the Automobile Manufacturers Association; subsequent years estimated by FORTUNE. Number of cars on the road (registrations) from Bureau of Public Roads, converted by FORTUNE to end of year estimates. Number of cars older than eight years from R. L. Polk and Co.

TOTAL CONSUMER EXPENDITURES ON TRANSPORTATION

	Billions of 1959 dollars		
1929	13.7		
1940	14.7		
1947	22.3		
1948	23.7		
1949	26.6		
1950	30.9		
1951	29.6		
1952	28.5		
1953	33.6		
1954	33.2		
1955	39.5		
1956	36.9		
1957	37.8	Cars	15.8
1958	34.8	Gas and oil	11.2
1959 *est.*	39.3	Misc. car expenses[1]	9.1
		Public transportation[2]	3.2
1965 *proj.*	50.0		
1970 *proj.*	65.0		

[1] Includes outlays for tires and parts; repairs, servicing, parking and rental; tolls; insurance premiums less claims paid.

[2] Includes outlays for local trolleys and buses, taxicabs, rail commutation; outlays for intercity railways and buses, airlines.

Source: Back data from Department of Commerce. Converted into 1959 dollars by FORTUNE.

Per Cent of Disposable Income Spent on Transportation

	Per cent of current dollars
1929	9.16
1940	9.39
1947	9.05
1948	9.40
1949	11.00
1950	11.87
1951	10.78
1952	10.54
1953	11.73
1954	11.42
1955	12.88
1956	11.60
1957	11.80
1958	10.62
1959 *est.*	11.70

Source: Department of Commerce.

	New Cars	Gas & oil	Misc. car expenses	Public transportation
1929	3.11	2.18	1.87	1.98
1940	2.91	2.99	1.82	1.67
1947	2.70	2.13	2.40	1.81
1948	3.02	2.34	2.34	1.69
1949	4.26	2.64	2.48	1.63
1950	5.17	2.59	2.67	1.44
1951	4.15	2.66	2.59	1.40
1952	3.72	2.81	2.66	1.38
1953	4.68	2.99	2.76	1.30
1954	4.42	3.12	2.66	1.23
1955	5.76	3.20	2.77	1.15
1956	4.59	3.26	2.66	1.10
1957	4.71	3.36	2.66	1.06
1958	3.64	3.33	2.65	1.01
1959 *est.*	4.70	3.33	2.71	.95

Source: Department of Commerce.

CHAPTER TWELVE

THE BILLIONS FOR DOCTORS, BROKERS, BANKERS—AND JUST FUN
(billions of 1959 dollars)

1929	35
1940	33
1947	44
1953	68
1959 *est.*	84
1965 *proj.*	108
1970 *proj.*	132

Source: Conversion of actual dollar figures into 1959 dollars by FORTUNE on basis of detailed price data from Department of Commerce and Bureau of Labor Statistics.

How the Billions Are Divided

(per cent of disposable income)

	1929	1940	1947	1948	1949	1950	1951	1952	1953	1954	1955	1956	1957	1958	1959 est.
Saving	5.0	5.5	2.8	5.8	4.5	6.1	7.8	7.9	7.8	7.3	6.4	7.8	7.5	7.4	7.2
Medical care, financial charges, insurance, etc.	12.6	11.6	9.9	10.0	10.5	10.5	10.5	10.7	11.1	11.7	11.9	12.4	12.7	13.2	13.2
Recreation and travel	4.7	4.5	4.9	4.7	4.8	4.5	4.4	4.4	4.4	4.4	4.5	4.6	4.6	4.8	4.8

Index: 1959 = 100

	1929	1940	1947	1953	1959
All consumer prices	57	46	78	92	100
Prices of recreation, medical care, etc.	52	51	67	85	100

Source: Actual dollar figures from Consumer Expenditures portion of Gross National Product data from Department of Commerce, including medical care, personal business, recreation, education, religion and foreign travel. Price indexes calculated from Department of Commerce and Bureau of Labor Statistics data.

CONSUMER EXPENDITURES FOR SELECTED ITEMS
(per cent of disposable income)

Used for:	1929	1940	1947	1948	1949	1950	1951	1952	1953	1954	1955	1956	1957	1958
Medical care	4.26	4.64	4.51	4.58	4.74	4.67	4.60	4.71	4.83	5.07	5.10	5.25	5.40	5.63
Insurance	2.35	3.78	2.73	2.44	2.51	2.36	2.32	2.50	2.48	2.53	2.53	2.53	2.27	2.36
Religion and welfare	1.43	1.33	1.19	1.17	1.17	1.13	1.09	1.12	1.10	1.16	1.13	1.18	1.20	1.24
Education	.79	.84	.82	.82	.88	.86	.85	.88	.88	.92	.94	.99	1.02	1.08
Legal services	1.27	.93	.71	.71	.74	.70	.71	.67	.67	.70	.69	.71	.72	.72
Cash deposits & gov't bonds	−4.20	4.10	2.83	.90	.99	2.67	3.07	4.84	4.21	3.70	4.42	4.52	4.43	4.56
Fin. services	2.45	1.22	1.05	1.08	1.15	1.13	1.11	1.19	1.26	1.33	1.36	1.44	1.45	1.49
Interest	.70	1.07	.52	.64	.79	.92	.94	1.04	1.24	1.30	1.41	1.53	1.60	1.60
Corp. stocks & bonds	7.63	−.38	.52	.72	.50	.54	.91	1.01	.65	.44	1.24	.89	1.23	1.15
Active Sports	.91	.98	1.34	1.32	1.30	1.31	1.34	1.35	1.32	1.31	1.40	1.45	1.48	1.56
Spectator sports	1.11	1.25	1.33	1.14	1.11	.96	.86	.82	.77	.79	.76	.73	.68	.69
Books & mags.	1.02	1.07	1.04	1.04	1.10	1.05	1.03	1.04	1.03	1.02	1.02	1.01	1.05	1.08
Travel	.76	.22	.35	.38	.44	.44	.40	.43	.46	.49	.53	.55	.56	.60
Misc. recreation	.92	.90	.85	.80	.82	.77	.76	.77	.78	.79	.79	.81	.82	.83

Source: Breakdown of savings data from the Securities and Exchange Commission for 1940 to 1958. Breakdown for 1929 based on figures in *Individuals' Saving* by Irwin Friend and Vito Narrella, John Wiley & Sons, 1954.

Index